KT-568-934

CATCHING A
SERIAL
KILLER

GREENWICH LIBRARIES

3 8028 02336126 1

CATCHING A SERIAL KILLER

My hunt for murderer Christopher Halliwell

FORMER DETECTIVE SUPERINTENDENT
STEPHEN FULCHER

with Kate Moore

EBURY
PRESS

Although this book is based on real people and real events, some names, places and identifying features have been changed in order to preserve their privacy.

3 5 7 9 10 8 6 4 2

Ebury Press, an imprint of Ebury Publishing
20 Vauxhall Bridge Road
London SW1V 2SA

Ebury Press is part of the Penguin Random House group
of companies whose addresses can be found
at global.penguinrandomhouse.com

Penguin
Random House
UK

Copyright © Stephen Fulcher 2017

Stephen Fulcher has asserted his right to be identified as the
author of this Work in accordance with the Copyright,
Designs and Patents Act 1988

First published by Ebury Press in 2017

www.penguin.co.uk

A CIP catalogue record for this book is available
from the British Library

ISBN 978-1785036279

Typeset in India by Integra Software Services Pvt. Ltd, Pondicherry

Printed and bound in Great Britain by Clays Ltd, St Ives PLC

Penguin Random House is committed to a
sustainable future for our business, our readers
and our planet. This book is made from Forest
Stewardship Council® certified paper.

To Sian and Becky,
and the girls who haven't been found

GREENWICH LIBRARIES	
CO	
3 8028 02336126 1	
Askews & Holts	12-Jul-2017
364.152	£7.99
5449945	

*'Rules are for the guidance of wise men
and the obedience of fools.'*

Harry Day,
Royal Flying Corps fighter pilot (1898–1977)

Prologue

Friday, 3 January 2003

The steady thrum of music from the Destiny & Desire nightclub could be heard even on the street outside. It seemed to pound through the pavement, pound in time with the girls' heartbeats as they stood there chatting, their noses nipped by the cold night air.

As the two young women waited on the street, a car's engine joined the cacophony: another noise to add to those irking the residents who lived nearby, who complained that the nightspot was the bane of their lives. Yet the engine's purr soon faded as the car pulled up smoothly next to the kerb. The driver, unseen in the shadows, beckoned one of the young women to his side.

She went, somewhat unwillingly, and was clearly not interested in whatever it was he had to say. She returned quickly to her friend, perhaps with a toss of her bright blonde hair, leaving the man to his own devices. The new hope of the New Year was still tangible in those first few days of January 2003 – and auld acquaintances, in some cases, *were* best forgotten, after all.

But the driver disagreed. The silver Volvo stayed unmoving at the side of the street, so the young woman once again went to speak with the man behind the wheel.

At 20 years of age, she was a gentle character, yet she also had a reputation for being feisty when she needed to stand her ground. Her petite frame – she was only four foot eleven – belied her strength of character. It wasn't long before a row erupted: raised voices disturbing the sleep of those beleaguered neighbours who had been disturbed too many times before to bother looking out of their windows to spy the source of this latest commotion. They didn't see the girl shouting through the Volvo's window or storming back to her friend – or the way the car remained, despite all this, by the side of the road, its presence commanding and insistent, its driver unswayed by the wishes of the woman.

She had said no once. She had said no twice. But, the third time, she told her friend she was leaving, shrugged her shoulders in a huff and slipped hurriedly inside the rear of the vehicle, slamming the door shut behind her.

It closed with a decisive click: a punctuation point to mark the end. The car pulled swiftly away, its tail lights glowing red in the dark. With a final burst of acceleration, it rounded the corner and vanished from sight.

PART 1

Cat and Mouse

1

'Night, guv'nor.'

Looking up from my desk, I raised a hand in farewell as my colleague ducked back out of my office and went whistling away down the corridor, the jauntiness of the melody signalling his delight at getting out of the nick relatively early on a mild spring Friday night.

I turned back to my computer with a sigh: there would be no such early doors exit for me. As director of intelligence for Wiltshire Police, I had my work cut out – I was responsible for all intelligence across the entire force, with a particular remit for fighting organised crime. I was often the last one out of Wiltshire Police HQ on a Friday evening.

As I settled into my work, however, I found the time passed quickly. Much as I often narked on about the constant cuts or the tedious politics of modern-day policing, the truth was I loved my job. I'd been a copper since 1986, starting out as a bobby on the beat in a big hat and boots; Yvonne, then my girlfriend, had told me I'd have to become a detective as I looked utterly ridiculous in the uniform. But I didn't need any urging: almost from the moment I joined the force I wanted to deal with proper crime and make a real difference. I liked serving the public and trying to do my best for them, and I felt best placed to do that in CID, where I earned my stripes as a young detective from the age of 23.

The funny thing about policing is that it starts out as a job like any other: you're working to live. Somehow, though, over the years – particularly for detectives, I think – that equation turns on its head and you live to work: the job becomes the life. Being part of the police force in some ways is like being part of a family, and I relished the teamwork and the camaraderie, that sense of pulling together to bring in a result. Even though there seemed to be more and more bureaucracy the higher I climbed – moving first from constable to sergeant, then to inspector, and finally, in 2007, to the heady heights of detective superintendent – I still lived for the cut and thrust of operational policing. Detective superintendent was the highest rank for that and now, aged 44, I wasn't sure I had the appetite or the inclination to climb any higher, for it would mean leaving the real job behind. In addition to my role as director of intelligence, I headed up major crime enquiries as an SIO (senior investigating officer). That involved the intellectual challenge and down-and-dirty work of solving crimes and bringing offenders to justice – and those aspects of the job moti-vated me like nothing else.

Sat at my desk in HQ, I yawned widely and checked my watch: nearly 7 p.m. I smiled wryly to myself; our chief constable, Brian Moore, had a well-worn catch-phrase – 'There are two seven o'clocks in every day and I expect you there for both of them' – and it seemed I was destined to fulfil his mandate once again. I gazed around my office as my ancient computer started its laborious process of shutting down for the night.

The intelligence team resided in the bowels of Wiltshire Police HQ: hot-water pipes ran all through the department, a less-than-glamorous backdrop to the filing cabinets and whiteboards of our trade. As my screen flickered to black, I found my gaze resting on the noticeboard beside my desk. It was where I kept bits and pieces from old cases – personal items that wouldn't end up in the official files, such as notecards or thank-you letters – and my eye was caught by a woman's smiling face on an order of service. She was a murder victim; one of the more recent cases that I'd solved. I'd attended her funeral and pinned the booklet to the board afterwards; I couldn't tell you why, really, other than that it never seemed right simply to chuck them away. I guess her presence there, by my side every day, was a worthy reminder of why I did the job.

There were no pictures of my own family: my wife of nearly 23 years now, Yvonne, and my two teenage daughters, Elsie and Jennifer. My whole career, I'd never brought family photos into work; I had always compartmentalised and kept the two very separate. In fact, my desk was entirely bare; not even an in-tray on it. Such was the sensitive nature of my intelligence role that I always kept a clear desk and locked files away in the secure cabinets that lined the room.

I stretched and shrugged on my grey herringbone coat, hastening now to get out of the office and back to my girls. I knew I was lucky to have them; divorce is endemic in the police force. Yvonne was really easy-going, however, and – perhaps more importantly – a black belt in karate, so she had always managed to keep me in check. The anti-social aspects of police work – the late nights and the cancellations of long-scheduled events – had become a way of life for us both by now. Mercifully, ours remained a supportive, egalitarian marriage.

As I locked the office door behind me, I felt the weight of work lifting – but only so far. I patted my pocket deliberately: yes, the force-issued standard Nokia mobile was safely ensconced in there. I couldn't leave work without it because I had volunteered to be the on-call SIO for the coming weekend.

There were about three or four of us qualified to do that job in the force – we'd be on call once every three or four weekends, on rotation. It wasn't actually due to be my call, but one of the other SIOs, a good mate of mine named Bob who ran the major crime team, was deep in preparing for an upcoming rape trial and was swamped by paperwork. He'd asked if I'd mind swapping and I'd said I'd be happy to help out.

The Nokia phone weighed next to nothing in my pocket as I made my way outside to my car – and the responsibility across my shoulders felt about the same. There was nothing to suggest it should be a fraught weekend ahead. In fact, with Yvonne and the girls planning to visit her parents from tomorrow morning onwards, I was rather looking forward to a quiet few days at home.

What's that saying again?

Famous last words.

2

Saturday, 19 March 2011

The roar of jubilant Ireland fans discharged from the TV and I tutted in disgust. I usually watched the Six Nations rugby with Bob down the pub, nursing a few pints of Wadworth's 6X as we put the world to rights, but as you can't drink alcohol when on call, for this all-important England–Ireland match I was at home alone instead – with a sensible mug of tea. I sat back on the sofa in abject despair as half-time came and went; we were losing 17–3 and England showed no signs of improvement.

Other than the execrable display from my team, that Saturday, 19 March, had been just as I'd planned: a bracing walk with my wire fox terrier, Pippa, on the Bratton Downs in the morning, then after I'd waved the girls off to the in-laws I'd chilled out with the newspapers. Being on call meant I couldn't leave the county, which was why I hadn't gone with them; instead, I was a somewhat willing prisoner in my own home, with column inches for company.

With it now being early evening, I was on pretty safe territory that I wouldn't get a call from the nick. If a job happens, you tend to get called in on a Saturday or Sunday morning. But my day had been undisturbed, and

I knew from experience it would be an unusual time to get a call at 18.45.

So it was unexpected when the Nokia sprang suddenly to life with its incongruously cheerful ringtone – incongruous because, whatever news awaited me on the other end of the line, it was never good. I muted the TV and sat forwards on the sofa, immediately attuned to whatever crisis needed my help.

It was the control room of Wiltshire Police on the line, connecting me with the duty detective sergeant at Swindon CID.

'DS Fulcher?' she asked. It wasn't an officer I knew well; I only knew the Swindon team in passing professional terms, being based at HQ in Devizes myself.

'How can I help?' I said.

She outlined the reason for her call. At 09.49 that morning, the force had received a report of a missing person. Sian O'Callaghan, aged 22, hadn't come home the night before. She'd gone clubbing in Swindon's Old Town on the Friday night with some friends, but become separated from them at 01.30. It was her boyfriend, Kevin Reape – with whom she lived, just half a mile away from the nightclub she'd frequented – who had raised the alarm. He'd last heard from Sian by text at 01.24 that Saturday morning: 'Where are you?' He'd been asleep, in bed, and replied to that effect when he woke to find her still not home at 03.24.

But she didn't reply to that text, nor to the second message he sent at 04.40 which simply read: 'Worried X'. Kevin and other members of her family had been ringing her all day – until her phone battery had died at 14.36 – but had received no response. Her behaviour was completely out of character.

Reports of people going missing are not an unusual occurrence. The police receive more than 300,000 missing-person calls a year and most cases are resolved swiftly, with most people returning home within 24 to 48 hours. Perhaps because of that, there are some schools of thought within the force that dismiss all such calls as uniform jobs: go check the hospitals and ask them to phone again in 24 hours. But I was not a subscriber. Each case needed to be assessed on its merits to gauge the level of investigation required and, where necessary, I felt an active rather than passive approach was essential to prevent harm.

I listened as the officer told me more about Sian's disappearance, the hairs on my neck lifting slightly: copper's instinct assessing the probability of there being a criminal component to this incident. On the face of it, it could be entirely innocent. She could have met an acquaintance and stayed the night with them. Perhaps she'd got lost, gone the wrong way in a drunken fug of confusion, even though the club was so very close to home. Maybe her phone had been stolen and that was why she hadn't answered any of her family's increasingly desperate calls. She could have been knocked over by a car and bowled into some bushes, rendered incapable of calling for help.

Or maybe, just maybe, something more sinister had happened.

The guys at Swindon are very good; in fact, the standard of frontline police officers generally is excellent. Swindon was a busy town with a diverse population and as a consequence the team was switched on. They'd spent the day since the call had come in doing all the obvious things: searching the route from the Old Town to Sian's house as well as the house itself, phoning hospitals and taking statements from her friends. As the day had drawn on and there was still no sign of the missing woman, they had grown progressively more concerned, first elevating the enquiry to a Level 1 Missing Person and then escalating the case to a more senior officer. That was where I came in.

Notwithstanding my belief that every missing-person enquiry needs serious attention – after all, when your loved one vanishes, it *is* serious – it is an approach that requires some skill. If an officer's starting point is to think *major crime* at every report of a misper, that ups the ante. It places the responsibility on senior officers to assess the situation, otherwise the force would be setting up a major crime enquiry for every repeat misper from a care home, which would be nonsensical. And, as I listened to the DS, I made that assessment now.

It's hard to describe what it is that tells you when something is off: that this girl hadn't just failed to come home, but that her disappearance had criminal characteristics. It smelt wrong to me. The character of Sian herself and her propensity for doing this kind of thing was key. Being a detective in part is about reading people: by all accounts she was a sensible, family loving girl and she had just vanished into thin air. I requested that, if it hadn't been already, the CCTV from the club be located and that cell-site analysis on Sian's phone should begin: the telephony team should be able to pinpoint its last known location from the 'pings' that every phone emits when it periodically checks in with the nearest mast. And I told the officer something else, too.

'I'll be with you shortly,' I said. 'I'm coming down to Gablecross nick.'

3

I changed hurriedly, throwing off my scruffy jeans and yanking one of my typical navy CID suits out of the wardrobe. You never quite knew what you were going to encounter in this job, so my MO was always to be prepared. It was a matter of minutes before I was locking up the empty house and slipping into my beloved Alfa Romeo GT Spider, a gunmetal-grey beauty with a red leather interior that was my pride and joy.

I pulled away from our house on the hill in Bratton and set off for the nick. The bare facts I knew to date had me so concerned that the only option was to attend in person to progress the case. I was acutely aware of the 'golden hour' principles around serious investigations: the more time that passes following an offence, the more likely it is that evidence is going to be lost, compromised or destroyed, so pace is of the essence when it comes to investigating any crime. Detectives call it the 'golden hour' as traditionally it's the first 60 minutes after an offence has occurred that are crucial – but I went beyond that and applied it to the first 96 hours of a major crime enquiry. Whenever you had a live job come in, you had to get on the back of it swiftly, get the parameters of investigation set and get people out there on the ground trapping your evidence. If an

SIO failed to get a grip, enquiries lasted months or even years rather than days, and oftentimes those long-running cases ultimately went unsolved.

In my experience, if you moved fast, you got a result. It meant working like stink for those first four days – giving up on admittedly rubbish rugby games to spend your Saturday night in the nick, for example – but if you nailed the case, if you helped the victims, then all the hard work was worth it.

As I drove, I let the facts of the case so far percolate through my mind. As it stood, I had no way yet of knowing if Sian O'Callaghan's disappearance *was* criminal in nature. But, if it turned out to be, we were potentially looking at a kidnap case here: a crime in action.

I had dealt with lots of kidnappings over the years – but they tended to be kidnap-and-extortion cases, based on the notion that the offender has taken a hostage in order to gain a financial advantage. If you received an extortion demand alongside your report of a missing person, then you had a pretty reasonable chance of getting the victim back safely. That end result, as per the force's official kidnap manual – and basic humanity – is always the number-one priority in any kidnap case, above all other considerations.

As I pulled off the M4 motorway towards Swindon, I wondered if extortion could be the reason for Sian's disappearance. Yet I knew that extortion demands traditionally came in soon after the abduction; at times, they could be the first signal you had that the person was missing. It was now more than nine hours since Kevin Reape had dialled 999 to report his girlfriend's disappearance and no such message – requesting money in exchange for the safe return of Sian O'Callaghan – had been sent.

It was close to 19.30 by the time I made the turning into the nick, which was based on the outskirts of Swindon. It was a three-storey red-brick building set beside a busy A-road.

As soon as I'd parked the Spider in the front lot, I made my way inside to locate the detective sergeant who'd called me earlier. We caught up in a CID office so she could brief me fully. I was struck by how busy it was: normally there is a lull at the weekend and at that sort of time on a Saturday night the nick would be relatively quiet, but there was a bit of a buzz about the place: the team had clearly recognised the potential seriousness of Sian's case. Good.

The DS slid a photograph across the desk towards me: this was the girl we were trying to find. The woman in the picture was smiling: a very fresh-faced, attractive young lady with dark-brown hair cut into a sharp asymmetric style. She was white, with sparkling green eyes that were full of personality. I couldn't help clocking how young she looked, just 22 years old; she was only a couple of years older than my own daughters.

I didn't want her image to end up on my noticeboard at HQ.

To my practised eye, although I had never met Sian personally, the snapshot seemed to be quite an accurate reflection of her – of who she was. Her friends had described her as a bubbly, instantly likeable person and the smiling girl before me had that character. That was good: for policing purposes, we wanted this image to engender sightings, to remind people if they had seen her. The DS told me that the picture had already been released to the media, and the on-duty chief inspector had done a piece to camera at 19.00 hours to appeal for Sian or any witnesses to come forward. At this stage in the enquiry, we needed all the help we could get.

Sian seemed to have disappeared off the face of the planet. She had made no cash withdrawals since 18 March; her last Facebook entry was on the Friday morning. The DS gave me the names and statements of the friends she'd been out with the night before and, with a lurch, I realised that one of them was the daughter of a colleague. It made us all appreciate how very close to home this was.

Sian had been out with a handful of good friends after finishing work that Friday; she was employed as a personal assistant in an office. They'd had a meal at the Harvester before moving on to Suju, a popular nightclub on the High Street. It was a very typical nightspot, without a rough reputation. Sian, clearly, had not felt worried: she was a sociable girl who regularly went out and she usually walked home: it was just a 15-minute stroll to the house she shared with Kevin.

Sian had become separated from her friends at 01.30 on the Saturday morning. She was last seen in the toilets with a white woman of about five foot four – just an inch taller than Sian herself – who was in her early twenties and wearing a khaki-green jacket. Less than 45 minutes later, Sian's friends had left the club without her at 02.12.

I scribbled the timings in my daybook. The CCTV from Suju showed Sian O'Callaghan departing alone at 02.52, picking her way down the internal staircase with careful steps, having had a few drinks, but she was easily able to manage them: she wasn't falling down drunk. What had happened after that was anyone's guess.

But we did have one clue to help us: the cell-site telephony. And here the puzzle became yet more complex. Sian's phone was pinging in Swindon's Old Town for most of the evening, just as I would have expected. But at 03.24 – half an hour after she left Suju – her phone came to life to receive the text message that her worried boyfriend had sent her, having woken alone in their bed. And at that moment, as Kevin Reape messaged her to express his concern for her safety, her phone signal had bounced off the Cadley mast, some 14 miles away in rural Wiltshire.

Why was Sian there?

4

The primary role of the SIO on a major crime enquiry is to devise lines of enquiry for your team to follow. It's a heck of a responsibility: make the wrong call, and you send everybody haring off in the wrong direction. It's crucial to assess the evidence before you and, on the basis of it, devise sensible hypotheses to fit the circumstances that can then be tested, confirmed or dismissed on the basis of further investigation.

Looking at the evidence before me, I concluded that there were three hypotheses about what had happened to Sian. All we knew was that she'd left the club at 02.52 and at 03.24 her phone had pinged off the Cadley mast. What could have happened? One: she could have met an acquaintance and voluntarily gone there with them; she had subsequently failed to make contact with friends and family for unknown reasons, but was none-theless safe and well. Two: she could have become separated from her phone, which was taken by persons unknown to the Cadley area, and Sian herself had met with an accident in Swindon's Old Town following her exit from the club. Or, three: she could have been abducted with her phone, perhaps enticed into a vehicle and driven into the countryside, and there rendered incapacitated.

Perhaps she was still there now, just waiting for us to find her.

For all that the SIO role is something of an autocratic one, because you're the one calling the shots, if you have any sense at all you get good people around you. Immediately following the briefing from the DS I summoned the on-duty officer from the major crime team, knowing that for this kind of enquiry their professional expertise would be essential.

I was pleased to find that the on-duty officer was DS Sarah Bilston, an excellent detective with roughly eight years in the job with whom I had worked many times. Sarah was an up-and-coming star: an exceptionally bright woman in her late twenties.

With Sarah and the original DS by my side, I called an immediate formal briefing on Sian's case in the conference room on the top floor of Gablecross, pulling together the small team of detectives and on-duty uniform colleagues who had been conducting enquiries throughout the day. We gathered at 20.00, the 25-odd officers finding seats around the large conference table that furnished the functional meeting room. I wanted first-hand knowledge of precisely what had been done to date and by whom, so I could start formulating immediate strategies for the night ahead. If Sian had been snatched off the street and was even now lying bound and gagged somewhere, she deserved for us to be working every minute of the coming hours to bring her home. There wasn't a moment to lose.

From my seat at the head of the table, I began by discussing the significance and repercussions of Sian's phone pinging off the Cadley mast. These days, telephony is the first recourse in any missing-person enquiry because, generally speaking, everybody has a phone now. That element of investigation, what we call passive data – the traces left behind by people's mobile phones, Sat-Navs, on CCTV and similar – has changed policing beyond all recognition. In circumstances like this, where there was an immediate threat to life, we had the ability to get a live trace on Sian's phone through her telecoms provider and the data from her mobile was a crucial lead.

With Sian's friends and family having spent the morning desperately phoning her, it had been many hours now since the missing girl's phone had registered any sign of life; her battery had long since burnt out and, currently, there was no signal. But we knew that, since that initial 03.24 ping off the Cadley mast, her phone had consistently bounced off the same mast until the signal vanished at 14.36. If both Sian and her phone had made it out of Swindon, chances were they were still in the same location now.

Usually in telephony, you can use several masts to pinpoint a phone's position and easily narrow down the search area, sometimes to within a single metre. But in this case, as is Sod's Law, the remote Cadley mast was located on its own, in the heart of the Savernake Forest – an area which comprised not only your typically hard-to-search woodland, but also villages and towns, such as Marlborough and Ramsbury. Now, I was told, the signal from Sian's phone did give us a defined search area, but a defined search area that had a radius of 6.7 *miles*.

I shook my head in disbelief and concern. A traffic cop, also attending the briefing, piped up to inform me that the forest's roads were closed off at night, meaning you couldn't drive a car all the way through. It was helpful local knowledge – the kind you wanted the guys on the ground to be sharing – because it at least gave us some specific entry and exit points to this vast area to start our search. I ordered that a 200-metre radius of all entry and exit points to Savernake Forest should be conducted immediately using search dogs – and then I upped the ante and requested that the force helicopter be utilised to scan the entire 6.7-mile radius with heat-seeking equipment to see if Sian could be located from overhead.

There was a ripple of reaction around the room. Using the helicopter was no small decision – it cost £1,500 just to get it in the air – but obviously we had to use it when it might save someone's life. It was a decision that would ultimately be green-lit by officers above my head, however – I might be the SIO, but I didn't hold the purse-strings when it came to that kind of expenditure – yet I knew it was something we must and would do for Sian.

The telephony data had given us a big area to search – but there was an easier place to look for the missing girl: her home. My attention next turned to those uniformed officers who had searched Sian's house and the surrounding area. They were both young policemen, keen thrusting types just starting out in the job. I tried never to let myself forget what it was like to be in their shoes, doing thankless tasks and getting ripped to shreds by ungrateful guv'nors back at the nick. So I attempted to be understanding as I grilled them on the outcome and thoroughness of that search: 'Would you bank your careers on the fact she isn't there?'

I didn't ask it lightly: there'd been a couple of recent cases where searchers had missed bodies later found in the vicinity of the victim's home. I was mindful of that, and didn't want it to occur in this case: we needed to be sure that Sian wasn't in an outbuilding, a loft or garden shed.

'I'm not criticising you,' I said, more gently. 'Just go back and do it again.'

To their credit, they immediately – and amenably – acquiesced. It was a good attitude, and one reflected in the whole team: let's do everything methodically and get this right.

Despite my request to the young lads, I was still struck by the telephony results. Why was Sian's phone in the Savernake Forest area? One of the most striking things about the data was the speed at which Sian – if she was with her phone – must have travelled from Swindon. I asked for a test to be conducted that night to see how long it would take to get from the High Street, Old Town, where Sian had left the nightclub, to Savernake Forest. Perhaps that would help us to pin down with more accuracy the potential timing of any accident, assault or abduction that may have occurred, as well as giving us a possible route to search for further clues.

It was plain to me that I needed to designate two areas of focus: Savernake Forest, where Sian's phone had pinged at 03.24, and the High Street, where she had last been seen leaving Suju at 02.52. I couldn't ignore the fact that she might still be in Swindon somewhere, so those lines of enquiry had to run simultaneously. I tasked the team with collecting CCTV from the commercial premises on the High Street, a job to be combined with house-to-house enquiries along the parameters of Suju to Sian's house. We needed to get as many people as possible involved in sightings of her.

And we had an idea as to how we could make that happen. The chief inspector who'd done the media briefing earlier had already managed to get some flyers printed with Sian's photo on – and we determined to hand these out widely in the High Street throughout that Saturday night. By going back to the same area in which she was last sighted, especially to those pubs and clubs where some revellers may have returned for a second night in a row, we were hoping to prompt a witness to come forward who could explain this young woman's troubling disappearance.

We were still talking through the flyer campaign when a cheery ringtone broke the intensity of the discussion around the table.

'Excuse me,' I said after a moment, glancing down at the battered screen of the Nokia handset and responding instantly to the name it showed, 'I have to take this call.'

5

Brian Moore, the chief constable of Wiltshire Police, was on the line.

'Evening, Steve,' he said when I answered, then dispensed with the pleasantries as he asked to be brought up to speed on all I'd done so far to find Sian.

I wasn't surprised he was calling. He was a remarkably hands-on CC and was, quite rightly in this case, taking an interest because it was the biggest incident occurring at that moment in time for Wiltshire Police. Brian had a bit of a reputation as a Tartar – he famously kept a big brass crocodile on his desk at HQ, perhaps a symbol to say to any subordinate officers summoned there, 'You're here to get chewed' – but I'd always got on reasonably well with him. Despite his ascension into the highest echelons of British policing, he still saw himself as a detective by trade, so he and I were cut from the same cloth in that regard. Brian had wavy ginger hair and sharp features set into a thin face. He was extremely fit: he used to run to work and back every day, a direct contrast to my own more lackadaisical approach to exercise. He was a man of the people: he went out on patrol a lot and naturally the guys on the frontline thought that was fantastic; actually, for a CC, it was unheard of.

I quickly filled Brian in on the case so far. It was plain from the number and scale of lines of enquiry that I outlined to him that I was putting considerable resources into the search for Sian – which came, of course, with considerable costs attached. It wasn't just the use of the helicopter: if Sian remained missing, the amount of officers needed to fully investigate her disappearance would be significant: you could easily spend ten grand an hour just on people. Of course, I needed the right officers to be working on this, those personnel with the relevant expertise. My attitude was that you couldn't put a price on a girl's life.

But it wasn't my call to make. I told Brian I was putting the balloon up on this one: I was designating the disappearance of Sian O'Callaghan as a category-A enquiry, which meant I suspected her life was at threat. It transformed the enquiry into a major investigation of significant concern – and meant that I expected all possible resources to be made available to me. To my mind, although one of my current hypotheses was that Sian could be safe and well and happily with an unknown party, with every minute that passed the likelihood of that hypothesis being right diminished. Everything I and my colleagues had discovered to date told me that Sian was either in difficulty or in danger: we needed to expend every effort to help her.

Brian, understandably, quizzed me on the basis of my concerns. It was in his power to overrule me – he could have said, 'No, Steve, we'll treat it as a misper and send out one PC to interview the family sometime tomorrow.' Instead, he listened carefully as I made the case for Sian.

To my relief, Brian backed me all the way. What was gratifying was that, because I had a long-standing reputation for getting good results, I could articulate as little as this – 'a girl's been missing for less than 24 hours and these are the reasons why I personally am concerned' – and he trusted my professional opinion and supported it.

His backing meant a lot because, at that time, all was not well for the Wiltshire Police hierarchy. In recent months Brian's deputy, DCC Dave Ainsworth, had been removed from his post because of allegations of sexual harassment. Though some of his female colleagues loved working with him, he clearly made others feel distinctly uncomfortable and had been known to make inappropriate remarks that were laced with sexual innuendo – such as 'Nice buttons' to one woman who had worn a tailored blouse. I'd seen him just a few weeks ago, when he'd agreed to review my dissertation for me – I was currently studying for a masters in applied criminology and police management at Cambridge University. He'd appeared very much on edge, unshaven and dishevelled in the wake of his professional disgrace.

Because Brian was Brian, it wouldn't have been his way to close the call without adding his own tuppence worth to the investigation. Detection ran through his blood and old habits died hard. He too had been struck by the timings of the pings of Sian's phone and he had a solid theory as to how she might have been transported to the new location. And, perhaps, a suggestion for a cohort of possible offenders.

His voice sounded louder in my ear than I expected as he pressed his point home: 'Make sure you consider the taxi drivers.'

6

With Brian's sage words ringing in my ears, I terminated the call and faced the 25 officers still sitting round the conference table. Ordinarily, of course, I wouldn't have interrupted the briefing for love nor money, but when it's the chief on the line you tend to break off.

I relayed what Brian had said and asked the teams heading out to the High Street to concentrate on cabbies with their enquiries, making sure to alert as many drivers as possible to Sian's disappearance. Cabbies, after all, have by trade a nocturnal, rather anti-social lifestyle, and in terms of potential witnesses they were the one group of people that we knew would have been moving around at the times central to this case. Even if they didn't pick up Sian, they may have seen her. Equally, a cabbie might well have taken her to Savernake Forest, or to another location thereafter, and we needed to know ASAP if that was the case. She may have requested such a fare – or, potentially, a taxi driver could be our kidnapper, if the young woman had indeed been abducted, as I increasingly feared.

Without wishing to malign an entire profession, taxi drivers can be quite strange people. Though some have no choice in their career, others actively seek it out, flourishing in the little kingdom of their car and revelling in their ownership of the roads after the rest of the world had retired to bed. Being out at such anti-social hours offers opportunity if nothing else to commit crime, while the nature of the job gives them intimate knowledge of the geography. They know their way around, cabbies; they know every back street, every random rural track, every nook and cranny and side street like the back of their hand. Useful knowledge, if you happen to harbour more nefarious predilections than simply outwitting the rush-hour traffic jams. The job also gives cover: no one thinks twice if a taxi is cruising the streets of Swindon late at night, they'll simply assume the driver is looking for fares, when in fact they may be looking for targets, assessing each solo woman or inebriated man to see if they might become their next unwitting victim.

I was conscious of the time and wrapped things up quickly. I wanted officers sent out to Sian's boyfriend, Kevin Reape, as a priority and an initial assessment made of him in the morning. If Sian's case turned darker, and in time became a murder investigation, I knew from the stats that most murders were domestic in origin, about 70 per cent. Shockingly, two women a week on average are killed by a violent partner or ex-partner, which constitutes nearly 40 per cent of all female homicides. While in all likelihood Kevin was an innocent party, we couldn't, for Sian's sake, make that assumption.

My final directive of the evening briefing was that I wanted a major incident room (MIR) set up first thing in the morning and for the case to be given a HOLMES account. As I dismissed the various teams and set them to work on their overnight actions, it was coming up to 21.00 hours.

HOLMES stands for Home Office Large Major Enquiry System. It's essentially a computer system that becomes the brain or memory of a major crime enquiry and captures the masses of information that can be generated by the multiple lines of enquiry, ensuring that nothing is lost.

As clever as the system is, though, to get it running well you need people who are skilled and use their minds. It relies on detectives thinking like detectives to get to the next line of enquiry – otherwise, like a drought-stricken pond, the ideas dry up and the cascade of clues abruptly ceases.

Consequently, as Sarah and I continued our work at Gablecross, our priority was to assemble a team for the enquiry who would be ready for action first thing the following day. We needed a specific HOLMES team – inputters and analysts – plus an exhibits officer to deal with any physical evidence, a disclosure officer and much more; not to mention a crack team of detectives who would be going out on the ground to search for Sian or at least those critical clues that might lead to her safe recovery.

While Sarah set about mobilising the troops, I made a few calls of my own. Though my deputy was soon appointed – a detective inspector called John Eldridge, whom I liked immensely and who confirmed he was able to attend the next day – perhaps my most important appeal for help went to Deborah Peach, a civilian employee of the force who was the PA of my boss and who also assisted me.

Debs had been employed by Wiltshire Police for nearly two decades. When I'd joined the force, I'd swiftly come to realise that she was the one who knew and observed everything. She was an incredibly efficient woman who played her role with a completely straight bat. Surrounded by senior officers and working in a tough environment, she didn't suffer fools; and despite having a good sense of humour she was, at times, the harshest critic. One of her greatest assets was her ability to be blunt with me. Somewhat inevitably, in the heat of an enquiry, I would be so focused on the job in hand that I would forget to eat, sleep or drink – I'd developed a painful habit of getting kidney stones after major crime enquiries as a result – but Debs knew me well enough to make me have breakfast straight after the morning briefing, knowing that would carry me through the whole day. At the time we were colleagues, but she has since become a friend.

I wanted her to join the team as a scribe: an assistant who would follow my every move and attend every meeting to record the hypotheses, decisions and formal policy at every stage of the enquiry. Every major crime investigation has a policy book – an official record of the actions of the police team and in particular the SIO's decision-making – and I needed a scribe to maintain it. Debs was always my first choice when she was available; we'd worked on six or seven enquiries together at that point and she was very, very good. The scribe is almost an aide-memoire to the SIO in some ways and there was no one I trusted more to help me than Deborah Peach.

To my relief, over the next few hours she made herself available and was able to attend the nick the following morning. I would need her by my side throughout the day – and beyond, if necessary, though we both hoped there would be no call for that.

I worked long into the night, commissioning an intel cell (intelligence team) to join the MIR the next day and making a brief first contact with Sian's boyfriend Kevin by telephone to emphasise to him that, wherever Sian was, we *would* find her. After that, I waited fruitlessly for updates from the teams who were out there, right now, searching for Sian in the Savernake Forest and Old Town.

As I worked, I was always conscious of the young woman we were seeking. My fear was that Sian was injured somewhere, probably in the forest, and that there was, therefore, a race against time for us to discover her, using all the means available to us. The one advantage was the mild weather: if she was lying out on the ground incapacitated somewhere that was in our favour. I wanted to find Sian and find her alive, quickly, so I could return her safely to her family. Nothing else mattered.

I never forgot, on any of the enquiries that I worked on, that the people at the heart of those investigations were individuals: someone's daughter, someone's son. That was always foremost in my mind. Looking again at Sian's picture, at that bright smile of that bubbly girl, I made a promise to her.

I would do whatever it took to bring her home.

7

Sunday, 20 March 2011

A regular sleep pattern is the first thing to be abandoned
when you're leading a major crime enquiry. I got back
to Bratton shortly before 02.00 and went through the
motions of going to bed, but my mind was still on over-
drive, turning over the evidence and trying to calculate
the consequences of the police action taken so far. Where
was Sian? Where would the next lead come from? Had
I missed anything that might prove critical?

I was pleased, at least, that Yvonne and the girls were
staying at her parents'; I never liked to disturb my wife
when I was working late, and even though I found sleep
hard to come by, at least I was resting in my own bed. I
knew it was important to try to snatch at least a few
hours' kip, otherwise my ability to keep alert would
diminish, and Sian needed me to be on top of my game.

I was dozing fitfully, therefore, when the Nokia trilled
on my nightstand at 04.00. I'd drummed into the guys
at the briefing how significant the pace of this enquiry
was. The moment there was any news, no matter what
it was, I wanted to be informed immediately.

It was the team who'd been tasked with timing the
drive from Swindon Old Town to Savernake Forest. Their
best estimate was that it could take no less than

25 minutes to complete the journey. That meant that, if Sian had been abducted with her phone, whatever had occurred had happened in the eight minutes between her leaving the nightclub at 02.52 and the Swindon Town Hall clock chiming three. By then, she would have had to be on her way to the forest. It dramatically narrowed the window of time, which was a very good start.

By 06.30, I was already on my way back to Gablecross. I knew the guys I'd summoned yesterday were going to start coming in around half-seven and I needed to be there for them. Nothing filled my brain but the search for Sian. It was just the way it was when you picked up a case – you wrote off everything else for the foreseeable future. Assuming Sian didn't return safely today, that would go for my day job too. Everything got binned: being an SIO was a 24/7 commitment.

As I drove, I used the time to process my thoughts. It's not a bad way to do it, to take some quiet time just to work through everything I knew about the case. At that stage, we really knew very little: today was all about getting cracking properly on the job, trying to work out precisely where Sian was and bringing the full pressure of the police force to bear.

Every job is different. Sometimes you go in and get an early lead and the whole thing's tied up by lunch-time. Others, however, drag on, with no end point in sight. Only time would tell what would happen in Sian's case.

I still stuck by the three hypotheses I'd generated the night before. If pressed, my gut feeling was that it was an abduction: for me, the most likely scenario had to be that there was a concerning reason why she had not made contact with her family. I didn't like the implications of the telephony, either.

As an experienced SIO, I knew what the statistics said. The academic research on the subject indicates a depressing average of just six hours from abduction to murder. If a person was abducted and abandoned alive, the average person would be expected to survive for 72 hours without food or water. Yet statistics only tell you so much, and you can't use them as a rule: you don't want the exception to be the victim in your case, the one you failed to act on behalf of because you lazily assumed the worst. You have to work on the hope that the victim is alive – because, if you don't, she will inevitably die as a consequence of your failure to act.

So I refused to think in terms of worst-case scenarios. Instead, as I steered the Spider into a parking spot and strode into the nick, I felt only hope and a familiar focus. When I got the bit between my teeth on a job, with a good team around me and an operation running like clockwork, I knew we could cover an enormous amount of ground. We had a lot to achieve today and I felt a professional eagerness to get started.

I took the elevator from the back yard of the nick: a small steel box whose doors opened onto the third-floor corridor where the MIR was situated. As I stepped out onto the thin, bluey-grey industrial carpet, into the glare of the overhead strip lighting, I could already hear the low buzz of noise which meant a major crime enquiry was underway.

The whole of the top floor of Gablecross nick was given over to major incident room facilities. Such was the scale of this enquiry that we had staked a claim to two MIR rooms, as we had more people involved than could fit in one standard facility. And further rooms sprang off the corridor, which ran the full length of the building, all essential to our mission: a dedicated exhibits store lined with shelving to home any captured physical evidence; quarters for the intel cell; a conference room for mass briefings and press conferences; and an individual SIO's office for me.

I headed straight for the primary MIR, keen to see what Sarah and her team had achieved overnight. She was already there, together with DS Neil Southcott, a heavyset bloke who was a fixture on the major crime team: the two of them would be running the rooms as there were too many things going on simultaneously for just one person to control. I could instantly see the fruits of their labours: on the four whiteboards that lined the walls they'd already entered the key lines of enquiry and the salient information of the case. Sian's picture was pinned there too, smiling down on us all as we worked.

I murmured greetings as I moved through the room, pleased to see that the 20-odd computer terminals I had ordered for the HOLMES account were already in place. I slapped the back of our techie mastermind in gratitude as he sat tapping away at a terminal.

'Tiny,' I said in acknowledgement.

'Alright, boss,' he replied.

Tiny Rowland – obviously, as his name suggests – was a colossally huge bloke; and the friendliest guy you'll ever meet. He essentially owned the HOLMES set-up for the force and took a lot of justified pride in his work. He was a really dedicated guy – always the first one in and the last one out – and true to form he'd got everything up and running in fast time.

Assured the MIR was running slickly, my next port of call was the intel cell. If HOLMES is the brains of the operation, the intel cell is the heart. It's often from their work that you'll get your new lines of enquiry pumping out: to say, for example, 'This has popped up in the background of a person of interest and needs further investigation.' Their priority that morning was victimology: we needed to know exactly who Sian was and what had been happening in her life in the run-up to her disappearance. They'd be accessing her financial information, phone records, looking at her past and current partners and her personal life. It sounds intrusive, and I suppose in some ways it is, but everything we did was in Sian's best interests. If her case turned out to be a homicide, I knew most murderers were known to their victims. We needed to know if there was a jealous ex lurking about, or if Sian owed money to some dodgy dealers. She'd been described to us only in glowing terms, which is how most missing people are described, but we needed to dig down into that. Did she have a reason for running away? Did someone have a motive for hurting her?

'Morning, Steve.'

'Good morning, Jess.'

DI Jessica Ridgeway was running the intel cell. She was diminutive, with glasses and a brutally short haircut. She was very good at her job, a creative individual with unstoppable initiative, which is what you needed in a good intel officer. A forthright woman, she could very much hold her own and I found her an extremely useful person to have around on major crime enquiries.

Victimology wasn't the only thing Jess's team would be diminutive on. Following Brian's call last night, I briefed Jess to spend some time first knockings looking into Swindon's cabbies. At this stage it was one of the few positive things I could get the team working on: it gave us a definable cohort of roughly 60 people who were relatively easy to process and, potentially, eliminate. It was basic stuff to secure a list of drivers from each of the local firms and then the team could methodically run those names through the intelligence systems on the PNC (Police National Computer). If someone popped up with a proclivity for sexual offences, then we could go and find out where they were at 02.52 on Saturday 19 March.

In a similar vein, Jess's team would be scouring recent prison releases on the MAPPA system (Multi-Agency Public Protection Arrangements), which holds details for anyone who has come to attention for committing serious crime. If someone had recently got out of jail who had previous for this kind of thing, I wanted to know about it. The enquiry in some ways was a blank sheet at the moment: we were looking for that lead that would give us a take-off point – and hopefully take us to Sian.

Jess's team also covered telephony. I knew she would be prioritising the call list on Sian's mobile. Did a particular number keep coming up that couldn't be attributed to known friends and family? Who was the last person she had spoken to? Experience told me that you could get some very useful early leads from the simplest of investigative tools.

Just by dint of walking through the intel cell and the MIR, those sergeants and inspectors who were responsible for running the rooms and sub-departments gravitated towards me. A small group of us decided to grab a coffee in the canteen and have an informal briefing around 07.30. A formal briefing for all officers was scheduled for 09.00, but this informal chat would enable my investigative leads and me to get a head start.

We congregated in the canteen on the second floor of the nick, a huge open-plan room beneath harsh fluorescent lights. The canteen staff dished up cooked breakfasts and packaged sandwiches from a serving counter, and chocolate vending machines lined the pale walls, but I had no appetite. I simply grabbed a cappuccino from the self-service machine. I blew on the bit of froth that half-heartedly decorated the hot beverage, clasping my hands around the cardboard cup as the guys and I drew up chairs around a table.

Jess was with me, as well as Neil Southcott and some others. Debs had arrived too, clutching her favoured black tea. She was petite, with dark, shoulder-length wavy hair. True to form, straight away she got out her daybook to make notes.

And there were immediate updates to process. One of them came from the helicopter crew who had spent the night flying over Savernake Forest with heat-seeking equipment. Unexpectedly, as the chopper had soared noisily over the treetops, scanning the ground below for signs of life, the team had had a breakthrough.

A pair of live bodies had been picked up by the heat signature of the helicopter.

The only question was: was one of them Sian?

8

A team had already been dispatched to trace the couple. Sadly, we hadn't located Sian, but some friends of hers who – having heard that the last known trace on her mobile had come from Savernake Forest – had decided to camp out there and start a search for her first thing. News of the popular young woman's disappearance was already spreading on social media and her friends had been trying to help.

I also now learned that DS Rupert Brooks had visited Sian's boyfriend, Kevin Reape, at their shared home. Kevin was a 25-year-old, university-educated quantity surveyor. Like Sian, he was born and bred in Swindon. The couple had been together two-and-a-half years and had only recently moved into their current home, in January; Rupert had noted there were still a few unpacked boxes about the place.

Kevin had last seen Sian at 08.20 on the Friday morning – or so he said – when she'd dropped him off in her little blue Peugeot 106 on her way to work. He had spent the day at Cheltenham Races with friends, but he and Sian had been in telephone contact during the day. After a sit-down curry in Cheltenham, he'd caught the 22.00 train back to Swindon and eventually retired to bed. He had an alibi – but only until 23.30.

I didn't really know Rupert, a divisional DS, so even though he seemed a chap of substance, I requested that my own people do some kind of verification on Kevin: eliminating Sian's boyfriend was crucial to the enquiry. I directed that Simon Smith, an experienced detective, should be fed into Kevin as a family liaison officer (FLO) to make his own assessment, as well as to offer Kevin support. Although the cloud of suspicion had to fall on Sian's partner in these early stages, I knew only too well that he could also be a completely innocent boyfriend in fear for his girlfriend's life, and we had a duty to support him through those straightened circumstances. I added that I wanted to meet him myself later that same day.

Kevin had supplied a description of what Sian had been wearing on Friday night: a grey dress, dark bolero-style jacket and distinctive heeled boots. She had also carried a distinctive handbag: black with a big beige flower. These details were immediately circulated to the crew.

The traffic team now provided an update too. Following the timing test of the drive that they'd communicated to me at 04.00, they'd spent time looking at the possible routes from the Old Town to Savernake Forest that an abductor might have taken. Because the period of time between Sian's last sighting and the ping on the Cadley mast was so brief, they'd theorised that the driver must have taken a pretty direct route.

And here, finally, we got a piece of luck. The most direct route between the two locations passed by an ANPR camera.

ANPR (Automated Number Plate Recognition) records car number plates by taking a picture of the index plate as vehicles pass. When the licence-plate data captured by ANPR is linked to the PNC, it will instantly give you the registered owner of that vehicle.

The fact that the most direct route to the forest could possibly give us a suspect's name acted like an adrenaline shot to the enquiry. Abandoning coffees and teas in the canteen, we raced back up to the MIR. I quickly set the team to look for all vehicles that the ANPR camera had recorded driving in the direction of Marlborough from 02.52, and set another parameter to search for vehicles re-entering Swindon from that direction from 03.24 to 10.00. This was to try to capture all vehicles that could conceivably have taken Sian to that location and needed to return.

PNC is a slick machine. The action was completed quickly and within minutes we had a cohort of 14 vehicles – with 14 registered owners attached, together with their known addresses.

They were located all over the show. Some were locals, but others came from a considerable distance away, including a couple of long-distance haulage drivers. Wherever they lived, each of the 14 now became a TIE subject in Sian's case. TIE means to Trace, Implicate or Eliminate and this was set as a priority action. We needed to trace all the individuals passing that camera at those specific times and prove their alibis – or otherwise. What was their professed reason for passing that point at that anti-social hour? And, when my team met them, did the detectives believe whatever alibi was offered – or did they think it was a lie?

It's often said that the best detectives, given another set of circumstances, would have made the best criminals. Part of the job involved getting into that mindset and recreating the circumstances of the offence – or, in this case, of that lonely, late-night drive through an unlit forest – to try to work out the truth, or otherwise, of what we were told.

The necessity for the large team I had commissioned was immediately apparent. Imagine being one bloke on your own trying to eliminate 14 individuals who were located all over the country; it would take days. Luckily, we were able to investigate the TIE subjects simultaneously. We couldn't forget that this was a race against time. Sian needed us to work through this lead as quickly as we could.

I looked again at the 14 names on the list. They'd been in the area at the relevant time. They'd driven the most likely route we thought Sian would have taken. Why do you take a late-night drive through a forest at 3 a.m.? Work, insomnia, late-night revelry … or, just possibly, for something much, much darker.

I reviewed the names again, paying close attention. For I knew that, in all probability, whatever had happened to Sian had been directly affected by one of these 14.

We just had to work out who.

9

At 08.58 I strode along the carpeted corridor on my way to the conference room for the first proper briefing in Sian's case. The rumble of animated conversation was audible even before I entered the room. On a major enquiry you call everyone in, so the first briefing always has the atmosphere of a welcome reunion.

This room was also where we held media briefings, so it was furnished by the paraphernalia involved in such things. A free-standing blue backdrop featuring the Wiltshire Police logo hung about behind me like a spare part as I surveyed the team before me. I was gratified to note the scale of the turnout: some 50 officers, all of whom had binned whatever Sunday plans they'd held in order to come to work instead. The dedication was humbling. There was a real mixed bag of my profession: the detectives in their suits, the surveillance guys and FLOs in scruff order, the traffic team in their hi-vis jackets and slashed-peak caps, and the more traditionally uniformed contingent too. There was a detectable frisson in the air – of interest and anticipation. They were all coming in fresh to do the job they'd actually joined the force for. However, keen as they were, I realised that these officers needed me to give them an investigative plan.

The room fell suddenly silent and I began.

'The time is 09.00, Sunday 20 March. This is the first briefing of Operation Mayan,' I said. The major crime team had generated the operation name, working sequentially through the alphabet. 'Thank you all for coming. We're here today because we're looking for a missing woman: Sian O'Callaghan. Here is what we know so far.'

As I briefly ran through the evidence gathered to date and my three hypotheses, everyone listened intently: some nodding, a handful of eager types taking notes. We had one shot to find this girl and everybody's efforts had to be fixed on that same end.

Briefings are not just a one-way road, however: they were equally a chance for me to hear what the guys had discovered on the ground. As the search teams updated us on what was happening in the Savernake Forest, it turned out that the camping couple had been but the first snowflake in an avalanche of activity: first tens and now hundreds of people were gathering there to search for Sian. Already, the media were taking a strong interest in the mysterious disappearance of this pretty young woman and it seemed the press reports and increasing social-media messages about the case were striking a chord with the ordinary people of Swindon.

I considered my options. Ordinarily, I wouldn't want members of the public anywhere near a crime scene – if you can call an area with a 6.7-mile radius a crime scene – as the potential for contaminating evidence is just too great. However, given the urgency of the search for Sian, was it better to try to cover that vast area with a mere handful of trained officers or to make use of a willing public who wanted to help?

It was a controversial decision, but to my mind an obvious one. When you're racing against time to try to find someone who could still be alive but is incapacitated, you're never going to turn away such significant assistance. In the kidnap manual, too, the priority is to save the victim's life above all else, including evidential recovery. It was a simple bit of common sense that Sian's life was far more important than any future prosecution for how she'd ended up wherever she was. If she could be saved – if she was lying in a ditch somewhere in the forest, her life leaking away even as we spoke – then she needed to be found as swiftly as possible and I'd be a fool to turn away the public.

Consequently, we did what we could to methodically shepherd their enthusiasm. I ordered the deployment of a POD – a Police Observation Device, which simply means a police-marked trailer to provide a high-profile presence to the public – to be sited in one of the main car parks in Savernake Forest, so we could coordinate the searchers. We also used the same flyers employed the night before in Old Town to inform the volunteers in their hunt for the missing girl.

Speaking of Old Town, the briefing now moved swiftly on to discussing leads there. We still couldn't discount the possibility that only Sian's mobile had gone in the direction of the Cadley mast and that she may have remained in Swindon. As such, CCTV was a major line of enquiry. I now spoke directly to the team responsible for trapping the footage from all those businesses along the High Street who maintained cameras.

'I want you to find every premises that runs its own CCTV,' I told them. 'Knock on every door. Ring every bell. I know it's Sunday; I know a lot of these places are closed. But you need to get the key-holders out of bed this morning and we need access to that footage today. Never forget: this is a race against time. What is a mere 24 hours to them could mean life or death for Sian. So don't tell me that they'll try to pick it up on Monday when the office reopens – that is not good enough. You need to make sure they give you the tape today and if that means disturbing the bank manager himself, that's what I want done. Understood?'

There were nods of agreement from everyone concerned.

The CCTV from Suju gave us further lines of enquiry. Sian's friends had last remembered seeing her with a woman in a khaki-green jacket. By now we had viewed the nightclub's footage and printed grainy black-and-white stills of the female in question, which were already pinned to the whiteboards in the MIR. This unidentified blonde was the last known person to have been seen with Sian and as such she was an urgent TIE subject, sitting alongside the ANPR 14. It turned out, from the footage, that she had chatted with Sian not only in the toilets, but also in the smoking area in the backyard. Sian's friends remembered her trying to persuade Sian to dance; they said the woman was a lesbian and that her behaviour had been overbearing.

Sian, however, didn't appear to have been bothered by it. All the footage from that night showed her happy, having a grand old time. It was further proof of the naturally sunny disposition of the woman at the heart of this enquiry; and perhaps a further puzzle piece that raised the question: why would anybody want to harm her?

Detectives were set the job of tracking down the mystery blonde, as well as the other clubbers who'd been in Suju that night. We'd received a report that someone had been arrested at the club in possession of an electronic knuckle duster with a 'stun gun' element; an officer was duly assigned the task of interviewing the individual in case they and their weapon had been involved. Similarly, a uniformed officer spoke up to inform us that one of the people who'd been at the club had made a Facebook posting early on the Saturday morning that he was feeling suicidal. An unconnected incident – or an expression of regret from a guilty man? A detective was despatched to his home address to find out.

There was masses of information coming in, thick and fast. Undoubtedly some of these leads would prove red herrings, but nonetheless each had to be given attention. It's how these enquiries work: you have to seize on what little you know and try to make the most of it. You have to meet these people who are cropping up, make a judgment and do it simultaneously and as quickly as possible. You can't arrest them all: if you did, you'd still be doing the job months later and you'd have lost the opportunity to collar the real offender. Instead, you sift through the information, sorting the wheat from the chaff.

My attention was suddenly drawn by a community beat officer with a prominent nose, who'd been on duty on Friday night. I nodded at him to go ahead.

He'd seen something disturbing, he reported. In the early hours of Saturday morning, two black males had been apprehended while trying to entice girls to join them in their van. I nodded slowly, already knowing from the CCTV footage what he was going to say next.

'We have a witness, sir, who says she saw Sian talking to a black man inside the club.'

10

Were the two incidents connected? Were those black men the same people Sian had been seen talking to? We could only find out by investigating further. The black males were identified as TIE subjects and we made it an action to find the van too.

By now, it was coming up to 09.45 and I wanted to draw the meeting to a close. Morning briefings, in my opinion, should be rapid and focused: get the team clear on what we're trying to achieve and get them out the door quick-sharp. You don't want to get snow-bagged with information, otherwise you could end up with a three-hour meeting and no one gets out to work until midday.

Before I dismissed the crew, though, I wanted to say a few brief words. It wasn't so much a pep talk, because you never needed to engender enthusiasm on these kinds of occasions. These were professional police officers and a girl's life was at stake: of course they were chomping at the bit. What I wanted to do was impress upon them how important their work was and to give each and every one of them the confidence to speak up. 'This is a team effort,' I told them earnestly. 'I want us to put rank and hierarchy aside. You might be a beat officer in some remote location – but you've got just as much of a voice as I have as SIO. And, actually, if you're holding the information that could break the case, you are *more* valuable than I am. We need everybody's ideas on this. If someone – anyone – has some information they want to share with me, at any time, come and find me, or call me. Don't hesitate or delay for a single second.

'Because I can't stress enough to you all the urgency of this enquiry. Let me say it one more time: this isn't a reactive murder investigation, which I know some of you have worked on before. We haven't got a body in a ditch here: a dead person who is beyond any kind of physical rescue. All these lines of enquiry we're following, which are great – the black men, and the blonde woman, and the suicidal clubber and the 14 people from the ANPR – these are all great leads. But this is not about finding a perpetrator. It's much harder than that. This is about finding Sian O'Callaghan. We're trying to locate and bring home somebody who I think has been abducted. It's a crime in action because – make no mistake – Sian's life is at risk. If we don't move quickly, it may be forfeit. And the responsibility for that falls on our shoulders.

'Let's reconvene at 20.00 hours.'

As the officers clattered out, each heading off on their individual assignments, Debs and I went into the SIO's office to start the official policy book. The office was a small, impersonal room with a long desk and maybe six chairs; it was up to each SIO how they wanted to configure it. I rarely spent any time in it, but it was a useful facility for those odd occasions when you needed to pick somebody's brain or wanted a quiet five minutes to update the policy book.

Debs and I quickly fell into our usual routine. I would dictate and she'd write in the entry in her much-neater-than-mine longhand script. It wasn't long before the formal record was up to date.

My next priority was to speak with the family, and I had a first phone call with Sian's mother, Elaine, in which

I introduced myself and assured her that all possible efforts were being committed to finding Sian.

As a father, I couldn't help but empathise with her. On every case, I always think in terms of the victims – and not only the person we might be looking for, but those friends and family trapped in the uncertainty of their absence. This case was no different. Though I hoped very much we might find Sian today, if we didn't, a face-to-face meeting with the family would be scheduled for the following day. I wanted them to meet me, to know who exactly was looking for their daughter and to show them the level of commitment they would get from me – for as long as it took to bring Sian home.

As the SIO, I knew that my primary role in this enquiry was to devise, prioritise and set the lines of enquiry that the team would follow. However, I was by nature a copper who liked to get out and about. So much of policing is instinctive, and it was my belief that you got stale if you spent too much time stuck behind a desk in the nick. Mid-morning, Debs and I took a trip out to the Old Town. I wanted to see for myself the location of Sian's last known whereabouts.

It was only a ten-minute drive. I was soon stood by the Dammas Lane short-stay car park, opposite Suju itself. Already, evidence of the young woman's disappearance was everywhere: the posters we'd printed the night before were stuck up all around; you couldn't miss them. If there was a witness to what had happened, such high-profile activity would hopefully encourage them to come forward.

The black-beamed period building which housed Suju was sited next to the Co-op, the club's incongruously modern metal front steps bordered by a public telephone and a postbox. Sian's route home would have taken her left out of the nightclub, so that's the way I went too, passing Domino's Pizza and Wilson's butchers. For a moment, I paused just past Charlotte Mews, for here a stone arch curved overhead, giving access to a grassy thoroughfare that ultimately led to the expanse of Lawns Park. It was entirely possible that Sian – separated from her phone – could have been taken that way, and officers were visibly involved in line searches of the area. I acknowledged their endeavours, then walked on.

The High Street in Swindon is a typical English shopping boulevard. There was nothing out of the ordinary about it on that Sunday morning, but nevertheless I observed each building and each secluded alleyway with extraordinary attention, only wishing walls could talk. I was attempting to retrace Sian's steps – but, really, I had no idea if she had even made it this far. Had she walked past the Old Bell hotel, its pink-and-cream frontage friendly and familiar, its huge gold bell silent and still? Had she noted her reflection in the window of Lloyds Bank on the corner of the High Street and Steeple View, or traversed the front of the ivy-covered Goddard Arms? Until the CCTV came through, to my frustration, I simply did not know.

I glanced at my watch. It was an Omega Constellation, a beautiful piece with a gold automatic movement that Yvonne and I had bought in Singapore when we first got married. It brought me no pleasure on that particular morning though – it only reminded me, with every turn of its tiny cogs, that Sian's life could be ebbing away with every second that passed.

The field trip was over. It was time to get back to the nick.

11

'Good afternoon, Kevin. I'm Detective Superintendent Fulcher.'

Just as I had requested that morning, a meeting with Kevin Reape had been arranged. My colleague Simon Smith had spent the morning with him, but this was an interview I wanted to conduct myself. It wasn't about not trusting Simon's judgment: for me it was vitally important to know first-hand that the loved ones we were dealing with were genuinely concerned. This job can make you cynical, because in so many instances where people come to harm, it is the nearest and dearest who are to blame.

Consequently, I wanted to look Kevin in the eye myself and know for my own peace of mind that those instinctive alarm bells inside every copper didn't jingle one iota. It's a skill more than a science: a matter of judgment. On the basis of very little, I wanted to assess whether he was someone who should be treated with suspicion, or whether we could bring him into the fold. If he was innocent of any hand in Sian's disappearance, then he himself was a victim in terms of having lost a loved one and should be afforded all the care that any victim of crime deserves.

We met in an office at Gablecross at 12.45. Kevin had volunteered to come in, and had willingly surrendered his mobile phone and the key to his house. We'd already reviewed the telephony and knew that his phone had pinged off the nearest mast to his house throughout the relevant times.

But that, of course, didn't prove anything except that his phone had been at home. Kevin himself could have been anywhere.

He was sitting down when I first walked in and stood up to shake my hand. He was a very tall man, about six foot four, and skinny as a rake. With fair hair cropped close to his head, he had a noticeably pale complexion and appeared to be extremely nervous.

As a highly trained police interviewer, I was familiar with the most up-to-date research on advanced interview techniques. A lot has been written on body language and non-verbal communication: how tics and covering your mouth can be a sign of leakage, for example – clues a suspect may be withholding information or outright lying. I personally believe there is a lot in it, and that such tics are worth noting when they are exhibited, as the subject is clearly reacting to the tension of the interview.

However, I also believe that you can't rely on such non-verbal evidence exclusively because it is not definitive. After all, good-quality criminals will be able to disguise such behaviour, while innocent people trapped in the headlights of a major crime investigation may understandably exhibit it. If you were the boyfriend in a missing-person case being spoken to by a detective, and you knew from watching TV crime shows that you were probably the favourite, how would you react? So I took Kevin's pale complexion with a pinch of salt, and the same went for his anxious manner.

There were four of us in the room: myself, Kevin, Simon and Debs. Debs made notes, as she did at every meeting, but the interview was not recorded. That wasn't appropriate to this interaction as it wasn't a formal interview – Kevin was simply helping us with our enquiries. Nevertheless, I recall it being quite intense, almost like a suspect interview. It was imperative that we bottomed this out.

My mentor when it came to interviews had been an old-school detective called Howard Bostock. You learn by watching other people and Howard, in my view, was the best of the best. He was an archetypical jowly detective who carried a lot of weight around his waist, a joker of a man who wore fake tweed jackets and mismatched ties. But, terrible though his dress sense was, get him in a room with a suspect and he was pure dynamite. He was exceptional at forming a rapport with the most heinous individuals and drawing them out. Back in those days, officers were judged in terms of getting a cough, an admission, and Howard must have been one of the most skilled detectives at that particular part of policing; arguably, the most difficult part.

It was from Howard that I'd learnt a lot of my techniques around drawing out suspects through apparent empathy; a method honed by one particular job I'd had many years ago doing prisoner processing, in which, in the course of a day's duty, I would conduct six or seven interviews a day with different suspects. By the time I met with Kevin Reape, I'd interviewed thousands of people over the years.

Of course, the more interviews you do, the better you get at them because you learn from your experience. Many senior officers hadn't got in a room with a suspect in years, but for me it remained a critical part of the job. I liked to keep my copper's instinct razor-sharp.

Partly because of that practised empathetic approach that I learned from Howard, the meeting with Kevin – despite its intensity – was run along the lines of a fluid conversation rather than an interrogation. I knew only too well that if you went in hard and oppressive, suspects clammed up and gave you nothing. Far better to keep it natural, open, flowing. The technique was engineered to allow Kevin to expose his personality and his inner thoughts. I was trying to get him to reveal who he was, how his relationship with Sian worked and what he really thought of her, all while exploring the more obvious things, such as: 'Where were you on Friday night?' Such a line of questioning might lead us off in a tangential direction that would put Kevin more at ease, but it was always about trying to gauge who he was and what propensity he might have for doing some harm to Sian.

The primary objective of this meeting, however, was to pin him down to accounts that we could then either prove or disprove. If, subsequently, it turned out he had lied on any topic, then that would give us grounds for suspicion. We would be testing his alibi; we would be finding people who knew them as a couple in order to verify what he'd told me about their relationship. His phone, Facebook account and computer would all undergo a thorough check too.

Throughout our time together – and the meeting lasted a good hour – Kevin came across as completely genuine. He answered everything I asked him very fully and gave me every impression that he was eager to help. I could see that he was clearly in a very loving relationship with Sian and devastated by her disappearance. The telephony alone showed how close they were: despite being on separate nights out, they had messaged and called each other while apart. I formed the view that, as far as he was concerned, she was his lifetime partner; a likely future wife. He seemed a genuinely nice guy – a really decent person, in fact – who had been caught up in a nightmare.

When I asked if he and the family might be prepared to appear at a press conference to appeal for help in the hunt for Sian, he readily agreed. Both of us hoped such an appeal would not be necessary, that she would make it home well before such an event could be arranged, but preparations were nonetheless made for a televised appeal the following day, in case that proved not to be the case.

As I left the meeting, struck by Kevin's evident heartache and desperate concern, I felt a renewed passion to find this girl, as quickly as we could.

12

I came out of the interview with Kevin buzzing with a new idea. At 13.50, I ordered Jess's intel team to do a cell-site comparison of the known movements of Sian's phone, cross-referencing the data with any other numbers that could be shown to have hit the same cell sites during the time period 02.52 to 03.24 on Saturday morning. Hopefully, the passive data would show us all those individuals who had followed an identical route to the missing girl.

I wanted to stay in the MIR room all afternoon, processing the leads and clues as they came in from the teams on the ground – but management had other ideas. At 14.10, I was called to a meeting set up by my boss, Nigel, and chaired by Assistant Chief Constable Pat Geenty.

I found management meetings interminable. I don't know whether Wiltshire Police was a particularly bad example, but it seemed to me that if the bosses could have you in a meeting for your entire standard eight-hour day of duty, they would. Perhaps that was because *their* stock in trade was meetings; they weren't operational in any fashion or form.

There are a lot of people who have got to quite senior positions without ever conducting a major crime enquiry, strange as that may appear. That was just one reason why I didn't want to join their club. I had always been driven by the need to catch criminals. To my mind, the most senior echelons in policing today weren't police officers at all, they were merely puppets blowing with the prevailing political wind. The saying goes that there are lies, damn lies and police statistics, and in our modern-day performance-measurement mindset you could do quite well for yourself if you played the game.

I was most definitely not a game-player. I did myself no favours actually. Early on in my career, I even remember going against the grain when a bloke I thought was innocent had been charged on the basis of my investigation. The charging decision itself had been taken way above my head – this was back in my days of being a uniformed bobby, and actually the police aren't always involved in such deliberations – and this poor chap had ended up in the magistrates' court despite, to my mind, giving a perfectly reasonable explanation in our interview that I believed was genuine. I can't remember what the offence was now; it must have been something relatively minor – although not minor to this bloke, of course. Anyway, I remember going to court to speak up for him, to say, 'This guy is innocent, he shouldn't be here.' He thanked me afterwards: 'It's rare to find an honest copper.' But that gives you some indication that I wasn't one to tick the boxes some managers had in mind.

As such, it would be fair to say that Pat Geenty and I sometimes had what you might call a robust exchange of views. But, to his credit, he encouraged his team to have frank discussions with him. Some people might have considered a forthright expression of a contrary view insubordinate – because he was superior to me in rank – but he didn't. I liked that about him a lot, I always thought it was very healthy, and despite my unspoken grumbles about the politics at the top, the two of us had always got on well.

He was already sat at the head of the table as I entered the room for this unwanted tête-à-tête with a group of senior officers. Pat was a tall, stocky man, very jowly in the face with extremely thin dark hair; he hadn't yet gone bald but only had about one-in-five follicles occupied. He quickly got down to business.

It turned out that the reason my boss had convened the meeting was because Sian's case had started to attract national media attention: he wanted to be sure that we were delivering a proportionate and effective policing response given the high profile of the enquiry. For management, reputation is always critical, especially pondering the answer to the question: 'What will the public think?' That is important, of course, but to my mind it wasn't *as* important as finding Sian O'Callaghan – and I'd much rather have been *doing* the investigation than sitting around talking about it.

The press were already drawing parallels between Sian's case and the Joanna Yeates murder, which had occurred in Bristol just three months before. You may remember the case because it had blanket coverage over Christmas that year. Joanna, a beautiful 25-year-old land-scape architect, had disappeared on 17 December 2010 after a night out with colleagues. The subsequent search for her was one of the largest investigations in the Avon and Somerset Constabulary's history; tragically, she was found dead on Christmas Day. The case attracted wide-spread coverage, some of it critical of the police operation, and tensions between the media and police escalated to the point that ITV News was officially banned from formal press briefings. Under immense pressure to find the perpetrator, the police arrested Christopher Jefferies, Yeates's landlord, on 30 December 2010 on suspicion of her murder. Although he proved to be entirely innocent of any involvement, the media didn't wait for that truth to emerge but condemned him in a series of high-profile defamatory articles. Such was the censure of the media against him that two newspapers were later found to be in contempt of court as their negative publicity of Jefferies was so slanderous that, had he been charged, it would have affected his right to a fair trial.

The real killer, Vincent Tabak, was arrested on 20 January 2011 and was currently awaiting trial in the autumn. Now, on 20 March, it was only 16 days since Jefferies had been released from bail and cleared of being a suspect. The case was still very fresh in people's minds and it seemed that Sian's disappearance had captured the public's attention in a similar way.

That was already becoming evident both in the press and on social media. The campers this morning had been alerted by Facebook posts from friends of Sian's family and these messages were reaching a wide audience; 40,000 entries were ultimately monitored on these pages. The police's own media services department had decided to establish an official Wiltshire Police Facebook page and those posts were even more prominent – the stats later showed they were viewed 533,943 times in a fortnight. On the media side, more than 289,000 articles about the case would be captured online in the first fortnight.

It was pretty sobering to appreciate the level of interest, which was apparent even on this first full day of the enquiry, and I realised I had a really tough job ahead. Trying to conduct a crime-in-action enquiry was hard enough at the best of times, but to do so in live-time scrutiny under the full glare of the national media does add pressure, to say the least. Given the proximity of the Yeates case, too, where relations between press and police had become so strained, I didn't doubt that journalists would be hot on the trail of this case as well, ready to scent out another police failure with which to castigate coppers, given the debacle of the high-profile erroneous arrest of Jefferies. It was my job to ensure that it wasn't a failure.

But, I was now told, perhaps it wouldn't be my job after all. I had picked up the case on weekend call and my managers wanted to review my position, with a view to replacing me from tomorrow with another detective stepping in as SIO. I thought it was a nonsensical idea given what we were trying to achieve for Sian and, to be frank, I thought it was all politics.

Wiltshire Police had recently decided to merge their own crime investigation capacity with that in Avon and Somerset to create a Major Crime Investigation Team (MCIT), also called 'Brunel'. It would be comprised of one team in Wilts and four in A&S, so essentially the major crime team of my force was being subsumed into another's. The plan was that all future investigations would be dealt with by this new dedicated team, and SIOs appointed from a cadre of SIOs within that body. Therefore, to my frustration and dismay, there was some discussion about pulling me out and transferring responsibility to an SIO from Brunel, which was, as far as I could see, solely a bureaucratic and money-saving measure. It made my blood boil.

As calmly as I could, I outlined the reasons why I thought I should stay in post, trying to fight for the role. Frankly, I was surprised, given the parallels to the Yeates case, that they were even suggesting it. The problems in that enquiry were partly caused by the fact that – because it occurred over the holiday season – they had five SIOs in five days. Imagine going into an enquiry and having to pick up all those threads of investigation that were inevitably being pursued. By the time you'd been fully briefed, it would be the end of your day shift: thanks very much, I'm off now and someone else will be in tomorrow. It was ridiculous. As I've said before, the first 96 hours of any enquiry are crucial: you have to grip these things and work like stink, otherwise there is no point to anything you're doing. And those 96 hours shouldn't include a three-hour handover – or a management meeting, for that matter. This was a crime in action: every second counted. And here was the suggestion that this was a good time to swap the SIO. My mind just boggled.

Our forthright discussion concluded with a resolution of sorts. As it was Sunday, I was allowed to remain in post to work the weekend – very good of them, that – but it was decided my position would be reviewed the following day. My heart sinking, I had no choice but to concur. Yet I could tell that this might well prove to be an ongoing battle: a political distraction that both Sian and I could ill afford.

The meeting concluded at 15.00 and I immediately returned to duty in the MIR, trying to put the frustration of the SIO discussion behind me in order to focus fully on the job. My responsibility was to find Sian and I was determined to block the political situation from my mind and think only of what was truly important: Sian O'Callaghan.

Back in the MIR, my deputy, John, had been doing sterling work in my absence. John was a bald bloke with thick-edged, black-framed specs and a goatee beard. He was a fantastic deputy: whatever I asked for, he made happen.

It had been a busy afternoon. Updates were coming in thick and fast. I wondered if we knew any more yet about the guys forcing women into the back of their van late at night – from an abduction case point of view, that was clearly a critical lead – but the officers tasked with tracing those men had not yet returned to the nick. Of the updates we did have, the most important to my mind was that the CCTV team had successfully captured the footage from the High Street. Their painstaking enquiries had resulted in tapes being forthcoming from The Bell, the Baker Street pub, Barclays Bank, HSBC, Godwin Court and the Goddard Arms. There had been CCTV from Domino's Pizza, too, but regrettably this extended only to the foyer and would be of no assistance in our search for Sian.

While it was good news that the tapes had been secured, I knew it was only the start of a time-consuming task. Now the footage was back at the nick, the team had to sit and view the films. With such high volumes of CCTV being captured, I appreciated that it was going to take many hours for them to look through it all before any sightings of Sian – if they existed – would be found.

I could only hope that, when the breakthrough came, it wouldn't come too late.

13

'The time is 20.00, Sunday 20 March. This is the second briefing of Operation Mayan.'

As I opened the evening briefing, I couldn't help but clock that the guys before me seemed somewhat downbeat – and I didn't blame them. Coming up to 48 hours since Sian had vanished, we still had very little to go on. You always hope there will be an instant take-off – that the last number she dialled will lead you to the offender; that an evil relative or stalker is found lurking in the background with obvious motive and intent – but in this case there was nothing solid by which we could progress the investigation. We stood on sinking sands, trying not to get sucked into the mire of misleading lines of enquiry.

We began by running through the results of the day's activities. There were no leads from the crew looking at victimology. Sian had no dark secrets, no skeletons in her closet: she was just an ordinary person, who had apparently been swifted off the streets. If anything, the victimology only went to show how desperately unfortunate she had been. Kevin had told us that, lately, he and Sian had rarely been going out as they were saving for a planned holiday to New York; Friday had been a treat, a little splashing out after weeks of abstinence. Then there was that short walk home: only 15 minutes at most, along a relatively busy, well-lit road.

There were updates on the 14 people who had been picked up by the ANPR camera. Rupert had been in charge of that line of enquiry and outlined the results so far. Five of the vehicles were HGVs registered outside the county; the remainder were local. Of those drivers they had spoken to so far, all had been eliminated. While that was good, in a way, as it narrowed the group, it still failed to provide us with a lead to pursue. Investigation into the remaining TIE subjects would continue throughout the evening.

With every update, there were only further dead ends. I now learned that the men in the van had been eliminated: this wasn't a *Silence of the Lambs* scenario after all, with a woman fooled into entering a van late at night. Also eliminated was the suicidal clubber, and the blonde woman with whom Sian had last been seen. Officers had successfully traced her, but not only was she not involved, she had no further intel to offer. You never know what witnesses might say, and there had been a distant hope that perhaps Sian had told her where she planned to go after leaving the club, but there was no lead to follow from the interview conducted.

There wasn't much more we could be doing in the Old Town. Notwithstanding the team's efforts so far, we discussed CCTV capture again and I asked that my colleagues extend their search yet further; viewing of the footage captured thus far had begun but I wanted to ensure every scrap of video evidence was secured. I also directed that new flyers containing Sian's picture should once again be circulated to taxi drivers in the area that coming night. That action was mostly about keeping the profile of the enquiry as high as possible in people's minds, but in all honesty it was a bit of hit and hope.

Thanks to the media attention, however, it seemed we didn't need to do much to maintain people's interest in the case. There were reports from the press department that journalists were already knocking on doors, essentially conducting their own investigation into Sian's disappearance simultaneously with ours, so I asked that the team took this information on board when conducting their enquiries. I hoped that the press conference we had scheduled for tomorrow afternoon would help to feed the media beast and limit any journalistic activity that might hinder the investigation. I'd worked on one high-profile child-murder case in the past where the press were literally racing us to the body – it was completely chaotic and unprofessional stuff – and I wanted nothing of the sort for this enquiry.

The briefing continued – the evening meetings, in contrast to the morning, tended to be longer, an hour at least. Next, the crew in charge of telephony gave an update that, so far, they were unable to deliver the cross-referencing data I'd requested earlier that afternoon. I bit my tongue, frustrated. Debs always describes me as the most impatient person she's ever met, which I deny (then again, I don't know who she's met). I wanted that answer *now*. Yet it was hard to reiterate the sense of urgency without undermining people's efforts. Nonetheless, I knew my ability to motivate the team had to take precedence, so I tried to keep my gob shut while asking them nicely to keep trying.

There wasn't much yet from the team looking into taxi drivers, either. A booking had been noted with one firm at 03.38 – a perhaps unusual time to call a taxi – which was a pick-up from Marlborough, a town within the vicinity of our 6.7-mile search area, but this had already checked out.

Staying with the Savernake Forest, the search teams filled us in on their endeavours. Here too there was very little indeed. If this was to be my final briefing on the case, it was something of an underwhelming one. A black phone had now been found in the forest by the teams doing a line search, but it was a Nokia and Sian was believed to own a smartphone.

It was another frustration. I can't tell you how impotent you feel, how helpless, when you can't find a take-off point in these cases. We had all these lines of enquiry set, lots of people doing really good work, but there was nothing to grip on to. The atmosphere in the room was appreciably dour and sombre, the morning's keen energy slowly dissipating after a day's hard work with nothing concrete to show for it, notwithstanding the many eliminations we had managed to achieve.

Then the officer in charge of the forest search spoke once more.

'One other thing, sir,' he said.

A pair of ripped knickers had been found on the forest floor.

14

Were they Sian's? There was only one way to find out. I directed that the underwear be sent immediately for fast-track forensication.

It was an intriguing lead but, in all honesty, not one I got terribly excited about. The fact of the matter was, if you're searching a forest floor of that size, you're quite likely to find any number of such items. If you comb any wasteland, you will find that kind of thing. Nonetheless, I wanted the forensics done pronto. As with any of our lines of enquiry, this could be the one that was the breakthrough. With nothing else to go on, it was our best hope yet.

I called the briefing to a close at 21.12. Some officers went home, back to children long ago put to bed by partners, or to empty homes embittered by divorce. I was not among them; there was still so much to do. Debs and I retired to the SIO's office again to make a note of all the policy decisions that had come out of the briefing. I also spent time with Jess and the intel cell, as well as Neil and Sarah in the MIR, wanting to ensure that they were coping with the volumes of information and intelligence coming through. The high-profile nature of the enquiry meant that the public were providing leads, just as you would wish, but they were doing so in large numbers.

When I first started out in policing, pre-social media, you would perhaps get anything up to 100 letters from the public regarding a major enquiry – including ones saying, 'I'm a clairvoyant, don't think I'm mad, but have you thought of looking for the lost girl here?' It was a point of pride that I always responded to them and followed them up; because you could guarantee, if you didn't, that that little nugget would be picked up later and a guv'nor would say, 'Well, why on earth didn't you respond?'

But we weren't talking about a hundred letters here: we were talking hundreds of thousands of posts and tweets and emails. I wanted to be sure they could manage the processing task required to sift through it all. However, the team appeared to be working wonders.

Eventually, I determined that there was nothing more useful I could do at the nick that night and left, very reluctantly. After all, wherever Sian was, she didn't get to call it a night. Although I was heading home to snatch some rest, however, the police efforts continued on her behalf. The actions to interview the TIE subjects, the staffing of the POD in Savernake Forest and the search efforts were maintained throughout the night.

I used the time on my drive home to think. What could I do to change the equation from where we were right now? What else could I be getting people to do? Management had mooted my removal from post, but I felt strongly that this would be a hindrance to the case's progression. However, with no breakthrough in the enquiry so far, I didn't have much hard evidence to persuade them otherwise; except, I suppose, for my own track record. Yet I consistently pushed the management directive to the back of my mind: it was irrelevant, because, until they told me otherwise, I was responsible for finding this woman and nothing else mattered.

The most important skill of an SIO is to calculate alternative consequences. As I drove, I tried to assess every line of enquiry and decipher, from the mass of information, which direction we should prioritise. I continually asked myself the question, *Am I doing everything that can be done?* Because, if I missed something that it was later proved might have saved Sian's life, and I hadn't done it, I would never be able to forgive myself.

The time hung heavy as I drove the grey Spider through the country lanes on the way back to Bratton, the absent girl always in my thoughts. Forty-eight hours on, I still had no real idea what had happened to Sian. I didn't have a direction to pursue: all I had was a phone signal in Savernake Forest and a woman who was missing. How on earth could I outwit whoever it was who might be holding her if I didn't have a clue who they were, nor where she had been taken? At this stage, I conceded to myself, I still didn't even know if this *was* an abduction. This was not the position I'd wanted to be in, returning home tonight.

Yvonne's car was visible as I parked up on the steep hill in the village and traversed the few feet to the front door. I eased my key into the lock gently and inched the door open as quietly as I could, not wanting to disturb my family – but one member of the crew was nonetheless there to greet me.

'Evening, Pippa.'

The wire fox terrier brushed against my legs affectionately, wobbling about a bit having woken from a recent doze. Bless her little heart, she was always around on enquiries and would always come to greet me, no matter what time I came in. She had a snowy-white curly coat with brindly bits and a long snout that she liked to push into my palm, demanding attention. I thought she was a very handsome dog. She was lovely, too, with a friendly temperament, and also a bit of a character. Though most of the time she was very calm, every now and again she'd randomly do something totally inappropriate. Like many of us, I suppose.

I always found it a refreshing escape from police work to take the dog out for a walk. Now, as I wound down from the intense day at work, I led her out into the garden for a brief roam around, then settled her back in her basket. All around the ground floor of the house was evidence of my family life: snapshots on the mantelpiece and after-school commitments scribbled on the kitchen calendar. My girls were both very messy, as befitted their age, and prone to abandoning things all over the house. The detritus of their teenage lives – magazines and school books and bags – was splayed around haphazardly. I shook my head, but indulgently, far too in love with them both to much care.

As Pippa's gentle snores began to echo around the kitchen, I decided it was time for me to turn in too. One of the great benefits of this house was that we had five bedrooms, so at times like this I'd kip in a spare room, rather than wake Yvonne. One of the rooms had a couple of brown leather sofas in it and I decided I'd bed down there for a few hours' kip.

After brushing my teeth, I crept along the landing. I couldn't help but notice that my daughters' doors were closed, the bedrooms behind them quiet and still. There was a sense of peace about the place: of things being just as they should be. The girls had school the following day so I didn't look in on them, not wanting them to stir.

Yet the reassurance I felt personally in them being exactly where they belonged served only to remind me: there was another young woman who wasn't safe in her bed.

It was my responsibility to find her.

15

Monday, 21 March 2011

As I swung the Spider off the A420 at 06.30, into the grounds of Gablecross, I couldn't believe my eyes. Opposite the entrance to the nick was a mass gathering of the media. They were all banked up: a haphazard collection of press and TV vans, their satellite dishes sprouting like tumours on their sides. There were also a handful of journalists hanging around, preparing for their breakfast-news reports – the very first of the regular updates that would run throughout the day. This was quite literally blow-by-blow coverage, turning the public into armchair detectives as they too tried to figure out what had happened to Sian.

I clocked them, but I paid them no mind. I'd had a restless night, my fitful sleep broken regularly by calls from the team, largely focused on the pursuit of the ANPR 14. I'd told them I wanted to know the moment another name was cleared or otherwise, not to leave it to the morning. I'd heard back from the guys who'd gone to Newcastle, and a few others besides. Each call had contained an elimination rather than an implication, but it was still progress: another line closed off, which meant we could move on to the next one.

Despite the lack of sleep, I didn't feel at all tired. Rather, I felt I was in the grip of a continual adrenaline rush, fuelled partly by the impetus of wanting to get into the MIR and get going with a new day's work.

Nor was I the only one. As I walked into the major incident room, the HOLMES guys were already in situ at their terminals – perhaps some had never left. The inputters and analysts tended to get in very early, knowing that they had to get the latest intel onto the system in order for it to be turned into actions for the guys on the ground. I greeted them gratefully; then my deputy John, my investigative leads and I had a quick, informal catch-up. Having been kept updated overnight, there was nothing major to report.

What was more significant, for me personally at least, was bumping into my boss, Nigel. Though he reiterated yesterday's management message, that in all probability I would very shortly be replaced as SIO by someone from Brunel, I received a stay of execution: I would remain in place until further notice. It was a relief – despite the guillotine still hovering above my head – but I couldn't allow myself to become distracted by its gleaming blade. No date was given for when the swap of SIO might occur, so for the time being I considered myself fully in charge.

Nigel also informed me that an internal Gold Group was being established to oversee the enquiry. The purpose of this was to provide support to and governance of the investigation – another layer of middle management, but with a specific responsibility for this particular enquiry. In short, the Gold Group had two functions: to ensure the appropriate allocation of resources and to oversee my work as SIO; in addition, they would govern the media strategy because of their concern with force reputation. That was fine by me: they could worry about that, and I would worry about Sian.

As I'd mulled over the possible leads on my drive in, I'd given more credence to the ripped knickers that had been found the day before. Many if not most abductions have a sexual motive and I arrived at the nick with a renewed interest in that particular line of enquiry. Therefore, as soon as Nigel and I parted ways, I headed straight to forensics, wanting to discuss with Genevieve Fryer, the head of CSI (Crime Scene Investigation), the fast-tracking of the underwear that I'd prioritised the night before.

Forensics was based on the ground floor of Gablecross. In contrast to the shiny, scientific lab you might be imagining, in fact it was more like a big open-plan office, which housed only limited equipment: drying cabinets, UV lights, high-tech cameras and so on. Back in the day, forensic science used to be a fully funded government department but then – as with so many other things – the service was sold off to private companies, so these days most lab work was outsourced; at a tidy cost, of course. Though Genevieve and her team were still responsible for crime scene investigation, the lab work they themselves did was very low-level stuff.

Genevieve was in her fifties: a blonde, intelligent woman who wore spectacles. To my disappointment, there wasn't much more she could tell me about the knickers, other than that they'd been sent off to the external laboratory as I'd requested. To my mind, 'fast-tracked' was something of a misnomer: even with an item prioritised for forensication, it took days rather than hours for the results to come through. I had to keep the enquiry moving faster than that, and could only hope that the results would back up the direction I had pursued while we waited. As we had no discernible crime scene at this time, all I could ask Genevieve to do was to prepare for that eventuality.

At 09.06, the now 60-strong crew gathered in the conference room on the top floor for the morning briefing.

As we began, I sensed a rerun of the atmosphere of the evening before. I was personally frustrated that the telephony team were still unable to give me a suspect cohort from the data analysis I'd asked them to do. I understood that the cell dumps from the masts would be many thousands of numbers long, but we had computers that I assumed would be able to sift through that data to find the one or two mobiles that correlated. I believe I gave them quite a hard time about it, actually, but there was a motive behind my demanding approach. After all, it was no good having this data when Sian had been gone a week.

'This is not an academic exercise!' I expostulated. 'This is somebody's life! If she is bound and gagged some-where, in somebody's cellar or in the boot of a car, hoping and praying that the cavalry are coming, well, *we are the cavalry*. Either we get it right – or she dies.'

I was equally frustrated that our search area around the Cadley mast was so incredibly huge. With the search radius being roughly 6.7 miles, that meant the total area we needed to cover was 141 square miles. Thinking of all we knew of the lifespan of people who were inca-pacitated and had no access to water – 72 hours and no more – this would clearly not be covered by officers in any time period that I thought might save Sian, as by such a calculation she had only 18 hours left to live. Therefore, we desperately needed to try, if at all possible, to narrow the search parameters.

I was told there was a company who might be able to help. The private firm Forensic Telecommunication Services (FTS) had form in this field. They could go out physically on the ground with a device that pinged to the mast and attempted to put the likely location of Sian's phone into a triangular vector, which could potentially cut off anything up to 90 per cent of the radius. Although even 10 per cent of such a massive swathe of the countryside would still be a challenge to search, it would obviously focus the rescue effort in a way that might just make the difference. I directed that FTS should be sent to Savernake Forest as a matter of priority.

Running alongside our search for Sian herself was the search for a possible perpetrator. Update after update, the news had come back that first this person and then another had been eliminated. I was bitterly disappointed by our progress on this front – particularly with regards the ANPR 14. When, yesterday morning, we'd identified the most likely route from Old Town to Savernake Forest and then had the lucky break of the ANPR camera being on it, I'd been convinced that one of the drivers must be the person who could lead us to Sian. Update after update, I'd had to swallow down the news I might be wrong.

'Update for you on another of the ANPR TIE subjects, boss,' an officer said.

'Yes?' I asked wearily, not holding out much hope.

'This is the male driver of a red Skoda. He entered Swindon at 02.10 and left in the direction of the Savernake Forest at 03.01. We've done an initial interview. His reason for entering Swindon at that time was because he was bored. He said he'd decided to go shopping, at two in the morning – for some prawn cocktail crisps.'

Prawn cocktail crisps . . .? It was such an improbable answer, I think there might even have been a shocked, nervous titter of laughter that rippled through the room.

But I wasn't laughing. I was deadly serious.

'We're not happy with this bloke, guv'nor,' the interview team told me frankly.

And when my team wasn't happy, neither was I.

There was more. When they told me where he lived, you could have heard a pin drop in the briefing. His home was located in the heart of the Savernake Forest – in the exact location where scores of officers were even now scouring the land in search of Sian.

Was it possible that this guy was our man – and that he was, at this very moment, holding Sian O'Callaghan hostage?

16

Everyone instinctively realised that this could be the breakthrough we'd been waiting for. A frisson of excitement ran through the detectives gathered in the room.

'Right, we need to do more work on this bloke,' I said briskly. I scanned the 60 officers before me, my eye landing on Bill Dutton, one of my most trusted colleagues. He'd come from the national crime squad a few years earlier and was a Tier-5-trained interviewer: the highest qualification in that field. He had a certain George Clooney look about him that certain people found attractive; I'd never seen the appeal myself. What I did like about him was his sense of humour: he was a good conversationalist; and a very good detective. This was our best lead yet and I wanted to put my best man on the job. After all, the importance of this next interview could not be overestimated: the Skoda driver could be the person who'd snatched Sian on Friday night. I directed him to re-interview the driver ASAP that morning.

'Oh, and Bill?' I added. 'Seize the car.'

The briefing concluded at 09.38 and for the first time in a long time I had a spring in my step as I walked away. My officers shared my buoyancy: we had a firm lead now and everybody felt up as a result. It was still too early to put all our eggs in one basket, so work continued on all our many lines of enquiry, but given what the initial interview team had said – and the weak excuse the driver had offered – there was a certain smell about this that had us all feeling we were at last headed in the right direction.

After a management meeting that focused on the press conference to be held later that day, Debs insisted I ate some breakfast in the canteen, though the constant flow of people and phone calls meant it largely went cold before I could consume it. But for Debs's ministrations, I was living solely on coffee and cigarettes. If you'd asked my wife, she'd have told you I was desperately trying to kick my smoking habit, but, I must confess, during major crime enquiries my good intentions rather went out the window. The days went by so quickly that it was difficult to manage the basics, like eating, so the idea of giving up fags was utterly redundant; I would have gone mad. Instead, I took refuge in the habit, huddling outside the nick in the back yard with the other renegades, clutching my blue Rizla papers and loose tobacco to roll my own salvation.

In fact, I found smoking as an SIO a useful professional exercise. It was during my occasional fag breaks that a lot of good info was exchanged. Despite my pep talks in the briefings, I think the guys found it easier in some ways talking to 'Steve the fellow smoker' than to the SIO. Perhaps that was where I first heard the news of what was happening in the Savernake Forest.

Yesterday, I'd been impressed that hundreds of people had turned out to search for Sian. Today – and bear in mind it was a Monday – I started getting reports that the general public had outdone themselves. The day before had been an ad-hoc effort on behalf of local residents: today, they'd got organised and the search had taken on a life of its own. I now learned that coachloads of people were turning up to help with the rescue effort.

I assumed they were perhaps organised by community groups or church groups: coach after coach was rolling up in the car park in the forest and then armies of Swindon locals were pouring out on a mission to find Sian. It astonished me. This wasn't just immediate friends or family, who had an understandable, vested interest in seeing Sian come home safe. These were complete strangers. One estimate put the numbers at an extraordinary 10,000 people, all now being briefed and organised by the search teams.

I had never come across anything like it. I didn't know much about Swindon, but I guess I'd always thought of it as an anonymous commuter town that must be devoid of community spirit. Well, how wrong was I? Here were huge numbers of people, literally an entire community, coming together to do one thing: *find Sian*. I don't say it lightly when I say that such a thing restores your faith in humanity. And it shored up the hope in my heart, too. Surely, with such a fantastic response, we would soon get a break and find this girl who so many people wanted to come home.

The energy shooting through the team was palpable. And, mid-morning, we caught another wave when a second strong lead was identified. John, Jess and I convened to discuss it in my office as Jess had a somewhat sensitive development to bring to our attention. I had previously set the intel cell working on the cabbies of the town and a person of interest had now emerged from this cohort. One of the drivers, it turned out, had previous convictions for sexual touching. Could *he* be our man, rather than the Skoda driver? I told Jess I wanted to know chapter and verse on this character in quick-time, and I wanted to know what his movements were on the relevant night.

The fact that two such strong leads – the Skoda driver and the cabbie – had come in one on top of the other was often what happened in an enquiry. My job was to re-appraise everything constantly to ensure I didn't take the enquiry in the wrong direction and go haring off after a potential suspect who turned out to be a completely innocent bloke. I awaited the results of the further interviews with interest. In the meantime, at 11.03, I had what I considered to be one of my most important meetings of the day.

In one of the nick's formal conference rooms, I introduced myself to the family of Sian O'Callaghan. They had come in en masse: Sian's mother and father, Elaine and Mick; and her siblings, Lora and Liam, who were close in age to Sian. There was a family resemblance to the girl we were seeking; Elaine, like her daughter, was an attractive, dark-haired woman. Kevin Reape was with them, too, and I shook hands with him warmly as we all sat down around the table. Joining us were ACC Pat Geenty, who had been appointed commander of the Gold Group overseeing the enquiry, and Donna Andrews, the junior press officer assigned to the case.

The O'Callaghans struck me as calm and composed given these situations are always difficult for the family. Not only were they distressed about Sian, but they had been catapulted into a world they knew nothing about and were having to put their faith in others to find their precious daughter. The intense news coverage was an added pressure. It was a horrible position for them to be in anyway, but this was not a trauma happening in private but in the full glare of publicity, with Sian's disappearance front-page news.

I felt nothing but empathy for them. I suppose, in a way, the empathetic approach that I brought to suspect interviews informed my interaction with victims' families too. Though I would obviously deliver the same professional commitment on any enquiry, whether it was an old man or a young girl who had gone missing, as a father of daughters I was able to identify particularly with the concern they were feeling. It was my personal opinion that such empathy enriched my work and made me a better copper. It wasn't just a job. These were people's lives.

Given my appreciation of the position in which they found themselves, I was as thorough and transparent as I could be as I explained the progress we had made so far and the specifics of the work we were doing. The O'Callaghans understandably wanted to know how seriously we were taking Sian's case and asked how many officers were involved. In fact, since the morning's briefing the team had grown again, with more officers drafted in from neighbouring forces, so I was able to inform them that 140 colleagues were now involved in the search for Sian.

It was apparent the family had discussed what they wanted to ask me beforehand and come prepared. Sian's brother was by nature a dynamic individual and he took the lead on behalf of the family; he had a list of questions scribbled in a notepad. However, by the time I had briefed them fully, understanding their need for any information I could share, they commented, 'We had a whole list of questions, but you've answered them all. Thank you.'

'This is your enquiry,' I told the family earnestly. 'In these kinds of things, we work for you.'

I meant it. I worked for the police *service* – and, to me, the service of the public was the most important aspect of the job.

Donna then explained how the televised appeal would work; it was scheduled for 15.00. Bravely, Sian's family had agreed to read a statement. I think Elaine was nervous about doing so, so Kevin stepped up – to my mind doing the prospective son-in-law bit – and volunteered to make the appeal himself. Given his emotional condition, I thought that was a very noble thing to do.

Before I took my leave, I made them a promise: 'I won't rest until we find Sian.'

I was true to my word. As soon as I'd exited the meeting, Neil Southcott grabbed me in the MIR. There was an urgent message for me to go straight to the ground floor of the nick, where officers were viewing the High Street CCTV.

Heads swivelled as I entered at pace.

'Alright, boss,' an operative said in greeting. 'We thought you might be interested in this.'

It was the understatement of the century.

The CCTV footage they had found was about to blow the case wide open.

17

In a shoebox-sized room, on a small TV screen, I watched the grainy black-and-white image of a woman walking down the High Street, Old Town. She weaved slightly, zigzagging her way across the pavement. Her left hand absentmindedly adjusted a large black handbag with a big beige flower, cementing it more firmly on her shoulder as she walked towards home in the early hours of the night: the digital onscreen clock showed 02.56. She walked swiftly and relatively surely, her distinctive boots striking the pavement inaudibly on the silent camera reel.

We were watching Sian O'Callaghan, strolling down the High Street minutes after she had left the club.

She was on the eastern side of the street; she must have crossed the road once she came out of Suju, though there was no footage of it. She was walking away from the camera: we saw her rear view. She was alone.

I watched closely, my heart pounding. Sian had obviously navigated the main road safely: no accident there, as we might have feared. She had headed north – towards home. I *had* been retracing her footsteps yesterday, when I'd passed the pizza parlour and the butchers and the curving stone arch by Charlotte Mews. Sian had made it all the way to the Goddard Arms pub, some 125 metres from Suju, which was where we saw her walking now, and from where the footage had come.

What had happened next?

The tape continued to roll, numbers spinning sequentially on the clock in the corner. She was safe and well for another second, one more, and another second after that ...

Sian O'Callaghan had almost reached the very edge of the camera's viewpoint when a bright white light abruptly flickered on the screen. Car headlights. They glimmered briefly before they suddenly shone so vividly that they eclipsed Sian herself. I caught only a final glimpse of those boots as she walked straight into the headlights, before she finally vanished from view.

In her place, instead, the lights blazed, dazzling the camera. They completely obscured Sian from sight – and the vehicle, too, was anonymous behind the blinding glare of its headlights. The car was parked close to the kerb. Its hazards flashed a warning. The footage ran for one minute and four seconds before the car moved off, travelling in the direction of Suju.

By the time it pulled away, there was no sign of Sian.

'Play it again,' I said.

The officer pressed rewind and played the scene again. Once more I watched as Sian walked towards the car and was hidden by its lights. At various points I asked for it to be stopped as we looked hard at the image, trying to discern what make of car it was or what was going on behind the lights, but it wasn't clear what was happening. No matter how many times we played it back – and I asked for it to be played again and again – the glare from the headlights masked any further details.

By now, all ten operatives from the CCTV team were gathered round the screen, each of us squinting and angling our heads this way and that as we tried to decipher the undecipherable. These guys were the unsung heroes: they'd spent hours in this tiny, windowless room reviewing the footage, a pretty dull and thankless task, but it was thanks to them that we had this sighting of Sian. For the past two days we'd been trying to find out: what happened to Sian after she left the club? Now, we had an answer.

I phoned John to come and look at it, and he, Debs and I watched Sian's weaving walk countless times over. There was mass interest from the whole team, because this was the thing we'd been looking for. Before, we really hadn't known what we were dealing with. She could have fallen in a ditch; she could have gone off with someone she met in Domino's: this was the first clear indication of what had happened. And although we couldn't see much of anything at all once she walked into those headlights, it was the firmest lead we'd had so far. I felt a certain professional positivity that I had called this right in designating a category-A enquiry. Commercial CCTV often overwrites on a rolling monthly basis – if we hadn't got on top of this right away, the footage might well have been lost.

That said, there were still many unanswered questions. Did Sian get into the vehicle, or did she walk beyond it? She had been so close to the edge of the camera's viewpoint when the headlights appeared that it was entirely possible that during the one minute and four seconds the lights obscured the screen she had continued her walk uninterrupted. *Was* this where Sian had disappeared? Or did someone else accost her beyond the car with its headlights on?

No matter the answer, the driver of the car was at the very least a key witness and we needed to identify him or her urgently. I called the traffic guys in: all of us were desperately trying to identify the make of the vehicle and I needed their expertise on this. By this time there was a bunch of us in the shoebox-sized room, all crammed in together, a PC's finger constantly on rewind and play-back and several pairs of eyes straining to see what we just couldn't see.

There was more footage of the car driving up the High Street and this too was played and replayed. Eventually, we determined it was a dark-toned estate vehicle with chrome roof rails, but the make and model were beyond our capability to identify. Nevertheless, we all started guessing as to what car we thought it could be. There were enough conflicting views for me to realise that I would need to send the CCTV footage to an expert to see if they could give me a definitive make for the car.

'What's that, boss?' one of the guys suddenly asked.

As one, we all leaned in towards the screen. The PC paused the video. The grainy still showed a side profile of the car as it moved up the High Street towards Suju.

In fact, it wasn't anything so good as a side profile of the car itself: it was a reflection of it, caught in the pris-tine windows of the Lloyds Bank beside the Goddard Arms.

'There,' the copper said, his finger hovering over a smudge on the reflection.

We all squinted. There was something visible on the side of the vehicle, a blur that seemed a different colour to the rest of the car. Was it just a quirk in the way the light was playing? It was only a reflection, after all; the vehicle itself appeared as a ghostly presence, and it was hard to see exactly what it was.

Discussion continued, seesawing between viewpoints, until we landed lightly on one side.

We thought it was a taxi decal.

This raised more questions. On the one hand, there was Brian Moore's early suggestion that we should consider cabbies as potential perps. On the other, there was every possibility that Sian might voluntarily have got into a cab.

It was peculiar, though. The location where the car had been waiting on the street was not a taxi rank – that was further along. If Sian had wanted a cab, wouldn't she have gone there? And, if she was headed home, why bother with a taxi? It was such a short distance. In addition, the car had moved off in the direction from which she had come. It was possible that it might have been a friend driving, or that the cabbie had said, 'Jump in, I just need to spin round.' But it seemed unlikely.

In my view, that taxi – if it was one – wasn't taking Sian O'Callaghan home.

The footage resulted in a maelstrom of activity. In terms of eliminating lines of enquiry, we could now stand down the search teams working south of Suju and in Lawns Park because Sian evidently hadn't gone that way; interest in the other clubbers Sian had been seen talking to on her night out also diminished, though the team was so dedicated that, ultimately, I believe we did find everyone in Suju that night and take a witness statement from them.

The critical CCTV footage itself span out more actions. Identifying the vehicle was a priority: we sent the footage straight away to TRL (Transport Research Laboratory) over in Wokingham. They held a database of every model and make of car and would be able to give a definitive ID by comparing the CCTV images to their own photographs of cars in identical positions. They promised to work through the night and estimated a result by morning. I wanted teams working on any possible witness sightings of the estate vehicle, too, now that we knew the key time of 02.56.

Finally, I tasked the CCTV team with perhaps the most important job of all: sourcing and viewing the CCTV beyond this footage from the Goddard Arms. After all, if Sian had walked on beyond that car, this sighting was entirely irrelevant.

But, if she hadn't, it was my belief that we had just witnessed her abduction.

18

Given the hot developments in the case, it was agonising to tear myself away from those grainy images on the screen in order to attend the press conference at 15.00. But doing so was part and parcel of the enquiry and, in some ways, despite the maddening timing, I saw it as an investigative tool rather than a bind.

When I stepped into the conference room on the top floor, it was like a scene out of a movie. Every one of the chairs was filled by journalists and the camera flashes started immediately, as blinding as the headlights on the CCTV I'd just been viewing.

Regrettable though it may be, there is often an under-current of antagonism between the police and the media, centred on a lack of trust. At that moment in time, in the wake of the Joanna Yeates case, relations were particularly strained. I had no doubt that there was an element of the media who were looking out for another chance to kick the police.

That said, speaking personally, as an SIO I always took the line that I wasn't going to alienate the media. I'd always given them common decency and the time of day. My view was that I was a public servant who worked on behalf of the public and that – as we as a police force inform the public via the media – our rela-tionship with the press should not be about trying to disguise cock-ups or keeping people in the dark, but simply serving the public effectively. As such, my dealings with the press on major enquiries had always been positive. In Sian's case, I was hoping to engender witness sightings and the media briefing could only help in this regard.

I noted a few familiar faces in the press pack before me; I had always had a good, professional relationship with the local BBC and ITV journalists – such as Steve Brodie and Rob Murphy, who were the chief crime correspondents for those outlets respectively – as well as with many others, like the staff of the *Swindon Advertiser*, who were always very active.

Given my years in the job, I'd previously spoken at many press conferences and I'd completed the usual SIO media training. So I wasn't fazed as I sat down behind the desk in the room, the blue backdrop neatly in place, taking a seat beside the senior officer who was coordinating the event. Sian's family were also in attendance.

I spoke only briefly, delivering the press lines formally approved by the Gold Group. Essentially I gave detail of my knowledge of Sian's last movements, including her text exchanges with Kevin. The explosive CCTV we had just found was also released, so people could see it for themselves. I knew I needed the media's help now to find out what had happened after that crucial moment. I'd also directed that an additional Police Observation Device be sited 24/7 in the Old Town opposite Suju, hoping that this would aid in the search for witnesses to whatever had happened outside the Goddard Arms.

I needed help from the press and public alike – for one very good reason. Because even if my gut was right, and the footage showed the moment Sian was kidnapped, we still didn't know the answer to the most important question of all, the one that had driven this investigation from the very start: *Where is Sian now?*

What I needed in the wake of this press conference was for someone to come forward – to say they'd seen her being dropped off by a taxi at such-and-such location, or to report a light being on in a remote barn that ordinarily was dark, where perhaps she was being held hostage. If in fact she had walked past those headlights and was safe and well – and somehow unaware that every man and his uncle was looking for her – hopefully this televised appeal would encourage Sian herself to come forward.

Although I was aware of the necessity of attending the press briefing, my whole brain was focused on the latest developments in the case, on what felt like a break-through. I desperately wanted to get back to viewing the CCTV again. As soon as I'd given my statement and finished taking some questions from the media, I made a sharp exit to get back to my proper job.

As I recall, I didn't stay to hear the family's statement. Later, I learned that Kevin had had to fight back tears, but he did exactly what we needed him to: he did Sian proud.

'Someone out there must have seen or known where she is and we just want them to come forward and contact the police,' he said, his bottom lip trembling, the tears visibly filling his eyes. 'We all just want to know that she's OK ... She has been missing now for over two days ... We are praying for Sian's safe return ... It's not like her to not come home or contact any of us for such a long time ... We want her home, safe and well ... It's breaking our hearts not to know where she is.'

I agreed with Kevin: *Someone must know where she is.* Even though I knew it was pointless, even though I knew, no matter how many times I rewound the tape, I couldn't see what had happened in the glare of the lights, I kept on watching and re-watching all afternoon, hoping for some clue to show itself or for inspiration to strike.

Most of all, I tried to glimpse the driver behind those headlights. *Who are you?* I wondered. *What do you know about Sian?*

19

At 20.07, the team came together for the evening briefing. Now there was a buzz about the place. At last, we had something to grip on to. Lines of enquiry are like threads in a way, dangling tantalisingly above your head, sometimes just out of reach. At times, you tug on them and find there's nothing on the end: the ultimate short straw. At others, the tension snags along the line and you take a firmer hold, determined to follow it through to wherever it may lead. That was how it felt right now: we were in a labyrinth, following multiple threads, only hoping that one of them would lead us to the monster in the middle of the maze.

We'd just passed a pretty big signpost that told us we were headed in the right direction.

There were three key people of interest that night: the taxi driver with the previous for sexual touching, the red Skoda driver, and the driver of the car on the CCTV.

Yet – with the third driver and car as yet unidentified – could we be sure it *was* three?

The cabbie with the conviction, we had discovered, did drive an estate vehicle – and some of us thought the CCTV car was a taxicab. Until we had the exact make and model from TRL, we couldn't conclusively say either way whether they were in fact the same vehicle, and the drivers one and the same. Would this prove to be like the Yorkshire Ripper enquiry? Was one individual coming in and out of the investigation, and it was up to us to connect the dots?

The Skoda, meanwhile, had been seized. I put Genevieve on notice that, if we were able to trace the car on the footage from the Goddard Arms, that too would become a 'scene' requiring forensication.

Again, though, until we knew the make and model, was it possible we already had the car? The Skoda was red, it was true, and the car in the footage looked much darker, but it was grainy, black-and-white video, and we couldn't be 100 per cent sure. I was also aware that we didn't yet definitively know that Sian *had* entered the vehicle on the CCTV. Perhaps she had walked past that car and encountered the Skoda further down the road.

As for the Skoda driver himself, Bill was still dealing with him and I didn't yet have a firm answer as to whether he wanted to eliminate or implicate the man. If he ultimately came back and concurred with the first team that he wasn't happy about him, we would put further resources into the lead. We couldn't forget that his address put him in the last known location of Sian O'Callaghan's mobile phone – large as that area was – and that the ANPR showed him following the route we thought Sian and her phone had taken. Given the driver's paltry excuse for being in Swindon at the relevant times, he was a person of significant interest.

It was evident that the ID of the CCTV car was crucial. Until we had that, we were somewhat in limbo. I directed that the intel cell step up their work on the taxi drivers of the town. They'd had so many leads to pursue, they were still in the process of collecting the names, addresses and mobile numbers of all the cabbies from their firms. I told them that I now wanted this done as soon as possible.

Despite all the positive activity, I kept coming back to the stumbling block at the root of the enquiry. For even if we identified the perpetrator, *we didn't have Sian*. This was a crime in action: above all else, we were working to bring about her safe recovery. I asked the telephony team hopefully if FTS had had any luck narrowing down the search area in Savernake Forest, but as yet there was no news. Despite the 10,000 volunteers and the best efforts of the search teams, we hadn't found her yet.

The briefing drew to a close at 20.50. I ended by asking the team to be careful when driving home; given the hours we were all working, I didn't want anyone to end up hurt. The crew dispersed in a distinctly positive mood, much more upbeat than the previous evening; a feeling which I mostly shared.

After the briefing, John and I caught up with one another, then Debs and I completed the policy book and looked through our notes to identify any outstanding actions, which Debs was particularly good at spotting. By the time we'd finished, late that night, the nick was still surprisingly busy. It was actually one of the things I loved best about policing: the camaraderie of those long nights in the nick, when the light at the end of the tunnel seemed somewhat distant in the dead of night, and it was just me and this team of people working like stink. We'd either get a result or we wouldn't, but if we didn't, it wouldn't be for want of trying. It was very much a shared endeavour and everyone took pride in what we were trying to do.

As I made my way slowly through the MIR, checking on this or that line of enquiry, I made a point of speaking to those committed individuals still hard at work. I was aware that many of them had family that they would have been with, but for me dragging them onto this thing, and I always felt a personal gratitude for their endeavours. My colleagues' commitment was particularly commendable because the force was going through quite a savage reorganisation at that time, and redundancies were being made. Despite the fact that they knew they might soon lose their jobs, they worked on regardless; many without overtime pay.

I found the atmosphere that night convivial – the occasional burst of laughter punctuated the rapid tapping at the terminals. As coppers, we had to look for the humour somewhere, otherwise we'd all have been manic depressives long ago. I was pleased to note that spirits remained high, despite the late hour.

Although I urged the team to go home and grab some rest, there was a great reluctance to leave. I think people were aware that it was day three of the enquiry and we were yet to name a prime suspect. Despite everything that was being done, there were still too many lines of enquiry to follow; we hadn't narrowed things down enough to be able to say with confidence: 'This is what happened to Sian and this is our plan for finding her.' I understood their desire to work on, desperately seeking a solution; after all, I was still in the nick too. There was a genuine sense of urgency as we were now so close to the 72-hour cut-off point – though enquiries would of course continue well beyond that, as Sian had not necessarily been abandoned without water.

Down on the ground floor, the team of CCTV operatives were scanning patiently through the hours of footage, looking for Sian O'Callaghan on cameras beyond the Goddard Arms. If they found her, the 'breakthrough' from earlier would become redundant: another of the many red herrings. As such, none of the team wanted to go home, not while there was still work to be done. Like me, they wanted only to find Sian.

Nonetheless, I urged those who were not engaged in critical actions to leave. If this case was a long-runner – and we had no reason, at present, to anticipate an early finish tomorrow – then I needed them to stay focused for a good while yet. We couldn't burn out. We couldn't let Sian down in that way. Tonight, it was the TRL and FTS teams who needed to deliver, in identifying the vehicle and narrowing the search field. I felt it was better to take our rest while we could.

After a while, I tried to lead by example. I eventually headed home to Bratton, where I bedded down on the sofa again; another night without a single glimpse of Yvonne and my two girls. But when I was in the midst of a major crime enquiry, I never saw my wife and daughters – they were in bed when I got home and I'd be back at the nick before they even came to. It was just the way it was.

I was pleased I'd made the decision not to disturb Yvonne. In the early hours of the morning, the Nokia suddenly chimed its cheery tones, waking me from my doze.

It was the CCTV team, calling from the nick. They'd located footage from an old people's home further along the road from the Goddard Arms and had been reviewing it for the past several hours. Now, they told me, there was not a single trace of Sian on its cameras early on Saturday morning. She had not walked past the point of those shining headlights.

It could mean only one thing: Sian had got into that car.

20

Tuesday, 22 March 2011

The call from the CCTV team wasn't the only one I received in the early hours of Tuesday. The second came from FTS, who'd had a real breakthrough.

They'd been out on the ground in the Wiltshire countryside, using their equipment to read the vectors from the Cadley mast, trying to reduce that massive 6.7-mile radius for me. Now, they told me something extraordinary.

Sian might not be in the Savernake Forest at all.

She might never have been. What their readings told them was that the signal could have pinged from a high-ground area. That could mean a location much closer to Swindon: because of its elevated position the signal might have bounced to Cadley, rather than to a mast that was closer to the town.

I couldn't sleep after that. I got up and into the shower, using the time to think, even as the hot water refreshed me. It helped me focus.

Despite the fast pace of the enquiry, I always shaved and showered before heading back to the nick, dressed in a clean shirt and fresh suit. That's basic professionalism: I was running a big team who were looking to me to set the standard. In addition, I was hyper-aware that the media were camped outside the nick, following my every move; a shambolic-looking SIO would not do much for the 'force reputation' the Gold Group was so keen to uphold.

It was a quick shower: head in the water and work out what was what. And, as I turned beneath the spray and mentally turned over the implications of all I had learned in the past few hours, I thought I *had* worked out what was what.

That Tuesday morning, I devised a new hypothesis for what I thought had happened to Sian O'Callaghan.

At 02.52 on Saturday morning, Sian left the nightclub. She travelled on foot from there, reaching the Goddard Arms at 02.56. At this time, an estate vehicle drew up and the driver engaged Sian in conversation for one minute and four seconds, by some means persuading her to enter the vehicle. I now posited that the motive for that was likely to be sexual. Having abducted Sian for that reason, the driver took her against her will to an isolated place, possibly a local beauty spot, within the Cadley mast area.

If that was the case, I now mused, and Sian had been abducted for the purposes of committing a sexual offence, then it seemed likely to me that the offender would have driven for as short a distance as possible, due to the need to keep Sian under control while he drove. After all, if he had persuaded her to get into his car – perhaps, I theorised, under the premise that he would drive her home safe, in case something happened to her on her late-night walk – then the moment she realised he was not taking her where he'd said, he was going to have a problem on his hands. For him, therefore, the shorter the drive, the better, due to his likely need to incapacitate his victim.

I got straight back on the phone to FTS. We discussed probable locations, given I now thought the abductor would have selected the closest possible site to Sian's point of abduction.

FTS suggested Barbary Castle. The Cadley mast read all the way up there, even though the ruined fort was right on the border of Swindon.

I felt a tingling down my spine. *Yes*. It made sense. Barbary Castle was an ancient iron-age fort set on a hilltop. It covered a considerable area – about 12 acres – and had a significant valley dip in it, like a natural amphitheatre, as well as two deep ditches. It lay within the Wessex Downs and was more a country park than a castle.

I mulled it over in my mind, trying to think like the offender, trying to imagine what he might have wanted from this spot. Barbary Castle was remote – unlikely to have any witnesses. That was in its favour. Yet it was also only five miles from where the car had picked up Sian beside the Goddard Arms. Convenient: just a short drive. To reach it, you would not pass the ANPR camera we'd already identified, meaning it would allow the offender to keep off the grid.

I had been to Barbary Castle personally only once before, to my memory. From what little I knew of the location, it seemed a strong contender. The telephony fit. The proximity to Swindon fit. The isolation fit. It wasn't inconceivable that, even now, Sian was lying hidden in a ripple of the valley, in a trench or copse. The fort was rife with those hilly, hidden earthworks that are buried beneath grass, mounds that children run and play on during Sunday walks. Perhaps one of those was hiding the missing girl. Perhaps she lay at the foot of one of them, bound and gagged, just waiting for us to come and find her.

It was now Tuesday morning. If Sian had been abandoned alive and not visited to give her water in the time since she had been abducted in the early hours of Saturday, we were now approaching – if not past – the limit of her life. I ordered that a POLSA (Police Search Advisor) should scope the Barbary Castle area and devise a systemic search plan ASAP. I wanted that chopper back up in the air too.

There was a dynamism to my drive back to the nick that morning. Never had the fast pace of the enquiry seemed so relevant. I steered the Spider swiftly along the roads towards Swindon, thinking fiercely of another driver's route, of another man behind the wheel – remembering that faceless individual whose identity was shrouded by the blinding white lights. Who was he? Where had he taken Sian? *Why* had he taken Sian?

I still couldn't discount the possibility that she herself had requested the journey: if our guesswork was right, and the car was a taxi, it could still be an innocent fare. But if the driver's intentions were darker, then motive was significant. The most likely reason was sexual – but that was a broad church. Was this a one-off rape, after which he had let Sian go, or was the abduction a long-term investment on the driver's part? Was he holding her even now in some derelict building or a purpose-built prison inside his home? I didn't know. I had to find out.

First, though, I had to find him.

21

As soon as she saw me, Debs asked, 'Did you get *any* sleep last night?' Despite the shower, I must have been starting to look a little worse for wear.

'Not much,' I said. 'But I do have a plan.'

I'd come up with it on the drive to Gablecross. TRL had promised the results on the CCTV car's make and model that morning. Aside from the search efforts at Barbary Castle, our priority was to identify the driver as quickly as we could. So, as soon as we had the info from TRL, I wanted to run the details through VODS (Vehicle Online Descriptive Search) and the PNC. From there, we could start narrowing things down: coming up with a suspect list. You never knew, perhaps we'd catch a break: it might be a rare car of which there were only five in Swindon, and then it would be a simple enough matter of tracing those five individuals. But even if it was a more popular model, we would soon have a defined cohort of owners. From that point on, it was a classic detective manhunt to get out there and interview them.

Somewhere within that cohort, we would find our primary suspect.

At the nick, Bill had an update for me on the driver of the red Skoda. Bill had put him through his paces and now told me that, as ludicrous as the man's story sounded about going shopping for prawn cocktail crisps at two in the morning, it actually checked out. There was no mileage in it. As we'd already part-suspected from the colour of the car, Bill now said that from his enquiries he could definitely say it wasn't the Skoda driver on the CCTV. Given we now knew Sian had got into that vehicle, and not walked on to be accosted at another location, the Skoda driver had been eliminated and was no longer of interest to the enquiry; the taxi driver with previous, however, remained in the mix. The Skoda itself was still with the forensics team but would ultimately now be released.

I found I didn't mind, as I might have done a few hours previously, that it had proved to be another dead end. With the focus now on the CCTV footage and the person behind that wheel, I felt like a road was opening up for us.

As such, I was feeling positive as I ran through my new hypothesis with a senior officer in the SIO's room that morning, early knockings before the briefing. Until we had the TRL enhancement, all we knew was that we were looking for the driver of an estate vehicle. The officer was nodding along, concurring with my analysis of the case, when his mobile phone unexpectedly rang.

'Sorry, Steve, I've got to take this,' he said, and stepped out to answer the call.

When he returned, he was ashen-faced. He told me that Dave Ainsworth, the Deputy Chief Constable of Wiltshire Police, had just been found hanged in the garage of his home. He had taken his own life.

It was a shock. The senior officer told me that Sean Memory, another colleague, had been sent out to deal with the situation.

Suicide among police officers is frighteningly high. I could cite you at least half-a-dozen cases, just anecdotally. One of the firearms guys I knew took a gun to his head; somebody else jumped under a train; another officer murdered his partner and then blew his own head off; a woman inspector killed herself, too. That's just in the last few years; some of the stories are truly tragic. Now, Dave Ainsworth was one of them.

His death, understandably, was a topic of some hushed discussion that morning, including at my pre-briefing catch-up with Jess and some of the other department heads. 'Bit of a shellshock, that one,' we all agreed.

In some ways, though, if I properly thought about it, it really wasn't. After all, Dave had been removed from post because of allegations of sexual impropriety – his reputation lay in tatters to the point he had nothing more to lose. When I'd last seen him, a few weeks before, he was in a complete mess, unshaven and dishevelled. The whole thing had obviously been playing on his mind and affecting him psychologically. Evidently so: he'd now done this.

In the informal briefing, we didn't dwell on Dave for long – we wanted to talk about the driver of the estate vehicle. We potentially had an unhinged sex offender on the loose who had, for some unknown reason – perhaps work, perhaps a break-up, perhaps some sudden disruption from his normal routine – found himself tipped over the edge: prompted, perhaps, to act out a fantasy he had long harboured. That was the person we needed to talk about.

I don't know who it was who joined the dots. We were talking about the estate car, and one of us suggested, I think, that it looked like an Audi A4 estate.

There was a pause then, as the sure knowledge settled on our shoulders.

That was what Dave Ainsworth drove.

Earlier in the enquiry, a suicidal Facebook post from a clubber had had us investigating instantly, lest the expression of proposed self-harm was the symptom of a guilty conscience. Now we had a policeman, who was already under suspicion of sexual impropriety, who drove the exact kind of vehicle we thought had picked up Sian O'Callaghan, who had *actually* committed suicide – just as the net might be closing in.

My heart sinking, I dialled a number on my Nokia phone.

'Sean?' I said when the call connected, unable to believe I was saying the words. 'You need to seize Dave Ainsworth's car. There's a chance he may have abducted Sian O'Callaghan.'

22

You couldn't make it up. That was my overwhelming thought. This was proving to be one of those jobs where nothing went right, where nothing was easy, and the idea that the perpetrator could be one of our own seemed to fit in that black scenario.

I pondered what I knew of Dave. I knew him about as well as anybody knows a distant, senior colleague. But how well do any of us know someone, even our closest friends? There are many tales of people being hitched to killers for years and they never had the slightest inkling they were married to a murderer. If someone wants to keep a secret, it's surprisingly easy to fool the world.

I asked Jess to do some discreet but urgent intel work on Dave and his car. With a darkly comic wry smile, I realised the benefits of knowing the potential perp first-hand: we already knew his index number and his home address. I directed Jess to find out if the car had cropped up on any ANPR or CCTV, so we could try to pin down Dave's movements early on Saturday morning. This was about proximate events. We had a girl who was missing, and a man who felt so desperate about something that he'd committed suicide. Were the two linked?

Something had been niggling me. With the Skoda driver now eliminated, none of the other vehicles in the

ANPR 14 fitted the description of the estate vehicle we were looking for. I'd asked my colleagues to recheck the data, but that kind of car did not appear to have passed that way. That could be because my Barbary Castle theory was right – but that was not definitive: the ping didn't *definitely* come from there, it *might* have come from there. Savernake Forest could not be completely discounted as the destination to which the abductor drove his car.

In which case, how had the car slipped through the net?

Two explanations occurred to me. If the car *was* a taxi, then the one thing we knew about taxi drivers was that they knew the layout of the roads. It might be that, if they had gone to the forest, the driver had deliberately avoided using the most direct route. Was he clever enough to have intentionally kept off the radar, using his intimate geographical knowledge to pick a safer, much more secret route away from the prying eyes of the ANPR? The cameras were supposed to be covert, but if you knew the roads well enough, as a cabbie would, it was possible that the driver might have detected the permanent camera and planned a different route. That made it a very pre-meditated attack.

But, I now realised, those hairs lifting on the back of my neck, if Dave Ainsworth was our guy, then the fact the cameras were covert didn't matter one bit. As a police officer, he could find out exactly where they were and plot to avoid them. So far on this case, we had had no evidential breakthrough: no witness sightings, no passive data that connected Sian to an offender, no DNA traces on a bloody rag or weapon. Was that because Sian had not been abducted? Or was it because the offender was a copper – who knew only too well how to commit the perfect crime?

I considered the idea without fear or favour. That was my duty. Yet I was distinctly aware of how controversial such a scenario would be. I directed Jess and the others to keep the development within the four walls of my office, and for them to brief the actions around Dave's car on a need-to-know basis only. Until we knew more, this was too scandalous a theory to be discussed in public. Until we knew more, it was a speculative, sensitive hypothesis that I didn't want falling into the wrong hands.

After they left, hurrying to get to work, I wandered over to the window of my office and looked out for a moment. Massed below, in front of the nick, were the media vans like the day before – only their numbers seemed to have swelled. I could just imagine the journalists' reaction if they'd been a fly on the wall in the meeting that had just occurred. If Dave was our man, that really would be the headline of the year.

Given the developments, I felt somewhat unsettled as I opened the morning briefing at 09.05. Yet I couldn't let that distract me. My job was to get people focused, enthused and working as hard as possible to bring Sian home.

Top of the agenda was the fact that the CCTV footage proved that Sian had got into the estate vehicle. This clarified we were dealing with a crime in action. Now we'd seen her getting into a car – and knew she hadn't been in contact since – we could say that, in all probability, this was an abduction. A crime in action is one in which an individual's life is at threat as a consequence of an ongoing course of conduct by a perpetrator which creates that threat. Typically, they are abductions because, should we not be able to find the victim, the consequences can be loss of life.

It was hugely important that I stressed the nature of the offence to the team because priorities in a kidnap differ from those in other enquiries. Where life is at risk, the first and overriding priority is to take such measures as are necessary to preserve the victim's life – at all times.

It was Sian we were looking for. That was our ultimate responsibility. We might collar the guy who did it, or collect evidence along the way that confirmed his guilt, but nothing mattered more than finding the victim and bringing her home safe.

I was convinced the best way to do that was to progress our enquiries around the car on the CCTV. We hadn't found Sian yet through searching alone: we needed a link in the chain, for the person who knew where she was to guide us to her, and we knew the last person to see her was the person driving that car. The results from TRL hadn't yet come in, to my frustration, but I directed that I wanted our efforts around ANPR widened. After all, for whatever reason, the estate vehicle had avoided the most obvious road out of Swindon and wasn't on the ANPR camera we'd already examined. We now needed to widen our parameters to include locations such as Barbary Castle, and look for data-capturing cameras located on other possible routes.

I also directed that officers should approach car-valeting services to see if any estate vehicles had been cleaned after the material times; I was anticipating that the offender may have wanted to get rid of physical evidence. As such, another line of enquiry was that any reports of burnt-out vehicles should be identified, in case the car had already been trashed.

I had a theory that perhaps our man had been building up to the abduction. He might have made failed or smaller-scale attempts of a similar offence in the months prior to Sian going missing. Consequently, I requested that the team do a sweep on the system for any previous incidents of women being approached on the street and perhaps assaulted. Finally, I had a specific directive for the intel team: I wanted to know where all taxi drivers in the Swindon area were at that material time on Saturday morning.

In the course of the briefing, though I kept Dave Ainsworth out of it, I did share my new hypothesis devised that morning with the team, including the theory that Sian might not be in Savernake Forest, but some other location that also pinged to the Cadley mast. I was painfully aware that Barbary Castle was just one of several possible sites, so I asked the locally based search teams for their own ideas of areas to which Sian may have been taken. In the same way that, the day before, I couldn't direct all our focus to the Skoda driver, I wasn't yet willing to commit all our efforts to searching Barbary Castle alone, just on the basis of a theory. The guys threw out a few new ideas, including the lakes at South Cerney.

Though the off-the-cuff brainstorming demonstrated that our possible assault-site options were still multiple, the really good news was that – notwithstanding our inability to pinpoint the ping exactly – FTS had at least narrowed the search area. The new parameters had been sent out to the crews, and on-the-ground searching would continue throughout the day at the forest. I also had the POLSA doing an assessment at Barbary Castle.

There was still a lot to do, but I felt we were making some real progress at last. In my mind, I told Sian to hang on for just a little longer. We were getting closer to her all the time.

After the briefing concluded at 09.38, Debs wanted a word.

'You're looking tired and you need to eat,' she said sternly. 'You can't exist on cigarettes alone.'

I must have protested, because she became much more forthright and fixed me with a steely gaze that I knew from experience took no prisoners. 'You're no use to anybody if you don't eat,' she told me bluntly. She added as a sweetener, perhaps sensing my reluctance, 'I'll get John to come too ...'

That swung it. A working breakfast I could manage. Debs, my deputy and I decided to go for a big boys' breakfast in the Sainsbury's caff across the road. All three of us thought that getting away from the nick for a while might be a good idea. After crossing the A420, I loaded up on baked beans and hash browns at the self-service counter and then sat down with my deputy to chew over the latest details of the case. Debs looked pleased that I was eating without constant interruptions – but her satisfaction was not to last long.

From where it lay on the table beside my plastic tray, the Nokia suddenly blurted out its merry little tune.

It was the intel team. They'd picked up on a report that they thought I should know about. It had just been called into the Control Room of Wiltshire Police.

A girl had been walking along a minor road in Swindon a short while earlier. She had noticed she was being followed; the vehicle had prowled behind her for a little while. Then, to her shock, the driver had attempted to bundle her into the back – it was only through luck that she'd managed to get away.

It was the second abduction attempt in Swindon in a single week. And it raised a disturbing question: had the perpetrator struck a second time?

23

It was a horrifying thought. Did I have a madman running around Swindon, abducting girls off the street every few days?

It wasn't far-fetched. On occasion, you saw crime patterns emerging in this way. Sometimes, something happens in a criminal's life to make them snap. Where previously they'd lived a life without offending, once the first crime has been committed the floodgates open and a string of similar offences may follow. Such was seemingly the case of Steve Wright, the notorious Suffolk serial killer. He murdered five women in just six weeks in 2006, their bodies discovered over a period of only ten days. Had something similar happened here? Could it be our taxi driver with previous, escalating from sexual touching to full-blown abduction and rape?

Officers were immediately sent to investigate. The vehicle involved was a red van; there was no trace of it and search efforts began. The fact that it wasn't an estate vehicle didn't necessarily mean it wasn't our guy: criminals frequently change cars and register many vehicles to their name, so without knowing who owned the van and the car, we couldn't rule out the notion that it might be the same person. The teams were set the task of taking statements from the girl and any witnesses, analysing local ANPR and identifying the vehicle. We had to find out if the two incidents were connected.

As I headed back to the nick, peace and quiet forgotten, identifying the estate vehicle on the CCTV was foremost in my mind. If this morning's incident was committed by the same individual, then it was imperative that we found out who that person was before anyone else got hurt.

But no matter how long I lingered in the major incident room upon my return, hoping to be there at the moment the news came in, the expected morning call from TRL failed to materialise. We were still in the dark on this most important issue. I was simply itching to get that cohort of owners; I was painfully aware it could be huge. With time of the essence, the sooner we got it, the sooner we could start the painstaking work of narrowing it down in order to identify the driver of the car that had taken Sian O'Callaghan.

In the end I gave up and retired to my office to pick up on other lines of enquiry. I was still there when, at 13.30, Gary Hale burst in. He was an earnest, eager detective inspector in his mid-thirties. And he was certainly eager to share this particular piece of news. He had just taken the call from TRL.

He didn't beat about the bush: 'Boss, the best fit for the image is a Toyota Avensis Estate, produced between January 2003 and October 2008, dark in tone with chrome roof rails. They think it was likely to be an end-of-production run as there were door mirror-mounted indicators. They couldn't find any other vehicle with such identifiable features and would be surprised if it was any other vehicle than the Toyota Avensis.'

Gotcha. It was the take-off point I'd been after. And it told us something else, too: neither the taxi driver with a previous conviction for sexual touching nor the tragic Dave Ainsworth were likely to be responsible for picking up Sian, as neither owned such a vehicle. When combined with the work Jess's team had done that morning, it ruled the idea of our fellow officer being the perp right out of court.

I felt relief that we could put it to bed. In hindsight, it was never going to be him and the whole idea was highly improbable, but naturally we had to consider everything, no matter how outrageous. Subsequently – much later – I would feel grief for my colleague, but in that moment I had neither opportunity nor time to think about the enormity of what had happened to him, nor the reasons why he might have taken his own life.

No: in that moment my priority was getting that cohort of Toyota Avensis owners. The fact we thought the vehicle was used as a taxi would help us reduce the numbers. We needed to find those people, do intelligence checks into their backgrounds, work out who they were, confirm their alibis and their movements on Friday night. I instantly ordered a VODS and PNC check to be run. Without a number plate, all we had was the make and model: the cohort could be many hundreds of people deep.

I was still in the process of digesting the news from Gary when I suddenly heard a pounding of footsteps racing up the carpeted corridor towards my office. Before there was even a moment to begin the VODS search, another officer flew through the door: Marcus Beresford-Smith. He was a tall, bald uniformed officer; I didn't know him well, but I recognised him from the traffic team.

Though he was naturally pale, I couldn't help but notice that he looked extremely flushed. It turned out he'd just pelted up two flights of stairs, where he'd been working on the ground floor in the CCTV viewing room.

'Boss!' he heaved, trying to catch his breath. 'You've got to see this!'

I could tell in an instant he was excited – he was on to something. I felt a familiar tightening in my gut.

'I was thinking,' he went on, 'did any of the patrol cars operating in Swindon near the Goddard Arms on Friday have ANPR fitted?'

I nodded in appreciation of the lead: smart idea. It was genius, in fact. Some police cars have ANPR mounted on them, so as they drive they snap the index plates of passing cars. If a police vehicle was near the Goddard Arms early on Saturday morning and had the technology in place, it might have caught the Toyota on its camera. It was a brilliant piece of thinking.

Through his gasps for breath, I realised Marcus was grinning. He wasn't just bringing me this as an idea, he had already run with it. It was the best way police enquiries worked: not just me or a few senior officers thinking hard, but everybody, no matter their department or their rank, sparking off each other.

'I found one, sir,' he said now, the words tumbling out of him. 'I found a patrol car in the area that had ANPR and I viewed the footage.'

I was halfway out of my seat, my legs ahead of my brain, my eagerness transporting me. I locked eyes with Marcus as he said the words that shot a bolt of exhilaration straight through me: 'At the time Sian went missing, a Toyota Avensis passed the patrol car – and gave a full index.

'We've got his number plate, sir. We've got him.'

24

As fast as our coppers' legs would carry us, Marcus and I pelted back down the two flights of stairs and once again a gang of us gathered round the boxy computers in the shoebox-sized room, where the operatives were viewing the footage. On the way, Marcus babbled out how he'd snagged on the idea. The team had viewed *all* the footage they had sourced from *all* the various High Street premises. To begin with, we'd had no idea if Sian had gone left or right out of the club; if she'd popped into Domino's and only walked home at 04.00; if an assailant might have been recorded loitering in an alleyway further down the street. So they had viewed it all. And as Marcus had sat numbly watching the hours of footage from HSBC, a vehicle had whizzed by: just a flash in the corner of the screen that someone else might have missed. But Marcus, as a traffic expert, recognised from the small snatch of it that was visible that it was a patrol car. *I wonder ...* he had thought. *I wonder if there were any patrol cars in the vicinity with ANPR ...*

The fact that there had been, and that the patrol car had happened to drive up the High Street only moments after the Toyota Avensis had pulled away from the Goddard Arms and driven the opposite way, so that the vehicles' paths crossed, was the sort of stroke of luck you prayed might happen. Any number of things could have stopped that interaction from occurring at that exact instant, or it could have happened but not been captured. But, to my relief, it *had* been recorded, in grainy black and white. Marcus now showed me the evidence, gesturing towards the screen at the picture of the index plate that the ANPR had taken.

Well, he *said* it was an index plate. To my untrained eye, the digits were pixelated and the numbers looked like gobbledygook. Without Marcus, I wouldn't have been able to tell anything from it, but his traffic expertise enabled him to interpret the fuzzy digits. I could tell, at least, that the vehicle was an identical shape to the car that we'd seen on the Goddard Arms footage: the one we knew Sian O'Callaghan had got into.

All around me the guys were buzzing. I shared their excitement, and my pulse started to race at a familiar frantic pace. The game had changed. For the past three days we'd been pushing at innumerable doors and finding nothing gave: now, the entrance had swung wide and we'd found a new way to surge forward. I was 100 per cent clear: this was the moment we'd been waiting for. Now we, as detectives, could get going with everything we'd wanted to be doing when we'd been desperately searching for a take-off point.

And, thanks to Marcus, we didn't even have to do VODS or narrow down a suspect cohort: as though served up on a plate, here was the candidate's licence number – the needle that we could have spent days searching through the haystack to find. In the course of a morning, we'd gone from having next to nothing to having something concrete we could seize on, and it was an even better lead than I could ever have hoped for. I felt a sense of hyper-focus and clarity. From information overload, there was sudden simplicity. The innumerable possibilities we'd been battling now crystallised: one path, one lead, one man.

'Run a PNC check,' I ordered.

For now we had the licence plate, we were seconds away from knowing his name.

When it came through on the computer, it was pretty ordinary, to tell the truth. It didn't really tell you anything about him, but for his identity.

The man's name?

Christopher John Halliwell.

He was 47 years old; a Swindon local. He had a criminal record, but only for a handful of property offences; the last offence, way back in 1986, had incurred a custodial sentence for burglary. Yet for the past 25 years he had not come to police attention at all; he appeared to have gone clean. As we could perhaps have predicted, he now worked as a taxi driver; he had been employed with his current company for only a couple of weeks.

A handful of aliases also popped up for him on the system from this time: Christopher John Bentley, Michael John Davies, Peter James Mann. I found that very interesting; it tended to indicate he had told a few lies in the past. As his last conviction was so very long ago, there was no DNA record for him on the system. Nor was there a photograph. For the moment, that was all we had.

Immediately, however, Jess and her intel cell started putting some meat on those meagre bones. The process was almost seamless. Our expertise as an investigative team kicked in: we knew his car, we knew his name, and from there it didn't take a genius to work out where he lived, where he worked, who his associates were, what his background was – and the intel team were on that in fast time. Another crew was sent out as a matter of urgency to interview the taxi manager who employed him. At 15.00, I formally nominated Christopher John Halliwell as a TIE subject in the case.

We didn't rush out and arrest him, nor was he formally named as a suspect. After all, what would I arrest him for? Potentially, picking up a taxi fare on a Friday night – well, that was his job. There was another niggle, too, although not necessarily one I voiced loudly in the midst of Marcus and the crew's celebrations. Nevertheless, as the SIO it was one of which I was critically aware.

Marcus had done an unequivocally amazing job in identifying the patrol-car ANPR footage – but there was just one problem with it, to my mind. The index plate wasn't captured *exactly* outside the Goddard Arms, but slightly further up the High Street. Therefore, there was a possibility – a slim one, mind you, but still a possibility – that there were *two* Toyotas: the one on the CCTV and the one on the ANPR. *They might not be the same car.* Halliwell could have pulled out from any side turning onto the High Street and into the path of the patrol car which took his photo, but another Toyota Avensis might have been the one that picked up Sian. As we were soon to discover with further intel work, the Avensis was a popular vehicle with taxi drivers and there were several operating in the town. So, although it was *probable* the vehicles were the same, part of me registered that it was not *definitive*. As such, all we really had at this stage was the knowledge that Halliwell was a taxi driver who drove the same *type* of vehicle that had pulled up next to Sian, and who was on the High Street at the relevant time. If you blew just a little, the whole house of cards could come tumbling down.

As the SIO, it was my job to direct the focus of the investigation. To date, we'd had so many lines of enquiry that even with the enormous team now working on the case we were really up against it to work through them all. I now had a choice. I could continue with that thinly spread direction – or I could bite the bullet and put my eggs in one basket. We would be able to work faster and produce more in-depth results that way, but it was also a high-risk strategy. For if I called this wrong – if Halliwell turned out to be another red herring, like the Skoda driver or Dave Ainsworth – then I'd be taking the enquiry in completely the wrong direction.

I was acutely aware of the race against time. Perverse as it may sound, I desperately hoped that whoever had abducted Sian was still holding her hostage and that she was bound and gagged somewhere (with the usual caveat: we didn't know for sure she had been abducted; all we knew was that she had got into the car). With a hostage scenario in mind, it was imperative that we rescued her as quickly as we could. Yet with time so tight, we only had one opportunity to get this right. I had just one call, and if I made the wrong one, I could potentially cost Sian her life. It was a heavy responsibility. But I knew that, if I didn't make the call at all – if I wasn't brave enough to bite the bullet – then with limited resources and the clock counting down we might not chase down this lead in time to save her.

With a deep breath, the kind that all SIOs take at this point, when you're plunging into a decision and you haven't the faintest idea what you'll find once you've jumped off the board, I made the call. Wherever Sian was, to my mind Halliwell had to be the step in the chain that could get us to her. If he was an innocent taxi driver and had picked her up, he would be able to tell us where he dropped her off. If he was guilty of abducting her, then he was now the only person on the planet who knew where she was. I therefore ordered that all resources be diverted from other directions I'd been pursuing hitherto.

I needed those resources desperately. Because at 15.12 Debs and I minuted a decision in the sensitive policy book: I was placing Christopher John Halliwell under covert surveillance.

25

The team deployed with immediate effect and we had operatives in place outside Halliwell's home in minutes. He was at home, his dark-green Toyota Avensis parked on the drive outside.

Halliwell lived in Ashbury Avenue, Swindon. It was a quiet residential street of mainly semi-detached houses in a good area; it didn't have a high crime rate. Mostly blue-collar workers lived in its peaceful environs, where neighbours were friendly and tended regularly to their small front lawns.

The surveillance commander was Charlie Cheadle. He was a front-end commander, out on the ground directing operations from the command car most of the time, but he also took responsibility for personally briefing me by mobile or in person on what was happening during the surveillance operation; updates that came whenever relevant. An earnest DI with little glasses and thinning fair hair, he was a really good guy.

I briefed him that I wanted a GPS tracker put on Halliwell's car pronto, so we could follow his movements and map them remotely; I also requested that his home be covertly searched.

Yet I stressed to Charlie that 'covert' was the key word – it was imperative that Halliwell didn't know we were on to him, otherwise we might as well just nick him there and then. He couldn't know that we suspected he had some knowledge of Sian's disappearance. I had a particular reason for ordering this covert surveillance, beyond wanting to understand Halliwell better.

I wanted him to lead us to Sian.

That was why the tracker – the lump, as we call it in the trade – was so important. Once in place, it would emit a constant signal that we could then follow remotely on a map. Search teams would subsequently be able to follow any route Halliwell had taken, whether in live time or more surreptitiously after the event. So if, as I hoped, he drove up an isolated country lane to a secluded barn, we would have the ability to follow him to that lonely location, where – I hoped – we would see Sian O'Callaghan through the window, burst in and bring her home.

The lumps themselves come in all different varieties, cue balls and teleloggers and deep-fit microphones, and it was the latter I was especially hoping we could plant in the Avensis, so we could not only track Halliwell's movements, but also pick up his conversations in the car. Of course, all these activities were subject to authorisation by an independent officer.

While the surveillance team plotted up to get first eyes on Halliwell, work continued in the MIR. The interview team had made fast work of meeting with Halliwell's employers and information was flooding in from the taxi firm for whom he worked. The company was extraordinarily helpful, I have to say, and it was a relief: we had to take quite a lot on trust with them, because we were alerting them to the fact that we were interested in Halliwell, at a time when we needed him to remain ignorant of it – exposing our hand, as it were. But it was critical to find out what his movements were and what records the company had kept of them. Luckily, they were very obliging.

The firm ran a messaging and tracking system, called Cordex, which recorded all customer calls and, operating a GPS tracking system too, sent the nearest driver to pick them up. It was possible to track the drivers and where they went – as long as their systems were switched on.

Records at the firm showed that on Saturday 19 March, the day Sian went missing, Halliwell's GPS tracking system was switched off at 02.13 and was not reactivated until 18.53 on Saturday evening. From records, Halliwell's last pick-up on Friday night/Saturday morning was at 01.10, when he dropped a passenger at Haydon Wick. He had left his system live and reported in at 01.58 to say he was going home in half an hour. From the records in the system, we were able to see that he drove down Groundwell Road at 01.53, into Princes Street and on Fleming Way, reaching Farringdon Road at 01.59. By 02.07, he'd covered Corporation Street, Manchester Road, Drove Road and Wood Street. He did a loop at Newport Street and at 02.13 stopped at the junction of Tismeads Crescent and turned his system off. When the system went live again at 18.53, Halliwell rang into the office saying, 'I'm starting work at 10ish, ring me on my mobile, I'm not at home.' This showed him at Covingham.

I studied the details of his route carefully. If he was the offender, these were his last known movements before he chose to make his strike outside the Goddard Arms. What was going through his mind as he made such looping turns around the streets of Swindon late at night? Was he just a taxi driver sharking for pick-ups?

Or was he purposely looking for a woman to abduct?

The name of one of the streets jumped out at me: Manchester Road. I knew of it because it was notorious as the town's red-light district, a place where narrow terraced houses cramped together and desperate girls hung about on corners, ready to do business in the back alleys behind the graffiti-scribbled homes. It was a grubby place, though ostensibly normal-looking enough, with launderettes and off-licences, but clients of the sex workers knew the score and kerb-crawled their way about the roads at night. Was Halliwell looking for a prostitute that Friday, then? Was using sex workers something he regularly did?

Despite the route, however, I kept an open mind. Manchester Road was a stone's throw from the train station; perhaps that was just the way he went on the lookout for a last fare before he called it a night. I had to remain objective. Until we knew more, we couldn't make a call on whether he was the right suspect or simply an innocent cabbie.

That said, I was very interested that he had turned off the tracking system at 02.13 – because the patrol car's ANPR conclusively showed that he was still out and about in Old Town 45 minutes later; even though he had told his boss almost an hour earlier that he was about to head home. To me, it seemed he had made a particular effort to get himself off the grid.

The taxi firm were helpful in another way, too. They supplied us with a photograph of Christopher John Halliwell.

It was a small one: a passport-sized snapshot from his driver ID. And, now, as I stared at the tiny photograph in the MIR, I laid eyes for the very first time on the man who might be holding Sian. I somehow had to find a way of finding her through him.

Christopher stared arrogantly at the camera with a somewhat haughty and dismissive demeanour. He had dark thinning hair and a sallow complexion. The image showed only his head and shoulders, but physically I could see he was quite thin and gaunt. Despite his rather unappealing appearance, I felt drawn to him, in a way, because he had the most distinctive eyes. They were deep set, with a dark ring around blue irises.

I stared at that photo for quite some time, wondering at his personality, at what he might be capable of. He hadn't come to police attention for 25 years. If he had snatched Sian, why now? What for? Or had he just been doing his job on Friday night, and was completely innocent of any crime?

I was desperately trying to work out if we'd got the right guy, knowing that Sian's life hung in the balance, but you can't tell that from a photograph. You can't get a feeling for whether someone's innocent or guilty from bits and pieces of gossip and an early-doors intel report. His own behaviour would hopefully tell us more, now we had the guys in place to track his every step.

As if summoned by my train of thought, my mobile rang with an update from Charlie.

Halliwell was on the move.

26

He was dressed in a grey jumper, a smart white collared shirt and dark trousers. One of the snippets we'd learned was that Halliwell always dressed very smartly for work, and was known by the other local drivers for the fact that he often wore a suit. It was probably reassuring to his passengers, I reflected. First impressions count: the image of a suited-and-booted cabbie probably put many people at their ease, confident that they were with an upstanding, professional person who took the nature of his job – safely transporting passengers to their desired destination – very seriously.

The surveillance team took their job very seriously too. Unfortunately, however, Charlie now informed me that since we'd last been in touch there had been a problem with the brief. To my dismay, I learned that it had proved impossible to fix the lump on Halliwell's car.

Part of the issue was that we ideally wanted to employ the deep-fit microphones – but they required mechanical interference, which ran the risk of setting off the alarm. That was a complete no-no, given the need to keep the surveillance covert. Although there were other techniques we could employ, the risk of showing out – being spotted – was deemed too great. The priority had to be to keep our distance and give Halliwell – if he was the abductor – enough rope to hang himself. Because Halliwell was a driver by trade, too, the guys had found he never left the car long enough for the specialists to have the opportunity to try a different, safer method of getting a lump up there. They simply couldn't get to the vehicle without alerting him.

It was a bitter blow; I could almost taste it. Yet you have to rely on people's professional expertise in that field, and Charlie told me frankly it had been impossible and I accepted the team's advice.

They had not implemented the covert search of the house, either, which I'd requested to ensure Sian wasn't on the premises, right under our noses. That was because Halliwell didn't live alone: he had a partner, Heather, who had her own children. Having watched the house for several hours, the team had determined that it was highly improbable Sian would be in there – because, if she was, the whole family would have to be in on it, and that seemed less than likely. Nonetheless, with Fred and Rose West in mind, we did run some basic background checks on Heather just in case, but it was soon apparent she was completely innocent.

Heather had been with Halliwell since 2005, we learned. They had met first as neighbours; Halliwell had originally lived a few doors down with his wife, Lisa, whom he married in 1991, and with whom he had two teenage daughters and a son. Heather and Halliwell had become close after she'd asked him to convert her garage, and in time he had left his family home to move in with her. The couple had been together ever since.

I was struck by the fact he had two teenage daughters. After all, so did I. Yet it was an especially striking thought given the offence I suspected him of committing: abducting a 22-year-old woman. His own daughters were only a few years younger than Sian. If he had done it, it showed a chilling lack of empathy.

Yet, on the other hand, did his daughters' existence therefore make it less likely he was guilty? Perhaps he was just a family man; certainly, those were the reports coming through to us from the intel team. All seemed well at home.

Because nothing truly could be discounted at this stage, I requested that the search team hold off on the covert search of Halliwell's home, but I left on urban CROPs (Covert Rural Observation Posts), whereby officers camouflage themselves and remain in situ, so that we could covertly monitor the property from the outside. Basically, people were hiding in bushes – but a little bit better than that.

Meanwhile, with Halliwell on the move but the lump not in position, Charlie told me that the surveillance crew were now going to extraordinary lengths to maintain our watch on him. Back in the day, we used to have double-man, 12-vehicle surveillance crews doing physical surveillance of people. Such methods had almost died out in our technologically advanced age but, given the circumstances, Charlie's crew had gone back to basics. I suspect in some ways they secretly enjoyed it, because it was what they were all trained in but very rarely got to do.

The 12-vehicle crew were going to use a technique called pivot peripheral surveillance. Understandably, we couldn't just have one car following Halliwell all the time because they'd show out almost immediately. Instead, all 12 vehicles would be involved, using Halliwell as the pivot. The team would then move north, south, east and west around him, so they always had eyes on, but with different cars coming into the equation. They'd swap the front lead; they'd take parallel routes. It's very skilful.

But it was risky. In an ideal world, what I'd wanted to achieve from the surveillance was a nice neat map with all of Halliwell's routes plotted, giving us a raft of opportunities then to put search teams into those locations. I was hoping that, while under observation, Halliwell would visit Sian wherever he was holding her – perhaps to bring her food and water – and in so doing lead us straight to the missing girl.

But that nice neat map, digitally plotted by a GPS signal, wouldn't be possible now. Instead, each car would keep a handwritten running log, which would be amalgamated by Charlie into a master document. It wasn't quite the same, and the risky method of surveillance was a real concern.

Yet the dedicated team were doing the very best they could. To their credit, they were immediately on the back of Christopher Halliwell once he started to move that Tuesday evening, 22 March. And it was a good job they were – because relevant intel started coming in immediately. Very quickly, Marcus's brilliance in identifying him on the patrol-car ANPR proved even more critical – for without that breakthrough, we wouldn't have had eyes on Halliwell for many more hours, if not days, and none of what followed would ever have been seen.

At 18.29, Halliwell made a quick stop-off at a store, purchasing a roll of Sellotape. Four minutes later, he parked up in the car park by the Old College and busied himself with the sticky tape and some papers in the rear of his vehicle. The surveillance guys squinted to see what they were as he pasted them up in the back windows of his cab. When they recognised the pictures, I received a call from Charlie.

Halliwell had just placed two missing-person posters for Sian O'Callaghan in the rear of his cab.

The development gave me food for thought. Was that normal behaviour for someone who was directly involved in her disappearance? Did his actions make it more or less likely he was our guy? I still couldn't discount the fact that it might not have been his car on the footage – although, on the balance of probability, it was. Even in that instance, however, Sian might still have been a paying customer, catching a cab.

The posters told us one thing, though: *he knew she was missing*. If he was an innocent taxi driver and he'd picked her up, why not come forward to say so? But people do stupid things sometimes, when they don't think through the consequences of their actions. Obviously the good and right thing to do would be to come forward and say, 'I picked her up at 02.56 and dropped her off here.' Then I, as the SIO investigating her disappearance, could move the enquiry forward and forget all about Christopher Halliwell.

I mulled it over. How would you react, if you had the slow, creeping realisation that you must have been the last person to see her, this girl who was suddenly national news? He might fear that the heat of suspicion would unfairly fall on him; he might feel guilty that he had dropped her off in the Savernake Forest and she had later come to harm. Perhaps, given the mass publicity, he just didn't want to get involved with such a high-profile case. Yes, it was wrong that Halliwell had not come forward with the information that he had. But it didn't necessarily make him the worst of all people. Maybe putting up the posters was his way of trying to help.

On the other hand, if he *was* guilty, his actions offered a disturbing insight. If he was guilty, he had no shame, just sheer brass neck. For he was copying the actions of his fellow drivers – all of whom had been very concerned by recent events – in order to camouflage his true self. He was professing concern for the whereabouts of a girl when he knew *exactly* where she was, because he was the one who had hidden her.

At 18.49, there was another update: Halliwell was cleaning his car. And not just chucking out a few discarded sweet wrappers or shaking out the footwell mats. The team observed him scrubbing the interior rear seating area, the rear of the driver's seat and low down on the offside door with a harsh-looking bright-blue chemical.

The moment the surveillance crew observed what he was doing, Charlie got straight on the phone to me.

'Boss, do you want us to intervene?' he asked urgently.

It was a crucial question. If Halliwell was guilty of abducting Sian O'Callaghan, then this avid cleaning could perhaps be his way of trying to obliterate the evidence. The surveillance crew could be watching as he scrubbed away the one forensic trace that put Sian in that car.

It was a major decision point. But, as a crime in action, this was not like other enquiries. The question I continually had to ask myself, as I assessed our options and the fallout of the consequences, was: will this action help us to find Sian? So I thought it through. If I told the guys to go in, and we seized the car and Halliwell and protected the forensic trace, what would I have? I might have some evidence against Halliwell that he had some involvement in her abduction, but I wouldn't have Sian. And even if the trace was there, it probably wouldn't be enough to convict him. After all, he could just say he had given her a ride.

'Do you want us to arrest him or not, guv'nor?' Charlie asked again, the tension in his voice audible.

If I wanted to, I could order Halliwell's arrest right now, stop him scrubbing the car and protect the evidence. But would arresting him give me Sian? No – so it couldn't be the right decision. Any idiot could storm in and arrest a bloke on suspicion of kidnap, but we had to play the long game.

Because I felt, in my bones, that if we didn't, we would never see Sian O'Callaghan again.

So I told Charlie not to arrest, but to keep on watching. I wanted to know what Halliwell did next.

27

Due to the timing of the information coming in on Halliwell, the evening briefing was cancelled; the team would meet again in the morning for an update. But a cancelled briefing didn't mean the work stopped – on the contrary, the identification of Halliwell as the likely driver of the car that had taken Sian acted as a power surge through the entire investigative team. There was much to do.

In the MIR, I set one team to focus on all sexual offences committed in the last 12 months in Swindon that involved taxis and/or estate vehicles. I was looking for a similar MO to Sian's abduction, as well as any forensic results. By now, the officers investigating the attempted abduction earlier that day had discounted any link to Sian's disappearance: the red van was a red herring, another crime that had no connection to this case. But that didn't mean what had happened to Sian was a one-off, and I wanted to know the ins and outs of all incidents that had a similar flavour, in case Halliwell had perhaps been building up to the abduction. There might be a pattern to his offending that, if we were smart enough, we might be able to decode. If he'd taken one girl to a particular location, for example, then the chances were he may well have returned to the scene of that crime with Sian.

I also passed on Halliwell's mobile number to the telephony team. I had remained frustrated that they hadn't been able to find those particular numbers that correlated with the pings of Sian's phone, but now we had Halliwell's exact details, it was an easy enough check to find out where he had been on Friday night. I asked them to prioritise it. Would the passive data show a correlation? Could I put him with the missing girl?

All the while, updates were coming in from the surveillance team. Halliwell was regularly picking up fares – but he was also regularly doing something else. At several locations, the crew observed him depositing items in bins. Was he having another clean-up of his cab?

Or was he dumping evidence?

Covertly, one team from the 12 vehicles circling our man moved in after each event. In a rural location, Halliwell was observed throwing something away in a dog litter bin beside a petrol station. Once he moved away, the officers retrieved it.

It was a woman's perfume bottle.

Once more, Charlie called it in. 'Should we arrest him, boss?'

But a perfume bottle wasn't Sian. The answer had to be no.

That didn't mean the deposition wasn't significant. Though I couldn't discount that it might be a lost-property item left behind by a careless passenger, I wondered if it belonged to Sian O'Callaghan. Perhaps, spooked by the media coverage, Halliwell was now getting rid of it. But that posited the question: why had he kept it in the first place? If he was the offender, I thought there was only one explanation: he'd wanted a trophy, to remind him of his crime.

It was a well-documented behaviour of criminals. In the USA and South Africa there have been many such cases where trophies were found; from my own experience,

I remember a case in Bristol where the offender kept his victims' knickers. We had to find out if that bottle was Sian's – my suspicions were that it had to be – so I ordered that the item be brought back to the nick and passed to forensics.

Christopher Halliwell continued his night's work. At 22.02, he turned into the car wash near the Aldi on Hobley Drive, Swindon. As the team watched, he slipped out of the driver's seat and deposited an item into the bright-orange industrial wheelie bin that was located there. Then, strangely, he got back in the car, rolled the car forwards, and then got out again just seconds later and once more placed something small in the wheelie bin.

Cautiously, the team moved in, some officers collecting the items while others continued their hawk-eyed watch on Halliwell as he drove off. This time, Halliwell had deposited an incomplete set of car seat covers; the crew believed the back seat cover to be missing.

I had two thoughts. The first was that the retrieval of these items gave us a real forensic opportunity in terms of establishing a direct link to Sian. The second was that it was suspicious activity. Why was he dumping seat covers four days after we knew him to have picked up a now-missing girl? With every report that came in, it increasingly confirmed my suspicion that Halliwell was the right bloke.

After the car seat covers were found, Charlie called again to ask if the team should make an arrest.

Once more I thought through the consequences of that action. We were slightly further forward than we had been when he'd first asked the question: we had the perfume bottle and car seat covers, which – I hoped – would provide an evidential case; it would be days, however, before the forensics team would be able to confirm or deny that. If there was a link, that gave me good leverage. If we arrested Halliwell, I could say to him in an interview: 'Look, we know Sian was in your car, and we've observed you dumping the evidence that would indicate your guilt in her abduction. So best you tell me where Sian is.'

But would that evidence be strong enough to elicit an account from him – to draw from him the key solution to the riddle: where is Sian? I thought not. His solicitor would be perfectly right in saying, 'I'm afraid, officer, that evidence of her being in his car doesn't constitute evidence of anything, does it? No crime has been committed here: my client is an innocent taxi driver.'

If we did arrest, we had only 96 hours in which to hold him before we'd have to let him go or charge him. But that would be 96 hours in which Sian – if he was holding her hostage – would potentially be left without food or water. I was very aware that if we intervened too soon, without enough knowledge to prompt Halliwell to reveal her whereabouts to us, then the chances were that she would die while we were holding him in custody.

I came back to the all-important question: how can I find Sian? Arresting Halliwell wouldn't help me. The best way to find Sian was to hope that Halliwell would return to her, so that we could follow him. I told Charlie not to arrest, but to keep on watching.

Halliwell, like so many taxi drivers, was a night owl. He certainly kept the surveillance crew busy as he went about his way that night. At 00.52, in the first hour of Wednesday morning, he was observed travelling on the Lambourn Downs near Sparsholt Firs, turning onto the B4507. He was coming from the direction of Hackpen Hill – just south of Barbury Castle – and from Ramsbury, north-east of the Savernake Forest, travelling at first along the B4001. The surveillance crews watched keenly as he drove about the country lanes, trying desperately hard not to show out.

It was a very, very hard thing for them to do. The rolling countryside of that region is largely open fields, stretching to infinity. Car headlights cutting through the pitch-black night were visible from miles away. Unlike in a built-up urban environment, where town-planners helpfully provided parallel roads and grid systems, there were fewer opportunities to engineer covert observation or to cross Halliwell's path surreptitiously. You were either on that country lane with the green Toyota Avensis or you weren't. The teams couldn't get too close behind him, yet the twisting nature of some of the rural roads meant it was hard to keep eyes on Halliwell at all times; with one bend or two between them, he came in and out of sight.

At that time of night, in such lonely locations, there were very few cars about too. At what point would Halliwell get suspicious that the quiet country roads were much busier than normal? At what point might he start to wonder about those headlights in his rear-view mirror, or the cars he kept on seeing up ahead?

The job got harder and harder. Above all else, the crew had to remember the key brief: *don't let Halliwell know we're watching*. If he was spooked, he might never return to Sian, and no one would ever discover where she was.

He was observed at 01.00 travelling from the direction of Kingston Lisle towards the Blowingstone Hill crossroads. At the junction, he took a right onto the B4507 again, heading towards Compton Beauchamp, Wanborough and Swindon. En route, he passed by Uffington Castle and White Horse Hill.

And it was there, in the dead of night, in the most difficult of all circumstances, that Christopher John Halliwell slipped fluidly out of sight.

28

Wednesday, 23 March 2011

For a professional surveillance crew, a loss is devastating. As the minutes ticked by with no trace of Halliwell, the team worked furiously to get back on plot. It wasn't their fault. Losses were known to occur with the technique they'd been forced to employ. From the moment they'd told me that the lump was a non-starter I'd been concerned that such a loss might occur. Now, my worst fears had come true.

Not that I knew about it right away. And I understood that: there was professional pride involved so they didn't cough to it the instant it happened. The last thing Charlie Cheadle needed at one in the morning was an irate SIO on the line who was chewing the furniture. I'd like to think that if he had called it in immediately I would have been very calm and understanding – and I don't recall making a massive issue of it even once I did find out – but I guess we'll never know.

The first I knew of it – as I recall – was shortly after 02.20 on Wednesday morning. That was when Charlie informed me that Halliwell had been off-grid for a total of one hour and eight minutes.

What Halliwell had been doing in that time was anyone's guess.

Charlie wasn't calling in to report the loss, though. It turned out that Halliwell had graduated from dumping things in bins.

The surveillance crew had finally caught up with him at 02.08. He was on the High Street in Wanborough – a large village about 3.5 miles south-east of Swindon – next to The Harrow Inn and the village hall, with his headlights illuminated. With eyes now on him, the crew carefully logged his movements. By 02.13 he was seen travelling very slowly along Rotten Row in Wanborough towards Kite Hill. His was the only vehicle in the area.

At the bottom of Kite Hill, Halliwell turned right onto Church Road, which in time becomes Pack Hill, heading towards the A419. He pulled away from the knot of houses clustered near St Andrew's Church and travelled steadily up the road. Pack Hill was an isolated lane, bordered only by fields; even more remote in the dead of night and right in the wilds. And it was on Pack Hill that the crew had seen him stop and get out – in order to fiddle with something on the ground.

By the time the crews got to it – having let Halliwell move along – it was burning brightly, the flames orange and lively. The team suspected an accelerant had been used to set the fire – all the better to destroy the evidence? It was a small bundle, about a foot square. As carefully as they could, the first officers on the scene attempted to extinguish the flames but, by the time they managed it, whatever the item had once been was charred beyond recognition. When they called it in, though, I had a hypothesis for what it could be. I thought it might be Sian O'Callaghan's distinctive handbag, with its big beige flower now black.

After Charlie's phone call, which I received at home, sleep evaded me for the rest of the night. When you're running a surveillance op of this variety, you're hopeful that the simple thing will occur – that he'll return to the scene of the crime, to Sian herself, and you can catch him red-handed. But as the night drew on, that wasn't happening – to the best of our knowledge. But I couldn't dwell on what Halliwell had or hadn't done during that one hour and eight minutes. What was important was what we'd seen him do and the pattern of his movements. What did I know about him now? Was the strategy working?

To my chagrin, all I had at this stage was a taxi driver cleaning his car. That was the long and short of it: it would hardly stand up in court. For all we knew, earlier on the Tuesday he might have picked up someone who had vomited in his cab; you would use a harsh blue chemical to scrub down a stranger's sick. All the intel reports coming through gave no cause for concern. He checked out: he didn't have a criminal history in the past 25 years, he was a family man, he was employed, he was in a stable relationship. There was nothing in what we were hearing to say that this was a guy who would snatch a young woman off the streets and render her incapacitated. The telephony teams also reported that the passive data on his phone didn't link him with Sian.

That said, although it didn't put him with her, nor did it clear him entirely by giving him an alibi of an alternative location, where his phone was pinging miles away. In the early hours of Saturday morning, Christopher Halliwell's mobile phone was switched off – just like his work GPS had been. There was no passive data. Perhaps he had deliberately got himself off the grid; or perhaps he simply was not there.

I turned the evidence and the facts and assumptions over and over in my mind. With this being a race against time, I felt in the middle of a whirligig, each piece of information another spoke in the wheel that spun faster and faster around me. I was trying to make sense of it all, trying to make the right call. Guilty or innocent? Was there even a crime? I was trying to do that most difficult of things: find an abducted girl when I didn't even know definitively that she had been abducted.

The forensics would take days to come through. What would they tell us when they did? Possibly – if there was any DNA to find and it hadn't been destroyed – that Sian had been in Halliwell's cab, and maybe left her perfume behind. That did not definitively make Halliwell her abductor. My mission was to find Sian, and I felt the only person who knew where Sian was, was the person who had taken her. At this point, I couldn't say that Halliwell was that man, nor that Sian had been snatched. Yet I listened to my gut. Despite all the 'ifs' and 'maybes', it said Sian was in danger – and Halliwell sounded right.

OK, so I was moving forward from that position. What was the best tactic to pursue from here? In a kidnap case, negotiation is a standard ploy. You don't arrest – because otherwise the 96-hour custody clock starts ticking – you put in a negotiator and you have a frank conversation: 'You've abducted person X, what do you want me to do to get her back?' I could make direct contact with Halliwell and show my hand, outside of arrest, and say, 'I think you've abducted Sian.'

I calculated the consequences. What happens next? If he says, 'No, I haven't,' we've got no evidence to charge him. And now he knows we're keeping tabs on him, so he abandons Sian to her fate and never goes back to the secluded barn or the cellar where he's keeping her. Consequence? Sian dies. Negotiation wasn't a tactic.

To my mind, there was only one way to find her – and that was for him to take us there. But from the activities we had witnessed so far, it didn't seem likely that he was going to do that. I had to change that equation. I needed to come up with some tactics to augment the surveillance. It was another critical decision moment: I couldn't just sit on the fence and watch him till the end of time, because

Sian's life was at risk and time was running out. I had to find a way to get Halliwell to focus on what I needed him to do, which was return to Sian.

What did his actions to date tell me? How could I use that to inform my next move? They told me he was dumping evidence: he was getting rid and clearing out. If the perfume bottle was a special trophy, then something had spooked him hard enough that it was more important for him to abandon it than keep it. I had to assume that he didn't yet know we were on to him, so what else had been happening that might have prompted this behaviour?

I didn't have to think very far before I had my answer. Sian's case was national news. There were 10,000 people in the Savernake Forest: potentially, 10,000 people all over his supposedly remote crime scene, getting closer to Sian every day. This was a major event. If you were the guy who'd done it, you would be spooked. And why are you spooked? *Because you think they're going to find her.* So what will make you go back? *If you think they're getting close.* If we found Sian before he did, he was rumbled. The best evidence on the planet would be a first-hand witness account where she could point a finger and say: 'It was him.' He would have to return to her if he thought she was about to be discovered.

But I couldn't rock up at Ashbury Avenue and tell him we were very close to locating her and he better nip down there double-quick or he'd be in trouble. So how could I communicate with him?

Again, it didn't take me long. Almost from the moment Sian had vanished, the media had been on to this. They were still banked up outside the nick, their numbers growing every day. Every time I left Gablecross they were desperately tugging on my sleeve: 'What's happening?' We knew from the fact that Halliwell had put up the missing posters in his car that he was engaged with the case and likely following the story in the press. So why not use their insatiable demand for developments to my advantage? I could use the media to put Halliwell under pressure to take me straight to Sian.

It was an unusual idea, to say the least. The notion that I would essentially be passing messages to one individual using public media was an extremely bold one; it was certainly never something I'd ever tried before, or heard other people do. But it was relevant to this unique set of circumstances.

Consequently, when Charlie asked me that same short question again in the early hours of the morning – 'Shall we arrest him, boss?' – I had my answer ready.

'No,' I told my old mate Charlie Cheadle. 'I have other plans.'

29

As I hurried into the nick that Wednesday morning, I watched the gathered journalists with a newfound interest. For once, the clamour of their calls for information wasn't unwanted. I felt a familiar impatience to put my plan into action. I wanted to issue a series of carefully worded statements to the media, drip-feeding their release over the course of the next 24 hours. Each one, in ever-increasingly overt statements, would be designed to say how close we were to finding Sian. This, I hoped, would spook Halliwell sufficiently for him to go to her. The surveillance crew, of course, would follow.

I turned my attention to the most pressing issue of all: what was I going to say?

First of all, everything I said had to be accurate and true. This wasn't about lying to the public: this was about persuading Halliwell to return to Sian. He needed to feel we were closing in on him – which we were: we had a 12-vehicle surveillance crew surrounding him, and urban CROPs outside his door. These were statements that needed subtlety and a certain psychological sensitivity too.

On my drive into the nick, I had realised something else as well. Currently, I had 10,000 people combing the Savernake Forest for Sian. Was Halliwell more or less likely to return to Sian if there might be 10,000 witnesses? Less likely, right? So the statements actually needed a two-pronged purpose: I needed the public at large to leave Savernake Forest, so that one individual could return under surveillance. That would be the implicit message, but clearly it wouldn't work if I said it in those terms.

Sitting in the SIO's office, I tried to get inside the mind of the man who had snatched Sian. What did Halliwell think was happening now? He, and only he, knew what had happened early on Saturday morning. What must he be thinking, given the evident size of the police effort coming for him?

If I was being brutally honest with myself, I was now giving credence to the thought that he might have killed her. But, if he had, her body was still out there somewhere. If we found her, could he really be sure that there were no forensic traces linking him to her? If he wasn't 100 per cent certain, he would have to return to her.

If, as I hoped, he was holding her hostage, then how would he respond in that instance? I assessed the consequences and let out a long, slow breath. The high-risk nature of the strategy was clear. The truth was, I didn't know how Halliwell would respond to the pressure, and I didn't know what he'd done with Sian. She could be alive right now, bound and gagged in a cellar somewhere. If he thought we were about to find her, what might Halliwell do? After all, if Sian was able to incriminate him, she was dangerous. I had to acknowledge that there was a chance that putting pressure on Halliwell might prompt him to return to a still-living hostage with an even darker motive in mind. I had to accept that I might be putting her life at risk.

Then again, there was a big difference between abduction and murder – perhaps Halliwell wasn't cold enough to kill.

Perhaps it would depend on how desperate he became.

I tried to reassure myself. If he did return to her, for whatever reason, then my guys would be close at heel and we would act before anything untoward could happen. After the loss last night, I knew the crews would be adamant that such a thing would never happen again on their watch.

I also assessed all my other options. Was there a safer way to proceed? It was now day five, and our on-the-ground searches had so far found no trace of the missing girl. It was all about equations again – so far, I had zero. If I changed the balance, I might get a result. The only way to find Sian, to my mind, was to get her abductor to lead us to her. I therefore had to take this risk, because there was no other way of finding her.

The message that went out to the public informed them that the enquiry was moving on at a rapid pace. I added that significant lines of enquiry were being developed, and that new technological techniques had successfully provided a tighter search parameter, so that large areas had been ruled out. Tactics, I announced, were being urgently progressed. I intended Halliwell to believe that we were sufficiently confident of finding Sian that he would have no choice but to lead us to her.

I directed that the first press release should go out at 09.00 for maximum exposure. A second was scheduled for 16.30, which would give further detail and make an explicit request for the public to stand down so that professional search teams could take over. To tell Halliwell: the coast is clear now, so best you get in there and clear your tracks.

Not content that the media strategy on its own was sufficient, I also devised a secondary tactic. I'd worked on a murder case a while back where the suspected killers had come from within the travelling community. During the enquiry, I'd been impressed that my undercover team had been able to infiltrate such a notoriously closed community. Not only that, they had drawn out incriminating statements that fingered the killers. It was quality policing. I therefore decided I wanted to adopt an undercover strategy for this job too. I directed that undercover officers should be briefed, ready for insertion that evening as passengers of Halliwell. The plan would be for them to have a carefully worded discussion about Sian's disappearance within Halliwell's earshot, in order to provoke a response.

I was entirely focused on Halliwell, entirely set on getting inside his mind, on working out how to push his buttons – pull his strings. Despite his late night, he was already up and about. The team had eyes on him outside Lloyds chemist, near some recycling bins in Covingham Square. He was cleaning again: the dashboard and front screen. More cleaning up of evidence? Or more evidence he simply liked to clean?

I brushed away the questions. For better or worse, I was committed to this course of action. Surely Halliwell was our man.

Just at that moment, the Nokia trilled – with an unexpected message. It was the custody unit. They had someone in custody for kidnapping Sian – because the guy had just made a full and frank confession.

His name wasn't Christopher Halliwell.

30

He was a black male. When I heard the news, I couldn't help but remember one of our early leads: Sian talking to a black man inside the club. Had we discounted someone who was in fact our guy? Could we have made such a critical mistake?

I despatched Bill Dutton to interview him urgently. I had to give the confession due credence. I was distinctly aware of how sometimes, in enquiries, you get a Chinese whispers effect once you've identified a person of interest, such as we had done with Halliwell. I'd made the decision to put him under surveillance, therefore highlighting to the team that I was highly suspicious. The surveillance team were consequently giving me updates on his behaviour that we all saw through the frame of that suspicion. Before you know it, you've created a whole story of your own generation, and an innocent man looks guilty. I'd seen it happen many times before.

While Bill raced off to the interview – the man had been arrested in a rural police station some miles from Gablecross – I strode into the conference room to begin the morning briefing at 09.03. The team was energised, all of us aware we had a big operation now running on a properly focused path. There were obviously lots of lines of enquiry being progressed around Halliwell.

The intel cell told me they had found a possible previous sexual assault that might be of interest to this case: a woman had been attacked in Savernake Forest back in February. I made a note and asked them to investigate further.

With so much to do, I brought the briefing to a close after only 12 minutes. The investigation was taking on a cracking pace now – so much so that a large contingent of the team was absent, as I had already set them the crucial task of following Halliwell's movements from the night before. The plan from the very beginning of the surveillance was that we hoped Halliwell would lead us to where he was hiding Sian. We now needed to retrace his steps to see if we could find her – a task given an added significance because of the holes in our knowledge of his movements due to the surveillance loss. He could well have visited her late last night. Why was he driving so slowly along Rotten Row at 02.08? Was Sian being held nearby? What significance did Wanborough hold, or Ramsbury, or Uffington? Did the fact he'd come from Hackpen Hill mean Sian *was* somewhere at Barbury Castle?

With a DC called Terry James in charge, I'd tasked the team to follow and methodically search – to the best of their ability – all the routes that Halliwell had covered while under surveillance the night before, taking the crews' log as their starting point. Perhaps, with a bit of luck, we might discover the missing girl. Halliwell had covered many miles, however, so it would be a painstakingly slow job. I knew Terry and his team would do everything they could.

For my part, as soon as the briefing finished I had only one destination: forensics. If Halliwell was our man, then I believed the items he had been dumping across town were crucial clues to his involvement. I wanted to see them for myself.

Genevieve was already there. The charred bundle that Halliwell had set alight on Pack Hill had been securely collected at 04.10 and returned to the lab for examination. It was now laid out on a plastic sheet on the floor of the office. Genevieve and her team had tried to arrange it as best they could, haphazardly piecing it back together. I'd scampered down the stairs rather eagerly, almost rubbing my hands in glee, believing the bundle could be Sian's bag – but when I laid eyes on the remnants for the first time, that zealous excitement soon faded.

The blackened bundle was literally just ash and charred plasticky stuff. You couldn't identify with any confidence what it was. Cold and completely burnt out, there wasn't even any smell to aid us. Genevieve, Debs and I stood around staring at it, trying to determine what on earth it could be. I bent down to get a closer look.

'Is that a flower?' I asked hopefully, pointing.

We all stared hard, trying to work out whether one blackened bit of the globular mess might just be the flower from Sian's distinctive handbag. But it was impossible to tell. Nonetheless, I asked Genevieve to get a scientist to examine it: sometimes they can do things to confirm identification that you wouldn't have believed possible.

Next, we turned our attention to the perfume bottle: the trophy I theorised Halliwell had kept as a reminder of his crime. I was much more hopeful on this item; I was pretty convinced that since Halliwell had decided to get rid of it, it must belong to his victim and Sian's DNA or fingerprints would be found. It was a long, thin bottle, made of clear glass. I'd tasked the family liaison officers (FLOs) with the job of finding out if it was Sian's usual brand, as well as asking them to get her fingerprints from home, so we could use them for comparison on the bottle. I requested that the item be fast-tracked: though it still wouldn't prove Halliwell had abducted Sian if the bottle turned out to be hers, it could be the first brick in the wall of an evidential case. Plus, if, in a few days' time, we came to the point of interviewing Halliwell, it could give me leverage to say, 'You've deposited Sian's perfume in a litter bin, Mr Halliwell. Now, pray tell me, how did this come to be?'

Finally, I reviewed the car seat covers that had been dumped in the orange wheelie bin. They were the detachable sort with elastic fastenings, made of a black fake-leather fabric. They didn't look at all incriminating, laid out on a table in the lab, but the scientific testing would tell us if in fact they held some secrets Halliwell had been hoping to keep hidden. These too were fast-tracked, but I knew it would be days before the results came back.

By now, it was coming up to 11.00. I called a quick meeting of my investigative leads, wanting to fill them in on the sensitive strategy of putting pressure on Halliwell. To my keen interest, Bill was back. He now revealed that the earlier confession was conclusively fake: the guy was clearly not fully compos mentis and Bill's verdict was that he had just been attention-seeking when he'd confessed to snatching Sian. At least we could rule him out and focus everything back on Halliwell.

And we now devised a further strategy to draw him out – and add to our own knowledge of this man. Much of the investigation had centred on taxi drivers to date. We now proposed that we would TIE (trace, implicate, eliminate) *all* the taxi drivers in Swindon, a process that would include taking a DNA swab. The plan was to send out teams to secure DNA samples, plus an account of the drivers' movements at the relevant hour. We would contact many if not all of the drivers, lending credence to the idea this was a general cohort – and that wasn't a bad idea anyway, given the slim possibility that another Toyota Avensis taxi had in fact picked up Sian – but our key focus, naturally, was on Halliwell.

I was very interested to learn what he would say, when given the chance to provide the police with an account of his movements on Friday night. Jess agreed to brief two officers who would go out to meet with Halliwell around lunchtime that same day.

So much of our efforts were now centred on Halliwell – but I hadn't forgotten about the most important person of all: Sian O'Callaghan. Despite standing down the public, we were still desperately looking for her. I directed that our key search teams be moved to Barbary Castle today. What with the hypothesis that the assault site would need to be close to Swindon, the high-ground reading from FTS and Halliwell's own movements the night before, on the balance of probability I thought it best to redirect our priorities to that location.

I stared at Sian's smiling picture on the whiteboard in the MIR. We were five days on, and we were getting closer, but I still didn't know where she was.

I was in the CID office when Terry James, who'd been retracing Halliwell's route, came in to grab me.

'Boss,' he said. 'Some news.'

He'd been out in Wanborough, following up on various leads from the night before. Halliwell had been seen making a slow pass past a particular location; he'd dropped something on the ground outside. Terry told me that they'd now discovered that 'something' was a handful of dirty tissues. They were blood-sodden, flecked with faeces. And the location where they'd been found was outside an abandoned house, right in the middle of the countryside.

I felt the hairs rise on the back of my neck. Had we finally found Halliwell's hiding place? Was Sian O'Callaghan in that house?

31

'Let's go!'

I could feel my heart racing. Suddenly, Terry had given me what we ultimately wanted: the chance to find Sian alive in a dirty garret somewhere. I fired off instructions as I flew out of the nick, directing that search warrants should be secured for the premises and that I wanted those tissues fast-tracked through forensics. Terry told me he had only done a cursory look round the place before alerting me, so the race was on to get back there and do a thorough search.

Terry was a wily, wizened old fellow who smoked roll-ups and was very sage. I trusted his instincts. And as the two of us pulled up outside the house in Wanborough, I could immediately see why it had caught his eye. Notwithstanding the bloodied tissues, it was a prime contender for being the hiding place of Halliwell.

Before us stood a large white detached property, set in overgrown grounds. It was located down a lane off the main drag, on the very edge of the village, where the houses were extremely isolated, set several hundred metres apart. The property had obviously fallen into disrepair: the stucco peeling off, the garden uncared for. There were several outbuildings dotted around and my heart pounded harder as I assessed the site with a detective's eye. Sian could be in any one of those outbuildings, or in the cellar or attic of the main house. The place appeared unoccupied and long-ago abandoned. To be frank, it looked like the archetypal property where a kidnapper would secrete his victim.

Officers were already combing the grounds, looking for a girl with an asymmetric haircut. It was likely Sian was incapacitated, possibly bound and gagged, so she wouldn't be able to call out to us: it was up to us to leave no stone unturned as we tried to find her.

Our footsteps crunched up the gravel driveway that led to the main house. My gaze flickered left to right and I felt a surge of hope that we would find her here. The weather seemed to reflect my mood: it was a bright, crisp day and the spring sunshine seemed to herald good news.

Terry was murmuring into his radio and turned to me with an update. To our surprise, it transpired that the property wasn't abandoned, after all. A little old lady resided there. It made our job slightly more delicate, requiring a bit of diplomacy with the householder.

But it didn't mean the search stopped. After all, Halliwell might have assumed the same thing: that nobody lived in such an isolated, run-down place. Perhaps, like us, he had only belatedly made that discovery, so that Sian had once been here, but had now been moved. It was a logical location, after all: close to Swindon yet secluded; close to where he had been spotted the night before. So, even if we couldn't find Sian, could we find signs to suggest she had once been here? Was that her blood on the tissues? Might there have been some clue left behind – perhaps by Sian herself – that would give us some inkling of where to look next?

I told the teams to keep looking. It was just like on day one, when I'd asked the young coppers about the search of Sian's home. Now, the question was: 'Are you 100 per cent happy that she isn't in the cellar or an outbuilding?' I told them to look, look and then look again.

Orders given, I left them to it, needing to head back to the nick. I'd requested a meeting with ACC Pat Geenty to discuss the sensitive strategy of putting Halliwell under pressure through the media. The more I thought about it, the more high-risk it seemed. I couldn't go out on a limb on this one and needed to talk it through with the chair of the Gold Group so he understood the strategy as well as the potential consequences. I had no idea what he might think of such an audacious idea, nor what the fallout might be for me.

Only that morning, before the formal briefing, my boss Nigel had reminded me that the chance of me being replaced as SIO was still very high. Would my unusual strategy make it more or less likely I'd be taken off the case? This would be the worst possible moment for the investigation to lose its leading detective, just as the net was closing in. Yet I stood by my conviction: this method was the only one I could think of to make Halliwell lead us to Sian.

Back at the nick, before the meeting with the ACC, Bill Dutton had an important update for me. As the interview expert, he'd taken over the management of the imminent police interaction with Halliwell: the informal approach, in the context of contacting all Swindon cabbies, that would request from him his DNA and an account of his movements on Friday night. Bill told me he'd selected a crack team of two officers to make the approach. They were Tier-3 trained, meaning they'd had in-depth schooling in how to manage conversations, recognise eye signals and so on. It was a male-and-female partnership. Dex Drummond was your archetypal DC: a thickset bloke with thinning hair and a chubby face who had a huge personality, very witty and sharp. I knew he had excellent interpersonal skills and I thought that if anyone would be able to form a rapport with Halliwell, it would be him. His partner was Bea Reiss, a senior detective who exuded an air of competence and control at all times.

The update from Bill told me that the pair were now on their way to Halliwell. At 13.00, the interview would begin.

32

'Thanks for meeting me, Pat,' I told the ACC as we each took a seat at the table in the management room at Gablecross. I'd summoned him from HQ in Devizes for this briefing, which was a pretty good trick, getting senior management to come running to me. But Pat was happy to do it – he knew I wouldn't have asked to see him if it wasn't important.

I outlined the latest updates in the case to him, including that, even as we spoke, a team were interviewing Halliwell and securing his DNA. I explained what I wanted to do with the media. My idea for the evening press release was to say that we were getting close to finding Sian, but that due to the loss of daylight, the search would continue first thing in the morning. This, I hoped, would spook Halliwell sufficiently for him to return to Sian, tonight, and take me to her. I added that, once he was out in his taxi, I intended to deploy undercover officers as passengers to engage him in conversation about Sian; a tactic that would be repeated twice.

We discussed arresting Halliwell. Why not make our move now? But if we brought Halliwell into custody before identifying Sian's location, such an action would almost certainly end her life – if she was still alive.

If I am honest, I did fear Sian could already be dead. Of course I did. If she had been abducted behind those blinding headlights outside the Goddard Arms, then statistics said that she was likely to have been murdered even before the sun came up on that same Saturday morning. If she had survived that long and then been abandoned somewhere in the wilds, we were now five days on from her abduction. No one could survive that long without access to fresh water. But perhaps she did have water; perhaps she did have food. Perhaps Halliwell had her holed up somewhere; not necessarily in the isolated house in Wanborough – and so it seemed from the searches we'd conducted – but maybe in some other, as-yet-unidentified location.

The truth was, I had no knowledge of whether she was alive or dead. I feared she was dead, but I hoped she was alive. And my duty in those circumstances was quite clear: I had to find and protect Sian if I could. I couldn't abandon her, not when there was a chance she was still living and waiting desperately for the cavalry to come.

'What are the risks of this media strategy?' the ACC enquired.

I took a deep breath. There were quite a few. If it failed, and we didn't find Sian, the media could turn on us: 'Why did you tell the public to stand down in the search when you haven't located the missing girl?' Perhaps they would even sense they had been used and react against it. Yet my biggest fear, ironically, was that it would work – just not in the way I intended.

My plan was to put Halliwell under immense pressure. I wanted him to fear that his whole life was about to come crashing down around his ears – that we were about to find the girl he had abducted, and that he would necessarily then be convicted and condemned. I wanted each press release and undercover tactic to make that pressure build and build inside him, until he shot off after Sian, unable to take the heat.

But the thing about pressure, and making it build, is that you can't anticipate *how* that tension and energy will eventually be released. This wasn't a 'controlled explosion' scenario: the pressure bomb I was intentionally constructing in Christopher Halliwell could in fact go off in any direction. The pressure *might* force Halliwell to lead me to Sian. Or it might force him to make another choice. I'd talked, before, about giving him enough rope to hang himself. *What if he actually did?*

'The biggest risk,' I told Pat Geenty, 'is that Halliwell might be sufficiently spooked to commit suicide.'

It would be the worst of all things. I believed Christopher Halliwell was the only person who knew where Sian was. If he killed himself, he killed her, too, because, when he died, he took the knowledge of her location with him. If he hadn't already murdered her, he would by implication do so the moment he took his own life. For if she was locked in a cellar somewhere, and only he had the key, then she would by natural consequence die a horrible death in that unknown prison after her captor killed himself. We would keep looking for her, of course, but the truth was she could be anywhere. The ping on her phone gave a location of five days ago. Halliwell could have moved her to another location in the intervening days and there would be no trace of that at all.

I told Pat there were implications for both the force and for myself. I was deliberately putting pressure on Halliwell. If he committed suicide under those conditions and while under police surveillance, we could be held responsible and the fallout would in all probability end our careers. I would have a dead suspect on my hands, and by extension a dead girl too – and I would be culpable for both. There would be no option but an Independent Police Complaints Commission (IPCC) referral for my actions because I would be seen to have driven Halliwell to his death. And, of course, even though you could argue that an innocent man wouldn't have topped himself, I wouldn't have enough evidence to say conclusively that he was guilty of Sian's abduction – so it would be an innocent member of the public I had done it to, as well.

Nevertheless, despite the risks involved, I was certain that, if I didn't take this step, we would never find Sian anyway. So even though I could have taken a hands-off approach, for I didn't have to try this tactic; even though I could have said, 'No, it's too risky, and I can do no more than what I'm already doing,' I didn't make that choice. For me, it was the simple mathematics of an equation: I was charged with saving Sian's life, and I thought this course of action was worth the risk – even if it did cost me my job.

I took a deep breath: 'There are so many things that could go wrong with this, Pat. I'll take full responsibility for it.'

The opportunity was there for the ACC to say, 'You can't do it.' Or: 'Here's a better idea.' But although we both acknowledged it was high risk, he acquiesced. He recognised that the course of action I had described was the best – I believe only – way of recovering Sian alive, if that was still possible.

He was understandably very concerned about it, though. After all, I had a duty of care to Halliwell, too. The police just can't go around employing tactics that might drive people to suicide. I would have to monitor him even more closely through the surveillance and try to prevent his death, if it looked likely to occur. Pat and I agreed that, because of the possibility of Halliwell's suicide coming as a direct result of the media strategy, it wasn't a tactic I could run indefinitely. We tacitly agreed that, if the plan didn't work and Halliwell failed to lead us to Sian, we would have to shut it down – and on a fixed timescale. I had until tomorrow night. If the plan had not succeeded, we would move to arrest Christopher Halliwell at 19.00 hours on Thursday.

There were several reasons why I didn't object to the deadline being imposed. And perhaps foremost among these was my duty to Sian. We had now been following Halliwell since 15.12 on Tuesday. If, by tomorrow night, he had not returned to Sian, she would have been abandoned by him for over 48 hours. If we worked on the premise that she had been alive at the moment the surveillance started, but had had no access to food or water since then as Halliwell had not returned to her, then we would need to change our tactics to give us time to rescue her before that new ticking bomb went off.

As Pat and I went our separate ways – him back to HQ, and me back to the MIR – I had only one thought.

Whichever way you looked at it, time – for Sian and for Halliwell – was inexorably running out.

33

'Boss? They're back.'

It was shortly after 15.00. Bea and Dex, the officers despatched to interview Halliwell, had recently exited Ashbury Avenue, having spent some two hours with him. I beckoned Bill Dutton into my office for an immediate debrief. Later, I would also speak directly to the officers involved, wanting to hear this account from them first-hand.

As directed, the detectives had gone to visit Halliwell on the premise that they were targeting all taxi drivers and he was just one of many. 'Nothing to worry about, sir, this is just routine.'

They began by asking him to give an account of his movements on the Friday night. I listened closely to the report of what he'd said.

Christopher Halliwell told the officers he had gone home at 01.30 on the Saturday morning.

My brain ticked over the evidence. His call to his boss at 01.58 to say he was going home *in half an hour*. The digital tracks of his own GPS system, showing him looping round and round the streets of Swindon – until he switched the tracker off at 02.13.

The ANPR photograph of his car on the High Street, moments after Sian O'Callaghan was last seen.

Halliwell is lying.

Dex and Bea next informed him they needed to take a DNA swab. It prompted an extraordinary reaction. As the officer took the swab from his mouth, Halliwell started shaking and became close to tears. His nerves were evidently shot to pieces. He tried to pass it off as emotion caused by the fact Sian was missing; he had two daughters himself, he said.

I couldn't help but reflect, *so do I* ... But I wasn't lying about my movements on the night she went missing. I wasn't dumping potential evidence and burning mysterious items on darkened country roads. I wasn't shaking and close to tears when asked to provide a DNA sample.

I tried to use the parallel to get into his mind. After all, Halliwell and I both had daughters of almost identical ages; the two of us ourselves were only three years apart in age. We would have gone through the same experiences of parenthood – and life – in the same sequence, and almost simultaneously. In many ways, we were now at the same stage of life.

For me, the account of his reaction strengthened my belief we had the right man. It still wasn't definitive – many people are nervous when asked to provide a DNA swab – but in terms of a gut feeling it felt like game, set and match.

No wonder, by the time they finished with him, Dex and Bea were sure: Halliwell had to be the prime suspect. And I agreed with them. At 17.00 on Wednesday 23 March, I formally named Christopher Halliwell as our suspect in the policy book.

Officially identifying a suspect is a major moment in any crime investigation. Until now, Halliwell had been a person of interest only: a TIE subject, like the ANPR 14. In naming him as a formal suspect, I was fully committing to him; and that went for the resources of the enquiry too. At my direction, everyone was working on the Halliwell lead; excepting those searching for Sian on the ground at Barbary Castle. I was dedicating all the means we had at our disposal – and all the hope – into Halliwell being our guy.

Even as I threw my weight behind him, however, I was painfully aware that there was no other avenue we could now pursue in time to help Sian. If Halliwell was innocent, and we turned out to be following a red herring in pursuing him, then by the time we retraced our steps and attempted to find another take-off point, the 'golden hour' would be over. In that case, it was likely we would never know the truth behind her disappearance. This was an all-or-nothing approach. The responsibility weighed heavy.

Yet the fact that Halliwell had blatantly lied to the officers and showed such extremity of emotion at the DNA swab steeled my nerves. I felt truly confident – in some ways, for the first time – that he was the right person to pursue and the only person who could lead me to Sian.

As such, as the light started to fade from the sky outside the MIR, the plans I had been devising all day were launched into action. The undercover officers were cast for their roles: I wanted a man and a woman for the first insertion, so that their interaction would look as natural as possible; followed by a second officer who would insinuate to Halliwell that they'd heard the police had found Sian. Scripts were commissioned so the teams would be ready to deploy that night.

We also issued the second message to Halliwell, via the media, that we were standing down the search teams at sunset. I seem to recall seeing an item on the news in response to it, saying that it was a bit of an odd update report from Swindon, but of course the message had been carefully worded for Halliwell alone. I could only hope that he was listening.

As we went about our work, Halliwell was at Heathrow, having taken a passenger to the airport. Following my conversation with Pat Geenty, I acknowledged my duty of care to him. I informed the surveillance crews that they had a new brief. While covert surveillance was still what we wanted, it was more important that Halliwell did himself no harm on our watch. I briefed them to anticipate the risk, and gave orders that if necessary they should get closer to him than they normally would, in order to mitigate the scenario I most feared. I could never forget: if Halliwell died, *so did Sian*. I asked them to update me if there was ever any indication from Halliwell that he would take his own life.

They did phone in an update, not long after their parameters changed. They had got close enough to hear him on the telephone: 'The police have been to see me,' he said. Recent events were obviously playing on his mind.

To hear someone's private phone call, you have to be operating pretty intimate surveillance. That was what I'd asked for, of course, but I hoped Halliwell hadn't clocked them.

At 18.23, the sun dropped below the horizon. Darkness settled around Gablecross, a blackness broken by the bright lights of the media vans outside. They were still watching our every move.

And we were watching Halliwell's. Was the plan going to work? Would he take the bait?

The surveillance crew trailed him all the way back from Heathrow, perfecting the pivot-peripheral method as the 12-vehicle team wove in and out of traffic. He drove closer to the environs of Swindon. The press report containing the message for him was the leading story on both local and national news that night. Had he heard it? Was he going to take us to Sian?

The green Toyota Avensis smoothly pulled off the main road – into a quiet residential street of mainly semi-detached houses. It was Ashbury Avenue. Halliwell was home.

And there he stayed: the door closed, the windows dark. In time, Heather left to go out for the evening, but he didn't take the chance, with his partner away, to slip out undetected. Instead, he remained at home all night, the house as silent and still as the dead.

34

In the MIR at Gablecross, I paced the floor, feeling sick. Charlie Cheadle would occasionally call with updates for me – to tell me there had been no change – but at times I was so frantic for news that I would phone him first. Yet there was never any alteration in the surveillance team's report.

Halliwell was alone at home and the house was completely dark.

What was happening in there? I was desperate to know. I tried to get an intercept put on Halliwell's phone in order to find out. If he was suicidal, he might try phoning his daughters or a friend to say goodbye. He might leave a message for someone in a fit of guilt, revealing crucial information that could give us the whereabouts of Sian O'Callaghan.

But, to my intense frustration, the authorisation was denied. I escalated the request through the senior echelons – given this was a life-and-death situation, both for abductor and abductee, I thought it was an entirely proportionate step to take – but despite me fulminating at every turn, I kept getting the brush-off. I was scandalised, frankly, given the circumstances and the threat to life. The refusal of the facility only added to the pressure I was feeling.

What made it worse was that I had once been involved in a similar case. It was another missing-person enquiry, but on that occasion the suspected kidnapper had been arrested. He was held in custody for 96 hours, saying nothing and giving nothing away. Though we were almost certain he had done it, we had no evidence and no trace of the girl. So we had to let him go, but did so with him under surveillance, hoping he would lead us to her. It was a similar situation to this case in a way – except the arrest was made first.

The man had returned home, and the surveillance team had plotted up outside the house – just as my team were outside Halliwell's home right now. They waited, and waited, and waited. Eventually, the decision was made to storm in.

They found him hanging from the rafters, up in the attic. He'd been swinging there, black in the face, while they all watched and waited outside. They found the girl shortly after: he had killed her, then buried her on a building site on which he worked.

That tragedy now played like a movie in my mind. I had a vision of Halliwell swinging from the rafters, each seesaw of his body a taunting reminder that it was the end of the line.

What do I do? I had the team there, ready and waiting to burst into the premises if it was necessary: if there was an immediate threat to Halliwell's life. If I'd had the tap in place on his phone, I might have had a better idea of whether or not that was required; at the first whisper of a maudlin phone call, we could swoop in and stop him from doing anything foolish. But I didn't have the tap, so I was on my own.

Nobody could advise me. It was my call to make. And it was a straight decision: I either blew any notion of recovering Sian by going in pre-emptively and arresting him when we had no evidence, or I held the line and held my nerve, hoping he hadn't done anything disastrous.

I kept staring at his photo on the whiteboard in the MIR. His dark-ringed eyes stared arrogantly back at me. *What is going on in your head right now, Christopher Halliwell?* I wondered. I had only my instinct and my very basic knowledge of him on which to rely.

Continually, I reviewed what I knew of him and how I thought he was feeling. I knew he was spooked: he was dumping evidence. I knew he was emotional: nearly crying with Dex and Bea. The physical shaking they had witnessed told me that he was scared, on edge, intensely anxious. The phone call we had monitored at Heathrow suggested our earlier visit was still on his mind. He knew, now, that we had his DNA. I had told him, via the media, that we were close to finding Sian. He was now alone at night, alone in the house. The odds he might take the one step I most feared seemed impossibly high.

I found myself persistently wondering if Halliwell was even still alive. I had a constant mental battle: should I direct the team to go in and arrest him, or should we sit tight and wait for the morning, hoping that Halliwell would emerge from his house? I couldn't stop my SIO's brain from calculating the consequences of his suicide. It was terminal for Sian; but what would I face in the morning if my prime suspect – the only person who had the answer to the location of that missing girl – was stone-cold dead? I would lose my career. I had no doubt it was on the line as every minute passed without an update from the surveillance team that Halliwell was on the move. If Halliwell died, my career did too.

I stayed at work, unable to leave, processing the updates from the intel cell and the surveillance crew, continually reviewing hypotheses and tactics. So much for my grand plan of this morning. Where yesterday Halliwell had been on the move throughout the night, now he was stationary. Without him out and about in his cab, I couldn't even deploy the undercover agents.

That night seemed eternal. Yet I knew that the sun would rise again, whether or not Halliwell was there to see it. If he was, then I had to think through the consequences of that. I planned another press release, a more overt one this time: a final attempt to persuade him that if he didn't want us to find Sian first, he had to return to her. Yet I knew that if the tactic failed – as it had failed so far – then come 19.00 hours on Thursday evening I was going to have to arrest him.

I called on Bill Dutton, interview expert, to advise me on what should happen if we reached that point. Together, we considered the options available to us to achieve the primary objective of this operation, which was to find Sian O'Callaghan and save her life. Bill suggested that we should employ what's called a safety or urgent interview. They're not used very often – there is very little case law – but given Sian's life was at risk (and, with every hour that passed, that risk grew more critical), Bill felt it was a legitimate option in these circumstances.

Under Code C of the Police and Criminal Evidence Act (PACE), once a suspect is arrested, they have certain rights – the right to a solicitor, the right to silence, and so on. The guidelines also say that suspects should only be interviewed at a police station or other authorised place of detention. However, there is a provision under Section 11.1 of PACE that says an urgent interview outside of these parameters may be conducted if not doing so would lead to 'interference with, or harm to, evidence connected with an offence' or 'interference with, or physical harm to, other people'. In this case, the latter exception applied because there was a risk to Sian's life. What it meant was that, if we had to arrest Halliwell, we could immediately ask him the question: 'Where is Sian?' without him having a solicitor present or being formally taken into custody in the nick. Essentially, if you're trying to save someone's life, the guidelines allow you to talk to a suspect. So, if we had to move to arrest him before we'd found Sian, we could ask him the question – and only hope Halliwell would be forthcoming with the answer.

Bill volunteered to write a script for the urgent interview and we agreed that we would assign it to Dex and Bea, the two officers who had already met Halliwell. Tomorrow morning, we would tuck the two detectives on the back of the surveillance crew following him. If we did have to arrest, then Dex and Bea would be ready to move in to conduct the safety interview at that point. The justification for the idea was the imminence of Sian's death if we didn't take that step.

It was good, in a way, to have a plan in place for what might happen on Thursday – but we had to get there first. If Halliwell didn't emerge from his house tomorrow morning, we might not have a suspect to conduct an urgent interview with. Again I kept calling Charlie Cheadle; again there was no news. I'd wondered if maybe Halliwell would wait until the small hours, then make his move and return to Sian – but the house stayed still and silent even as the night wore on, no shadowy figure slipping out to the green car parked upon the drive.

I paced the MIR; my office; the corridor with its harsh strip lights. Can you imagine the tension of the uncertainty? I didn't know what had happened to Sian, or what Halliwell might have done, to himself or to the girl I sought, and I was trying these tactics that had the potential to go so horribly wrong. I was mainlining coffee, buzzing on caffeine and fags and adrenaline and the sheer fear of all that could go awry, searching for some crumb of comfort where there was none.

One by one, colleagues, sensibly, started to head home. I was still battling to get the tap on Halliwell's phone, so I was right in the thick of it, waking people up at 2 a.m. and trying to explain that this was life or death. At some point, I noticed there were only the die-hards working on.

It was a surreal situation. Gablecross is a big police station: when it's empty, it's really quite an odd place. All around me were the entrails of people's crime files and bits of uniform kicking around, but there was hardly anybody there. It was a ghost town, shimmering with the spectre of absent coppers, haunted by missing girls and desperate men.

I think it was around 4 a.m. that I finally threw in the towel. The phone-tapping saga had run all through the night, until it had become irrelevant because the night had run out.

As I exited the nick, my head down, the black velvet collar of my herringbone coat turned up against my cheeks in the cool night air, I found microphones and cameras shoved under my nose: a handful of hardy journalists were still on the hunt for a good story. Even though my nerves felt balanced on a knife edge, I tried to remain pleasant.

'Just give me 24 hours,' was all I said.

For I knew, one way or the other, that this cat-and-mouse game with Halliwell would be over before the day was out.

35

I didn't even bother with the sofa that night. Having reached home, I had a shower, changed into a fresh suit and then came straight back to the nick, without a wink of sleep. There wasn't time for sleep. Today had to be the day I brought Sian home, and I had to be on top of her case from minute one.

As I drove back to Gablecross, I was trying to calculate the consequences of arresting Halliwell – as I knew must happen at some point today – in relation to finding Sian. I could imagine her so clearly, having dealt with similar crimes, with a rag stuffed in her mouth and her wrists rubbed raw with rope. But *alive* – still alive – and needing my help. How long could she survive if he had left her somewhere? When was the last time he would have been able to visit her? I could see no other equation but this: if I arrested him and held him in custody for the maximum 96 hours, it would surely secure her fate if she was still alive and he would not tell us where she was.

In the event of Halliwell's arrest, if he was not forth-coming about Sian's whereabouts, I foresaw that I would need to enlist the support of the public again to find her. Yet I also recognised that some missing people are never found. I didn't want Sian O'Callaghan to become another

Suzy Lamplugh – the young estate agent who was reported missing in 1986 and of whom there has never been another trace since. I had to do all in my power to rescue her and bring her home.

What else can I do? I wondered. *What other buttons can I push? Where else can I take this?* I contemplated deploying officers to question Halliwell outside of arrest, as one might do in a kidnap-and-extortion case. But if he refused to talk to them, it had the same effect as arresting him: we had shown our hand and blown our cover, and you cannot return to covert tactics once the subject is aware. I therefore still thought we had to carry on with Plan A: somehow persuade Halliwell to take us to Sian. It was our only hope.

I was already back in the MIR, hard at work, when Charlie Cheadle phoned in, just after 06.00. I held my breath as he updated me. What was the latest from Halliwell's house?

I can't tell you the relief I felt when he said that Halliwell had just got into his taxi to start his day's work. It washed over me, refreshing as iced water on a stifling summer's day. I'd spent the entire night frantic that he might have killed himself while inside that darkened house, but now I knew: the two of us both lived to fight another day.

I considered what it told me about him. After all, despite the pressure, he hadn't cracked. On the one hand, did that suggest his innocence? Perhaps the media messages had no effect because there was no guilty conscience to play upon. On the other hand, maybe he had a steelier character than I'd given him credit for. He hadn't crumbled on both counts: he had neither taken me to Sian, nor taken the 'easy' way out. If he was guilty, perhaps that brass neck he'd showed in putting up posters of Sian extended throughout his core, making him more metal than man.

In that moment, at 06.00 on Thursday morning, I couldn't be too disappointed that the plan to pressure Halliwell had not yet been successful, because I was far too relieved he was still alive. Nonetheless, the fact he hadn't cracked was sobering. Because, if he had the strength of character not to return to Sian when prompted to do so, and the fortitude to endure extreme pressure, then it didn't bode well that tightening the screws – as I planned to do that morning – would have any effect.

People were asking me the moment I got into the nick: 'What's the direction of the enquiry today? What's the plan, guv'nor?' Yet I didn't really have one beyond, 'Let's keep this strategy running.' I did still have the undercover officers to deploy, and I intended the final press statement in my media strategy to be released that very morning, which I hoped would act as a last lever to push Halliwell towards Sian. But, other than that, all I had was hope. I was hoping, hoping, hoping that something in the equation would change. A bit of leakage somewhere, a sighting of Sian's handbag or those distinctive boots, a witness who'd been abroad all week but came back today and suddenly said, 'I saw Halliwell snatch her.' Anything like that could tip the balance. Otherwise, beyond the strategies that were already underway, I could not think of any other tactic that could bring about Sian's safe return – except one, perhaps. A simple interview that said, 'Will you take me to her?'

At 09.05, the briefing began in the conference room on the top floor of Gablecross. I reminded the team that this was a crime in action, and told them that in all likelihood Halliwell would be arrested that day. Bea and Dex had their orders and were already with the surveillance team with Bill's urgent-interview script memorised. The fact that the situation *was* urgent was obvious: how long did Sian have left? The uncertainty was the major thing, because we didn't know what had happened to her. Even if it was statistically 99.9 per cent likely it was already too late, I had to fight for her to have that 0.1 per cent chance of life. If I didn't, I condemned her to die with my inaction. This was a race against time to give her that chance of life. I was painfully aware she might only have hours rather than days left to live. Given Halliwell hadn't yet returned to her while under surveillance, he might already have made the decision to abandon her to her fate.

It was at the briefing that an officer gave us a good strong lead to find her. He had remembered that there was a derelict café at Barbary Castle, nestled within its sprawling 12 acres of windswept land and within the narrowed-down search parameters supplied by FTS. Just as the house at Wanborough had been the day before, it seemed a likely place in which Sian might be being held hostage: an isolated 1950s concrete building to which nobody ever went any more. Search teams were already at Barbary Castle, but I now ordered that I wanted everything thrown at this: it was now the primary focus of our search for Sian. I just had this hunch that it was the favourite, and both the telephony and my hypotheses seemed to support the notion. A search team with dogs, as well as the force helicopter, were directed to be sent up there that morning.

The briefing concluded at 09.42. Just ten minutes later, I played my final hand. My last-ditch message to Halliwell was relayed to the media, in anticipation it would go out in the 10 a.m. news. It was an urgent appeal for witnesses, and I really pinned it down this time. I wanted Halliwell to feel that net falling over his head and beginning to tighten. I needed him to know he only had a very short time to get back to Sian before we made a move.

At 09.52, I appealed for sightings of a green Toyota Avensis in relation to the case of Sian O'Callaghan.

Yes, it was direct. Yes, it told him we were close to knowing who he was. But this was the last card I could turn over. It was now or never. In my mind I begged him: *Take me to Sian*.

It didn't take long for the message to have an effect. At 10.08, Halliwell was on the move. The surveillance crew followed him – into Boots, the chemist. He emerged at 10.11, throwing away the outer wrappings of small items he had purchased that he held in his hands, as though planning to use them instantly. Having thrown the rubbish in the bin, he got back into his car and drove away.

It was at 10.26 that the team recovered his receipt from the trash. What they saw had Charlie Cheadle reaching for his radio: Halliwell had purchased an overdose quantity of SleepEase and paracetamol.

When the news was relayed to me, I felt a crushing sense of abject powerlessness. All this time, I'd been plotting and planning, pulling this string and pushing that button, trying everything I could to bring about Sian's safe return. But with this development, everything was suddenly taken out of my hands. There was no question: under these circumstances I could not keep surveilling Halliwell without making an intervention. I couldn't allow him to commit suicide. Yet there was only one way to stop him.

And so – though I knew it was too soon; though I knew we didn't yet have Sian – at 10.28 I was forced to order the immediate arrest of Halliwell for the kidnap of Sian O'Callaghan.

36

I was under no illusions. In acting to save Halliwell's life, I could have cost Sian hers. If he didn't give up her location in the urgent interview, this was the end of the line. Now he had been arrested, he had rights under PACE, including the right to silence, the exercise of which right would cause the death of the party I'd been charged with saving – but I couldn't not arrest him because, if he killed himself, Sian would also die because he alone knew where she was. It was an impossible, catch-22 position.

At Gablecross, I paced the floor again, awaiting news from Charlie or Bill Dutton, who was also out on the ground overseeing the work of Dex and Bea. It can be frustrating to be an SIO, directing others to do the work in person, having to stay above the cut and thrust of a case and take an overview instead. But there was no question that it had to be my colleagues intervening, not me personally. For a start, Halliwell had just shown he was on the brink of taking his own life – for all I knew he was popping pills as he drove. There was no time for me to jump in a car and go after him. Primarily, though, SIOs try to avoid entering the evidential chain. You don't want to be the one actually putting a hand on somebody's shoulder, otherwise you'll end up as a bound witness when your case comes to court and you won't have a voice at the table in pre-trial briefings with the barristers. Instead, you utilise the big team of people working to your direction – that was *their* job – and I was fine with that.

It does leave you in the dark, though. As the minutes ticked by without an update, I wondered what on earth was happening. Had they arrested Halliwell yet? How did he respond? Would Dex and Bea get a cough in the interview? I was desperately hoping Halliwell would come across, that he'd hold his hands up and say, 'OK, fair play. You've caught me too quickly and I haven't had a chance to cover my tracks. This is where she is.'

But what if he didn't?

While we waited for news, Debs, John and a handful of other officers discussed the situation with me. It was hard to anticipate what the interview might throw out. Halliwell might make admissions; he might offer 'no comment'; he might say, 'I'm sorry for lying the other day, I was spooked when you came to see me, but I'm an innocent taxi driver and I dropped her off here.' People did sometimes lie when questioned by the police. Even though the intel cell hadn't yet come across a reason for him to do so (other than his suspected culpability for the offence), for all we knew he was having an affair that he didn't want to come out, and that's why he lied about his movements. His innocence, even at this stage, could not be discounted.

My brain was working in fast time, flicking through scenarios and calculating consequences. What would happen if Halliwell refused to reveal Sian's location in the urgent interview? I could visualise it clearly. He would be brought into custody, and the clock would start ticking – counting down the 96 hours to his release and to Sian's death.

And he would be released. We didn't yet have the forensics back on the perfume bottle, the bloodied tissues and the car seats, but there was a chance there would be nothing on them to link him to Sian. Even if there was, it was a very weak case. We'd have to present him with these items and say, 'I put it to you, Christopher Halliwell, that you abducted Sian O'Callaghan. Our evidence is that she was in your taxi and you got rid of these items when her case became a massive news story.' There wasn't a lawyer in the land who wouldn't laugh in my face. It was all circumstantial. Even if he'd killed her and we found her blood on the seats, without Sian herself to prove a murder had occurred, it clearly wasn't evidence beyond a reasonable doubt. She could have cut her finger on a broken bottle before she hopped out and went her merry way – that's what any lawyer could say.

If Halliwell refused to cough in the urgent interview, I could see no benefit to bringing him into custody to have such an exchange. All that would do was end Sian's life while the clock counted down. Yet we couldn't de-arrest him either: he was about to commit suicide. All hope for Sian seemed lost – but I thought, *That can't happen on this basis. We can't simply give up on her*.

To my mind, there was only one other thing we could do: talk to him. Talk to him again, in another urgent interview – this time, one that I would conduct myself, despite my desire to keep out of the evidential chain.

My colleagues and I talked it through. We were all actively engaged in the discussion, recognising the urgency of the situation. As I had done throughout the enquiry, I welcomed alternative viewpoints and people's advice. My deputy John was concerned about the idea, recognising that, while Section 11.1 of PACE allowed for an urgent interview, the idea of doing two seemed to breach the code. We'd all been in the job long enough to know that if somebody is under arrest they're required to be taken into the nearest police station. The way I was seeing the interaction with Halliwell, too, was of a frank exchange between two people, rather than a formal interview. John pointed out that such a move was likely to be frowned upon.

But the PACE guidelines are guidelines only: they are not laws. As in any code of practice, while the ideal is to adhere to it, sometimes its practical application in certain scenarios requires one to act in breach of it for the greater good. Since Code C of PACE had been incepted in 1984, it had attracted nine appendices – nine necessary amendments, in essence – once police officers started using it in their day-to-day work and realised that sometimes one size does not fit all. This felt like such a circumstance. The guidelines did not work in the interest of the victim whose life was being threatened. I felt it was my duty to put Sian first.

I knew that, should Dex and Bea not elicit a confession from Halliwell through the urgent interview, speaking to him myself after that event would not be illegal in any fashion or form. I was aware questions might be raised about the admissibility of evidence, but I also knew that, if I didn't do it, we didn't have a case anyway – and that Sian might never be found. An admissible 'no comment' was of no value whatsoever; this case wouldn't even get to court. My overwhelming thought was that we had nothing to lose by trying. If Halliwell came into custody at the nick, we had no other tactical options and no means by which Sian could be found. Although John remained unconvinced, others did not see any objections to the idea of simply asking Halliwell the question.

By this time, it was gone 11.00 and there was still no news. What were the teams doing out there? Unbeknown to me, it was taking a considerable period of time to get Halliwell into a position where they could make a safe arrest. I'd given the order at 10.28 and assumed that within minutes the arrest would be effected and Dex and Bea would commence the interview. In fact, none of that had happened in the intervening time. Left in the dark, hanging on a thread, I felt incredibly tense, pumped full of adrenaline, conscious that whatever happened next would make or break the case.

In the end, I bit the bullet and phoned Bill Dutton.

'What's happening?' I asked.

He told me that, a short time ago, Halliwell had been arrested in the Asda car park in Swindon at 11.06. It was now just gone 11.20. Even as we spoke, the urgent interview was underway.

37

He had already been cautioned by the officer who arrested him: 'You do not have to say anything, but it may harm your defence if you do mention when questioned, something which you later rely on in court. Anything you do say may be given in evidence.'

Then Dex Drummond stepped up to the plate, interviewing Halliwell in a miked-up police car in the Asda car park.

'The focus of the investigation is to find Sian O'Callaghan,' he told Christopher Halliwell.

That was always our prime objective; collaring Halliwell for her kidnap was a secondary concern if we could bring Sian home. It is what the kidnap manual directs. It's the most basic thing in it: you prioritise the victim's life. Nothing else matters relative to that; in fact, evidential recovery is fifth on the list.

'Tell me where Sian is,' Dex requested.

'I don't know,' claimed Christopher Halliwell.

'Can you help us with where Sian is?' Dex tried again.

'I don't know where she is,' Halliwell repeated. 'I don't think I should say any more without speaking to a solicitor.'

'Do you know if Sian is safe?'

'No comment.'

'Can you help us in finding out if Sian is safe?'

'No comment, not until I speak to a solicitor. Can I go to the police station now?'

Back at that police station, I still didn't know what was happening. The urgent interview lasted eight minutes, concluding at 11.28. Having heard no word since my call shortly before that time, I eventually called Bill back around 11.45.

'What's happening?' I asked again, the tension of the situation making me curt.

'Well,' Bill said, hesitating. And then: 'He's offered no comment.'

No comment. The expression 'my heart sank' does not do the terrible feeling justice. *No comment.* It meant no case; no cough; *no Sian.*

'We're bringing him back,' Bill added. 'We're on our way to the nick right now.'

I felt heat rising on my neck in an ugly red flush. That wasn't Bill's decision to make; I was annoyed at that. Though he was simply acting in accordance with PACE, I would still have expected him to notify me of the no-comment interview first, before *I* made the call to take Halliwell into custody. Because Bill might have given up – but I hadn't. His actions, however, added another layer to the pressure. For Halliwell was in a car right at this moment, on his way to Gablecross. The moment he got here, there really were no more options.

Because, if I let him come into custody at the nick, what would happen next? If he'd offered no comment to my colleagues just now, why on earth would he change his mind and offer an explanation once he had a solicitor by his side, whose job was to prevent him incriminating himself? If I took him into custody without knowing where Sian was, he would obviously offer no comment again and Sian would die.

I thought about what I'd suggested earlier: speaking to him myself. What were the consequences of that?

Well, there would be criticism, but if I could draw out from him the location of where Sian was being held hostage, I could save her life. That was evidently a far better outcome than her death, which was assured by my doing nothing.

There was a strange feeling of prickly heat. Even as Bill stayed on the line, having dropped his bombshell, my brain was racing, desperately trying to work out the permutations of this situation. I was in some kind of hyper state, I think, but actually in that state my mind was working really clearly. Everything was sharply in focus and my thought processes were crystallising to one essential realisation: either I went out now and intercepted Halliwell before he got to the nick, or I let Sian die. Notwithstanding the opprobrium that might come my way subsequently, I felt it was my duty to look Halliwell in the eye and ask him one question: 'Will you take me to Sian?'

'Stop the car,' I told Bill Dutton at 11.51. 'Hang fire. I'll call you back.'

I had only minutes to make the decision. Was I going to do this? Was I going to breach PACE in order to save a girl's life? It was literally a do-or-die scenario.

In that hyper state, with a clear mind, I assessed the situation. This was a crime in action. What did the kidnap manual and the law say? They were quite clear. The normal investigative priorities of securing evidence, arresting an offender and prosecution were relegated. The victim's life came first. In legislation, Article 2 of the Human Rights Act demands that the police take reasonable steps to protect an individual's life if they know there is a real and immediate risk to that person's life, and it imposes an obligation on the State to protect that right to life. It is a positive, not passive obligation. Officers can't just sit back and wash their hands of things: we have to intervene. If Halliwell had Sian O'Callaghan bound and gagged somewhere, as I feared, and his silence under Code C of PACE would cause her death, then Sian's right to life under Article 2 took priority and precedence: it had the prior claim over Halliwell's rights as a detained person (rights which were, after all, protected by guidelines and not enshrined in law). Essentially, I couldn't do nothing. It was my legal duty to intervene.

The law didn't give me carte blanche to do whatever I wanted, I will add. I couldn't hang him over a motorway bridge, beat him to a pulp or waterboard him – such activities were quite rightly precluded under Article 3 of the Human Rights Act. But I could speak to him; I could ask the question.

That didn't mean it was an easy choice to make. In fact, the easiest thing to do would be to let events take their course and simply say, 'Well, I've done all I can do under PACE and that's the end of it.' But could I live with myself if – next week, say, or the month after – we stumbled on Sian in some remote cranny of Barbary Castle, and discovered she had been alive at this very moment, but died because I personally didn't take every possible step to find her? Who would put their arm around my shoulder then and say, 'Well, at least you didn't breach PACE'?

On the contrary, they'd be saying, 'Why didn't you speak to Halliwell and beg him to tell you where Sian was? There's no harm in speaking to him, Steve. It's not against the law to talk to a bloke.' Could any professional police officer worthy of the name, given responsibility for saving someone's life under these circumstances, stop at the urgent interview administered by my junior colleagues and say, 'Well, I've never seen the bloke myself, but if he's decided to offer no comment then that's the end of Sian's life'?

The fact that I had never met Halliwell myself weighed heavily upon me. I could never forget: it might not be his car on the CCTV; even if it was, he could just have been giving Sian a lift, at her request, as part of his work as a taxi driver. His dumping of so-called 'evidence' could just be a spring clean. His shaking and lying yesterday could be a naturally nervous response to police enquiries – just as Kevin Reape, earlier in this investigation, had seemed pale and anxious when I'd interviewed him at the nick. Having spent an hour with Kevin, I could discount him: I'd looked him in the eye and knew he was a genuine, distressed loved one who only wanted Sian to come home. I hadn't looked Christopher Halliwell in the eye. Really, despite my policeman's 'gut', I had no sure way of knowing if he was the offender or not.

Even the fact he had offered 'no comment' just now to Dex Drummond didn't tell me a goddamn thing. I knew people watched TV and got the idea that you should offer 'no comment' upon arrest, and leave it for the police to prove their case. It was a response that could backfire spectacularly. There had been a case – on which I wasn't the SIO – where the lead investigator was convinced this young fellow had committed a murder because, when questioned about his movements on the night in question, he had offered no comment. The other evidence was circumstantial – he happened to be in the right place at the right time – but when he chose not to offer an account, the SIO determined that he must be the killer. This thing went all the way to court where, of course, the bloke was found not guilty because the evidential case was only circumstantial. And that was just as well: it turned out someone else did the job, later confessed and was ulti-mately convicted. But it went to show: saying 'no comment' might not be a sign of guilt, just a sign of senseless self-defence – batten down the hatches and 'I'm saying nothing to you, copper'.

The case I've just described was salient at this moment for another reason too. Was I doing exactly what that SIO had done? Was I adding two plus two and getting five? It was possible I'd built a whole balloon of hot air around Halliwell, fired by everybody's desperation to find an explanation for where Sian was, until it had taken on a life of its own and unstoppably sailed away. Strip it back, suck out the air that made that balloon billow, and all I had was a nervous bloke throwing away a bit of litter.

If that was the case, and Halliwell was innocent, what would happen when I took him into custody for the kidnap of Sian O'Callaghan? I didn't have to look out my window to know the media were out there, ready to beam images of the arrested man around the world. (In fact, as I was soon to learn, Halliwell's arrest in the Asda car park had been filmed by a member of the public on their mobile phone, and was already on sale to the highest bidder.) The media were hungry for stories and they would be all over the news of this arrest like vultures on roadkill. We were only two months on from the Christopher Jefferies scandal. If I called this wrong, then it would be a replay of that situation. I'd cause an innocent man untold suffering and loss of reputation, while the reputation of both the force and myself would be destroyed. Can you imagine the headlines once the truth came out? 'This man is innocent! This poor man! The incompetent wretched useless police officers have once again cocked up!'

It was sobering to realise, too, that even if Halliwell was guilty, at the moment I couldn't prove it. Unlike Jefferies, he could be the bloke who'd done this – but he might get away with it. Innocent or guilty, he might then have a case for wrongful arrest, and the damages would be incrementally greater as it would be an arrest that had occurred as the headline act in a media circus.

Speaking with Halliwell myself was therefore even more important. Doing so would enable me to test whether we had the right person or had made a colossal mistake. I didn't want to take him into custody in front of the world's media only for him to say that he was an innocent taxi driver; that wouldn't help him, and it certainly wouldn't help Sian if she only had hours left to live and we had to spend three of them in the nick waiting for Halliwell's solicitor to turn up. I wanted him to tell me now if he was innocent – and I wanted to look him in the eye while he did it.

There is no substitute for it. Without that interpersonal connection, it's very hard to get a feeling on an individual. Everything I knew about Halliwell had come to me second-hand. Unless I looked him in the eye and made a first-hand assessment, I was relying on a colleague's judgment – yet I was accountable, if they were wrong. Notwithstanding the general rule that an SIO stays out of the evidential chain, in this case it was an interaction I *had* to make myself. Not only for my own peace of mind that I had personally done all I could to find Sian, but also because I couldn't ask anybody else to breach PACE and conduct a second interview outside the nick. It had to be me; it couldn't be anyone else. My sole purpose was to appeal to him to show me where Sian was, with the intention of saving her life.

I took a deep breath. I could consult my colleagues on this dilemma – and I had – but ultimately it was my call. This wasn't a joint decision because none of my colleagues would ever be accountable in any fashion or form. The responsibility rested on my shoulders and mine alone. They wouldn't go to their graves – as I knew other SIOs had done, in similar cases where the hostages had died – thinking, *I should have done more. I was responsible for her life and I let the victim down.*

I could picture Sian in my mind's eye. She might be waiting for help to come, praying for it with every desperate thought she had. If I didn't take this step, she would die alone and abandoned, and I would be responsible.

I could picture her mother Elaine, too. 'I won't rest until I find Sian,' I'd told her. I had made her a promise. And I was not a man to break his word.

The skill of an SIO is to calculate consequences and that is what I now did. I knew what would happen if I let him into custody: Sian would die. What would happen if I didn't, and intervened to speak with him myself? As I saw it, there were four possible consequences.

One: he might offer 'no comment' to me, too, in which case there would be nothing else I could do but take him into custody – scrabbling around for some evidence that probably wouldn't convict him – but at least I would be able to look Elaine O'Callaghan in the eye and say that there was nothing more I could have done for her daughter.

Two: Halliwell could turn out to be an innocent taxi driver. Then I could move the focus of the investigation to the location where he had dropped off Sian.

Three: he might admit he had kidnapped her and lead me to his hideout, in which case I could rescue her and bring her home safe. That was the ideal scenario.

Or, four, he might have killed her. This was the only truly problematic situation from my own perspective – because, if he had, then the necessity for the urgent interview would cease, although only at the moment when I conclusively knew that she was dead. Nonetheless, if he was willing to reveal her location to me, then even in that instance, her family would not suffer the heartache of never knowing where she was or what had happened to her. Even in that instance, I could still bring Sian O'Callaghan home.

To my mind, any one of those outcomes was infinitely better than the consequence of doing nothing at all. I was crystal clear, even in that heated moment of decision, that if I didn't do this, Sian's life was over.

It was peculiar, in a way, I reflected as I picked up the Nokia and frantically dialled Bill Dutton. For the past six days, I had been juggling so many lines of enquiry; there were so many roads we'd wandered down, so many routes to take. But, now, I could see no other course of action but this one. It was a simple choice. I either accepted Sian's death, or I did my duty.

One last roll of the dice.

'Bill?' I said when he picked up. 'I'm going to speak to him myself. Take Halliwell to Barbary Castle.'

38

There was no time to discuss the decision further once it had been made. 'I'll get a car,' said my colleague Gary Hale, dashing out the door.

Debs and I left my office at a lightning-quick pace. The pressure was intense: I'd run all through the night with no sleep, on edge in case Halliwell topped himself, and the morning had offered nothing like relief. Now, in the blink of an eye, I'd had to weigh up so many conflicting arguments and condense them into a single moment of clarity. I felt pumped full of adrenaline. My thoughts were entirely focused on Halliwell and the extraordinary thing I was going to try to do: persuade him to take me to a girl he'd kidnapped so that I could save her life.

Which was why, when one of the press officers stopped me on my way out – a wizened old gipper of the most ghastly sort – I gave him short shrift. By now, the media had got hold of the arrest video and the officer was demanding to know why I'd made the arrest. I'd barely had time to assimilate the information myself and the media were on our backs already; it only heightened my concerns about nicking Halliwell if he was innocent. I knew why I'd ordered the arrest – because he was about to commit suicide – but I didn't want a public pronouncement on the subject; putting out a media statement was the last thing on my mind. The officer was insistent; in my memory, I remember it as him almost rugby-tackling me as I strode out to meet with Halliwell. In the end, I had to tell him forcefully, 'NOT NOW!' There may have been a few Anglo-Saxon expletives in there too, if I'm honest.

In hindsight, in some ways I think it was good we had the contretemps. It let a bit of the pressure out and in the wake of it I felt a steady climbdown from the adrenaline rush I'd been experiencing. As I stepped out into the back yard of the nick and Gary pulled up in his unmarked silver Audi, I felt this strange calmness descending on me, as though I was in the eye of a storm.

Debs and I fell straight into the car and Gary drove off at speed. All of us were conscious of the time pressure we were under: whatever had happened to Sian, it seemed unlikely she had much survival time left. Every second counted.

As we drove, the car was alive with the sound of ringtones. Debs was fielding calls from the nick, but every time she hung up another call would come in. We asked a senior officer to put out a holding statement to keep the media at bay. I took a call from Bill Dutton too.

'Are you sure you want to do this?' he asked. He was trying to offer me some sage counsel. But Bill wasn't responsible for Sian O'Callaghan's life. If it all went dark, it was on my conscience.

'Don't get wobbly on me, Bill,' I told him briefly. 'I'll see you up there.'

After the call from Bill, I sat locked in my own thought processes. I did think: *I could just stop the car and go back, then we won't have a problem.* But I also thought: *Then we won't ever have Sian again.*

It was a drive of some 15 minutes. After a while, the calls stopped coming from the nick and it was quiet, the countryside flashing by outside the window. I had an entirely open mind about the man I was about to meet. I had hypotheses and theories, but I didn't really have the faintest idea who he was. I didn't know what I was going to find.

By the time we were travelling up the country track that led to Barbary Castle and turning off it into the grey-gravelled car park, I felt almost eerily calm. I could see search teams dotted about the place: an indication of why I'd asked Bill to bring Halliwell here. My best bet was that Sian was here somewhere. Naive as it may sound, I thought that if he could literally point her out to us with a simple finger – 'She's over there beneath the floorboards in the café' – then she had a greater proportionate chance of surviving.

I suppose, psychologically, there was perhaps an element of wanting to impress him, too. I was almost laying my cards on the table: 'I think she's here somewhere and you know where that is.' Would he think I was a clever detective for having identified her rough location? Would that make him more likely to come across?

It was a clear, crisp day with particularly bright sunlight and cartoon-like clouds in the sky. We drove away from the search teams and pulled up in the main car park; there were one or two cars dotted about. We weren't near the fort itself, but a single green mound rose incongruously in front of the gravelled tarmac before the vista gave way onto a picturesque view of rolling fields.

We were there for only a moment or two before a marked patrol car driven by PS Danny Jones came up beside us; Halliwell was in the back. It was 12.11 on Thursday afternoon.

'Follow me and write down everything I say,' I instructed Debs before we got out of the Audi. Her role would be to record everything that transpired between us as best she could. This wasn't a behind-closed-doors encounter: I wanted a transparent record of what I was about to do.

I swung the car door open and stepped out. I think the police helicopter was clattering overhead, searching for Sian as I'd directed, but I was so focused on the man I was about to meet that I didn't even notice it. I walked the few feet between our vehicles and opened the back door of the patrol car.

'Hello, Chris.'

He turned his distinctive eyes on me. His complexion was sallow and there were bags beneath those eyes, as though – like me – he hadn't slept the night before. Up close, his eyes were a piercing blue, with a dark-brown ring around each iris. He was dressed smartly: black trousers and shoes with an off-white open-neck shirt. His hands were handcuffed at the front.

'I'm Steve Fulcher,' I said, introducing myself. I used my first name deliberately. If there was an opportunity to form a rapport with Halliwell, even in these extreme circumstances, I needed to take it. My old mentor Howard Bostock sat upon my shoulder: this was about empathy, not oppression. I needed to draw him out. Instinctively, I sensed that I couldn't be judgmental or antagonistic, nor attempt to impose myself or my agenda upon him. Going in hard would be counterproductive: he would instantly clam up and I'd blow any chance of forming a relationship with him.

As our eyes locked, Halliwell struck me as remarkably calm. Though there was tension in his frame, he held himself together unusually well for a man in his position. He looked quite sullen, but there was something else, too – a certain determination. I think he was calculating; calculating how to react. Exactly as I was doing, I believe he was asking himself, 'What's the best approach here?'

I spoke again. 'I'm running this enquiry and I'm looking for Sian O'Callaghan. I'd like you to get out of the car and come with me.'

He acquiesced, swinging his legs out of the vehicle and standing up. We were roughly the same height; he had a wiry build. Danny Jones had done a quick sweep for members of the public and indicated that the area was clear. So Halliwell and I walked a short distance from the car – about 30 feet – to stand at the foot of that strange green mound. Danny stood on top of it, keeping watch. And Debs just stood behind me, her blue notebook clutched in her hands. It was a smart decision on her part: she said, later, that she weighed up standing by the side of me, but thought it might be oppressive: two people standing shoulder to shoulder with Halliwell on his own. Also, given the crime we suspected Halliwell of committing, she thought having a woman present might prevent him speaking. She positioned herself a few steps behind my right shoulder, half-shielding herself from Halliwell's view.

It was just me and him. Halliwell and I were eyeball to eyeball. There was nowhere for him to hide: no lawyer to divert attention; no way he could obfuscate. This was a one-on-one exchange: the ultimate battle of wills.

As we faced each other at the foot of that hill, I could almost taste the words of the formal police caution. Even though I viewed this interaction as an extension of the urgent interview, I knew that because there had been a break in proceedings while Halliwell was driven here, the guidelines said that I should caution him again.

The caution begins: 'You do not have to say anything ...' Well, in these circumstances, I wasn't going to tell Christopher Halliwell that – because he *did* have to say something. I felt wholly justified in my approach because Sian's right to life was more important than a PACE-compliant interview. Simple as. Opening our conversation by telling him that he didn't have to say anything was counterintuitive: I believed he had information that would help her, I wasn't going to tell him that he didn't have to give it to me. I was prepared to do what I thought I should do: beg for the life of a young woman.

And so we began.

'Are you going to tell me where Sian is?' I asked. My voice was calm and low.

Halliwell was silent for a long time. Then he said: 'I don't know anything.'

His voice, like mine, was carefully modulated. And that calm exchange was absolutely right, because for me it was a very solemn moment. I was pleading for Sian's life – but, in return, I wanted him to give me his: for if he was guilty and gave up her location, he was going to jail for a very long time. That's not something you can demand of someone or get angry about. There should be a solemnity to proceedings.

After he spoke for the first time, I was silent too, thinking hard. Thinking that 'I don't know anything' wasn't an answer; he *did* know something, because I was 99.9 per cent sure that was his car outside the Goddard Arms. It felt like he was trying to buy some time; that he was not prepared to tell the truth. How could I elicit Sian's location from him, when he had every interest in not giving it to me?

'Are you going to tell me where Sian is?' I tried again.

He was silent. In the quiet, I tried to read him, looking for those non-verbal signals I'd been taught would mean I was dealing with someone who was anxious or duplicitous. Yet Halliwell showed none of the usual tells. He was very controlled. Throughout, his distinctive eyes stayed fixed on mine: there was no looking away or a flickering of his eyelids; he was able to maintain eye contact. If he was hiding something, he was clearly capable of fronting it out.

'What's going to happen is,' I said, 'that if you tell us where Sian is, that whatever you will be portrayed as, you would have done the right thing.'

If Halliwell had any conscience left, I knew I had to find it quickly and find a way of appealing to it. I needed to show him it was in his interests to help me. If we recovered Sian alive, it was not murder. He wouldn't have committed the most serious offence. Everything, in time, could be moderated and mitigated. Yet if he stayed on this path, he was doomed.

Once again Halliwell was silent. Then he said: 'I want to go to the station.'

He was stonewalling. I assessed him closely, trying to read him.

'If you're innocent, just tell me. Tell me and I'll take the enquiry from there.' I didn't want to take him into custody if he wasn't involved; this current line of his, of saying nothing, was bad for us both. 'Are you prepared to tell me where Sian is?'

I kept using her name repeatedly. She was a person, not just his victim. She had to seem real to him – as real as his daughters – otherwise he would feel no compunction at abandoning her.

Once more he was silent for a long period, coolly assessing me in return. In the quiet, both of us stared each other out, looking for leakage. Halliwell didn't know how much or how little I knew. Just as he didn't want to show his hand, neither did I. I deliberately made my questions focused yet vague, not revealing any information that I might usually give up in a classic quid pro quo. I didn't say to him, 'We have you on CCTV at 3 a.m. outside the Goddard Arms,' because then he could come up with a story to explain it. As things stood, he didn't want to cough to being the fella who picked her up, because he didn't know I knew that. Evidently, exposing what I knew would also expose what I didn't – and I didn't know so much. What I was asking him to do, in fact, was extraordinary: to roll over on the basis of no evidence at all. Yet I couldn't let *him* know that we had no evidence. I had to hold the line.

The silence continued. Halliwell stayed firm, those blue eyes boring into mine, no flicker of guilt or uncertainty to see. But, despite himself, there *was* leakage. The time he was taking to reply, for instance. His brain was working overtime and he was actively avoiding answering my questions. Yet an innocent person, in the same situation, would give an answer: 'Look, I really don't know where she is, it's got nothing to do with me.' Instead, with Halliwell, there was a disconnect. Our conversation was slow and strained; it was disjointed, because he was clearly trying to find a form of words that didn't implicate him – yet, in itself, that struggle signalled his guilt. An innocent person wouldn't have to think; they simply wouldn't have this conversation on these terms. Therefore – I concluded with an increasing certainty – I was having a conversation with a guilty person.

'You think I did it,' Christopher Halliwell said.

I held his gaze unblinkingly. 'I *know* you did it,' I replied.

I didn't – not for a fact. I was bluffing. But it was the only answer I could give. He was interviewing me as much as I was interviewing him and I had to hold the line.

How good is my poker face? I wondered desperately, even as I held his gaze. *Will he see through this? Will it shore up his determination to say nothing at all?* I felt we were both at the extremities of our intellectual manoeuvring. There was a strange, unspoken bond between us as we each mentally battled to win the upper hand.

There was a long silence as Christopher Halliwell stared me out. Then he said: 'Can I go to the station?'

'You can go to the station,' I told him, staying strong, trying to show nothing of my thoughts in my expression. 'What will happen is that you will be vilified in the press. Do you remember the Joanna Yeates murder and Christopher Jefferies? He was all over the papers. If you tell me where Sian is, they will know you helped me; you would have done the right thing.'

I was trying to throw him a rope. If he was innocent, he needed to know he could end up like Jefferies if he wasn't careful. If he was guilty, it was still in his interests to take me to Sian.

More silence; more leakage. Then: 'I want to speak to a solicitor.'

My heart was pounding as he said the words. PACE isn't just about cautions and being in a police station; the right to a solicitor is also key. I was supremely conscious that Halliwell had that right and that I was stepping over a line. Equally: at what point could I give up on Sian? In these circumstances, I thought asking again was reasonable.

'You are being given an opportunity to tell me where Sian is. In one hour's time, you will be in the press.'

He held the line. 'I want to speak to a solicitor.'

Halliwell was firm and in control. On this afternoon, on this windswept hill, there was no indication of the tears of yesterday afternoon or the suicidal man I'd heard about from my team. At this crunch point, he was maintaining his position in a very calm and resolute manner. We were two people locked in a moment in time.

Halliwell was undoubtedly calculating, *What do the police know?* He must have been pretty confident about the passive data; he'd switched off all his devices. Was he wondering about potential witnesses, about how close we were to finding Sian, about how much of his DNA he might have left on her?

I had questions running through my head too. *How long can I keep this going for? Can I do anything else? Can I change this equation?* The stakes were sky-high. For Halliwell, he faced lifelong incarceration. For me, this was my only chance to plead for Sian's life.

Yet I was conscious, too, that I shouldn't outright beg. We were equals in that moment, Halliwell and I. The whole thing balanced on a slim knife edge. I couldn't supplicate to him, nor could I overpower him. Every pause and word that passed between us felt like a hand in a game of poker.

I felt an aura around him. I looked him in the eye. I thought, *He is the right bloke and I'm not giving up.*

'You will speak to a solicitor,' I told him.

There was silence.

'I'm giving you an opportunity to tell me where Sian is.'

Silence.

'By the end of this cycle, you will be vilified.' It was a reminder of what I'd already said.

Halliwell and I continued to look at each other. Still he didn't blink, he didn't crack, he didn't cave. I felt a wrenching, crushing sense of failure. *This isn't going to work. He's not going to come across.* Every hour of the past few days I had channelled all my mental abilities into outwitting him, trying to find a way inside his mind – a way to persuade him to give up Sian O'Callaghan. Every move I'd made – the carefully worded press releases, the approach to get his DNA – had been calculated with an end point in mind. I had put him under pressure with reason. I had brought everything I could to bear. Yet now defeat was seconds away and I felt physically sick. I couldn't keep him here indefinitely. If I couldn't persuade him, it was over.

I fixed him with a gaze that tried to command, without words, that he *had* to do this thing. There were no more tricks. No more tactics. It was just him and me, each one of us calculating if the other was about to give up.

I swallowed one last time. I gave it one last go.

At least I would know that I had tried.

'Tell me where Sian is?'

We stared each other out. Sian's life hung in the balance – hung between us, teetering this way and that on a thin narrow beam. In my mind's eye, I could see her still, but there was nothing more I could do for her. I sent my thoughts winding skyward, to wherever she might be. *I'm sorry, Sian O'Callaghan. I'm sorry I couldn't save you. I'm sorry I let you down.*

Then Halliwell spoke, in a mechanical tone that had a sense of finality.

'Have you got a car? We'll go.'

39

I felt butterflies in my stomach at his words. I hoped he had made the decision to roll over, but it wasn't crystal clear. 'Have you got a car? We'll go' could also be a reiteration of his desire to go to the police station.

Whatever he meant, it was a decision that we acted upon. Side by side, we walked back to the patrol car and I ducked his head into the vehicle as he took his position in the rear behind the passenger seat. I swung in next to him and directed Debs to take the seat in front. I fastened Halliwell's belt across him.

'Are you sure it's not too tight, Chris?'

I was solicitous, trying to keep the bond between us on an even keel. It still felt like a knife-edge moment. What had Halliwell meant? I deliberately didn't ask him to clarify – didn't say, 'Are you going to take us to Sian, then?' I didn't want to break the moment, to focus his mind on the choice he'd made – if indeed he'd made that choice.

'Danny, just follow Chris's instructions,' I told the copper at the wheel.

At 12.20, the patrol car moved off and swung towards the winding road leading out of the car park. It was only at this point that I realised we had a massive audience. Halliwell, of course, was still under surveillance: there were at least 13 cars parked up a short distance away, and every man and his uncle was watching; there must have been the thick end of 30 officers. The sensitivity of the situation was such that I couldn't say a word: I simply crooked my finger as we passed and directed them to follow.

As we drove through the silver gates at the entrance to the car park, Halliwell suddenly seemed to take in his surroundings.

'Why did you bring me here?' he asked.

Later, that question would make me chuckle. I'd brought him to Barbary Castle because I thought Sian was here – evidently, that hunch I'd had that made it favourite was completely and utterly wrong. So much for the clever detective. I managed to deflect the question in the moment, not giving away my hand, only hoping that he'd think the search teams in the area were just there at this time because we were, too.

We drove on, heading sharply downhill as banks rose on either side of us before giving way to flat fields. And as Halliwell gave directions to Danny, I grew increasingly concerned.

We were on our way back to the nick.

I wondered if Halliwell knew it. Had this been his intention all along?

'Chris,' I said, having to interrupt, 'if we keep going down this route, you've got Sky TV vans and BBC sat vans ...'

Halliwell nodded. And then: 'We can divert round here,' he said. He directed Danny to take the three sides of a square to avoid the nick and then we headed out of Swindon on the A420. It was only at that point that I thought, with disbelief, *Bloody hell, it's worked. Halliwell is taking us to Sian!*

It was a surreal feeling. There was a sense of rising euphoria, of having achieved an impossible result, but it was tempered by the knowledge that, until we reached her, Halliwell could change his mind at any moment. We still didn't know where she was, so I remained focused. A misplaced word could turn him from being amenable to saying, 'You bastard, you're rolling me over, you take me back to the nick at once.' We were still hanging by a thread, and I had to be at the very top of my game to see this through.

The atmosphere in the car was tense, yet also calm. Halliwell seemed to be unburdening himself now he had made the decision – it was as though a weight was lifting from his shoulders as we drove – but he was not relaxed. Very few words passed between us in the car, just Chris giving directions to the place where he'd secreted Sian.

The police radio, too, was silent, and in hindsight that was thanks to the professional, switched-on response of my brilliant team. They appreciated the delicacy of the moment we were all in. One call from HQ, one radio transmission, and Halliwell might wake up and realise that taking us to Sian meant he was going to jail, but my team were on it and there were no comms.

In the moment, though, I paid that no mind at all. My attention was focused solely on Christopher Halliwell. At one point he asked for the heater to be turned on as his feet were freezing, to which we acquiesced. At another, I offered him a cigarette, which he accepted.

I made placatory small talk as I rolled him one, getting out the paraphernalia from my suit pocket and lining up the tobacco in a thin blue Rizla. For all that Yvonne disapproves, it's one of the things I'm really good at in life, rolling cigarettes, and Halliwell got the benefit of my expertise. We shared trivial, tangential information – how many we smoked a day – as we both puffed away, letting the nicotine do its work. We weren't laughing and joking – this was not a scene of blokey bonhomie – but the small talk was intentional. I was deliberately diverting his attention because the one thing I didn't want him to consider was the decision he'd made. I wanted to normalise what we were doing, for him simply to think – if he thought about it at all – *I'm taking Steve to Sian*, and for the enormity of that decision to be minimised. Chatting about our smoking habits made that decision part of everyday life. I knew, at all costs, that I had to hold him in the moment.

I had no idea of how long the journey was; no idea if we'd been travelling for 15 minutes or 5. I couldn't say, obviously, 'Where are we going?' because I couldn't give away that we were completely in the dark as to her location. Yet as the miles passed and the time ticked by, I was increasingly confident that we were going somewhere specific, that Halliwell alone knew of. That euphoric feeling built: we were going to find Sian, against all the odds.

We drove onto the B4000 Shrivenham/Lambourn road, then took a left towards Wantage on the B4507. I didn't connect the dots at the time. Only later did I realise that this very location was where Halliwell had given the surveillance crew the slip.

After a while, Halliwell seemed to recognise where he was and familiarise himself with the location. He asked for the car to slow down.

We were on a tiny road, almost a single track. On the left-hand side was a barbed-wire fence, with maybe three or four strands on thin wire, set against a rough grass verge. We were in the heart of the Oxfordshire countryside, near Uffington, and miles of expanse surrounded us. There was the occasional farmhouse dotted about, but otherwise it was a complete wilderness.

With a stark sensation, I acknowledged the facts: this location was any number of miles away from where we had been searching for Sian. This site had never been on our radar. It was a very sobering thought. *We would never have found her.*

The police car prowled along the road. We were all looking out the windows, looking for Sian. We passed a farm, and I wondered if Halliwell would direct us to pull in and indicate one of its outbuildings, but he didn't. Instead, we continued along this very remote country lane.

Beyond the grass verge, a steep bank sloped away from us. It must have been a 12-foot drop, with an abundance of trees, brush and brambles at the bottom.

Halliwell indicated towards it. He said he'd pushed her down the bank in the dark.

My breath came out in a rush; it was such a callous thing to do. I recognised, too, that there was no physical access to the bank below: no dog-walkers went that way; no farmers tilled that land. No one would have stumbled across Sian by accident, ever. But we were here now. We had come to bring her home.

'Is she concealed?' I asked, wanting to send the search teams in quick-sharp.

'She's not concealed,' he said.

'Is she clothed?'

'Mostly clothed.' He confirmed she had been wearing a grey dress.

As the car drove along the road at a snail's pace, Halliwell said he remembered the topography, but was uncertain about the exact location because it had been so dark when he'd left her here alone. We drove the length of the road, until we reached some crossroads where he indicated that we had now driven too far. Danny turned the car around and the search along the roadside began again. We wound down the car windows to see more clearly; the fresh air was welcome, as the warmth from the spring sun and the heater meant the car was stuffy. Above us, the force helicopter followed our every move.

Christopher Halliwell was fully engaged with the search for Sian; with the effort to remember and identify her location. I think, in the journey from Barbary Castle, that he had gone on his own personal journey too. From his denial of any involvement, he had finally reached a destination where he was fully contrite. In fact, he seemed agitated that he couldn't recall the exact spot where he'd left her. 'Further than this,' he would say, or, 'No, maybe it was back there.' We could have been having a conversation about something trivial: one bloke desperately trying to help another bloke find something he'd lost. But we were looking for a missing girl.

'Is this where you first brought her?' I asked. 'Or did you reposition her?'

'I repositioned her,' he said.

'Where was the original site?'

He replied to the effect that we'd been very close in our searches in the Savernake Forest area. Those 10,000 people might just have found her, four days before, if only we'd been lucky.

'When did you move her?' I asked.

'The Tuesday night.'

'It can't have been the Tuesday!' I protested, without thinking. 'We had you under surveillance then.' It was a stupid thing to say, giving away information. 'Perhaps it was the Monday,' I told him.

'Yeah, yeah,' he agreed idly. 'The Monday.'

Now, in hindsight, I think he was right the first time. He'd admitted we were close to finding Sian in our searches; both that and the high-profile media coverage must have had him spooked, so he'd had to move her. In that intense moment, I had forgotten that the surveillance guys had lost him for an hour and eight minutes on Tuesday night – only a mile or so from where we were – and only picked him up again in Wanborough, minutes before he set that fire. Now, I think that night is when he moved her. Perhaps the item he burnt was what he'd wrapped her in. If we'd been fortunate enough, I think the surveillance team could have caught him with Sian in the boot of his car.

'When did you last know she was here?' I asked.

'Two days ago.'

I did the calculations. From everything Halliwell was saying, I knew Sian O'Callaghan was probably dead. But I also knew I had to find her, to check, because otherwise she *would* be dead, and we were sitting here chatting while the last vestiges of her life leaked away. We had to put the facilities in place that would save her life if it was there to be saved.

Halliwell continued to scan the verge for any familiar markers, but after some time he conceded that he could not remember exactly. He had managed to identify a mile-long stretch of the road. I urgently directed that the officers following behind us should mark the search parameters at either end of the track. We needed to send in search teams and paramedics ASAP.

I glanced over at the man sitting beside me in the car. He was looking out the window. 'You've been helpful,' I told him.

'You will find her,' he replied.

And I knew we would. This wasn't a 6.7-mile-radius search area. This was a single-mile stretch. I was 100 per cent confident that Halliwell had been honest in his identification of it. We would find Sian O'Callaghan.

So I was grateful, as I thanked Halliwell for what he had done.

'Let's get you back to the nick,' I told him. 'We'll get you a solicitor and a cup of coffee.'

He had asked for another cigarette, and he blew the smoke out slowly as he looked at me, those distinctive eyes finding mine.

'You and I should have a chat,' he said.

40

I was thrown by the suggestion. My head was full of thoughts regarding everything we needed to do for Sian; as far as I was concerned, this chapter with Halliwell had ended. Though I hoped the search teams might find Sian alive, I knew from what Halliwell had now said that in all likelihood they would find her dead. The urgent interview was over. So when Halliwell asked for a chat, I thought, *Do I need the grief, really?*

I looked at him. I believed he had gone to a great deal of effort just now to try to recall and give me Sian's location. There was a clear exhibition of contrition on his part. The bond between us was palpable, and in that instant I interpreted it as having a quality of mutual respect.

Before, I had wanted him to speak to me. Now, he wanted me to speak to him. It was a quid pro quo. There was a certain element of gratitude and regard for him on my part, as a consequence of his having done the right thing. He'd given me what I'd asked for. Didn't I owe him the same?

I thought he was going to ask me to look after his loved ones. I didn't see any harm in that. So I nodded, and asked Danny to find somewhere to pull off the road; with all the vehicles in our entourage, we were blocking the country lane. He drove just a short distance, back the way we'd come, and found a single-track road leading up a hill. A brown sign pointed the way to the Uffington White Horse.

After we'd rattled over a cattle grid, Danny found a spot to pull over and all four of us got out. We were in the middle of the countryside, halfway up a sweeping hill that gave a stunning view of the patchwork of fields surrounding us. The sails of a wind farm spun lazily in the distance; the roads looked like ribbons from up here. We turned our backs on the view, however, and Halliwell, Debs and I walked 100 yards from the car up a steep chalk path that was cut into the hillside; Danny stood at the foot of it, ready to put off any members of the public who might be taking a lunchtime stroll in this pleasant environment.

It was quiet and still, peaceful. The sky was an electric blue and the sun was warm. Halliwell and I sat down on the raised bank beside the pathway, on a little grassy knoll, while Debs stood a short way off, still scribing our conversation. She told me, later, that she was wary of Halliwell's motives for this second chat, this desire to lead me off into the countryside: she thought he was going to make a run for it. Funnily enough, I never thought that. Perhaps it was the connection we'd made, but I had confidence in him.

Sitting there in the sunshine, we smoked another cigarette. We were seated almost on the tail of the White Horse itself, the grass was dry and it was a surreal moment. After all the tension and stress of the enquiry, all the urgency and pace, Halliwell and I were now sharing this tranquil moment, under this startlingly bright blue sky. I guess I was still assimilating and coming down from the notion that we'd found Sian; though the teams hadn't yet located her at the point we'd pulled away, I had no doubt they would. Finding her had been my sole mission for the past week, something I'd poured my heart and soul into. It was astonishing it had ended like this.

'What do you want to tell me?' I asked him. I still thought he was going to ask me to look after Heather and the girls.

'I'm a sick fucker,' he said, unexpectedly. He seemed distraught. My view now is that, in light of the circumstances and because of the bond we'd formed, he was clinging to me, like a life raft: his last hope and refuge. That was why he now appealed to me directly: 'Is it too late to get help?'

His words didn't surprise me, not by that stage. In the past hour, there had been a gradual progression in him, from implacable resistance at Barbary Castle, through the active effort to help me locate Sian, to his current state, which was contrition mixed with relief and despair – at least, that's how I interpreted it.

'It's gone beyond that,' I told him bluntly. I sounded austere and authoritarian, and in hindsight I think that was the right approach, although the truth of it was that I simply couldn't think of an answer at the time that could offer him any reassurance. But it asserted my authority – and Halliwell responded to it.

He spoke in a flat, low, modulated tone, as if moving on to another business item: 'Do you want another one?'

I stared at him. The implication of his words was clear. It was at that moment that my whole view of him changed. Because it's one thing to have abducted and – from his words I now inferred this – murdered Sian, but I had presumed that was an isolated incident. I was a professional detective: I knew from experience that lots of things can happen in the heat of the moment or due to extraneous circumstances; that people can become killers in ways you can explain.

This was different. This was someone voluntarily offering a second offence. I had set out to meet Christopher Halliwell on the understanding that he was the last known party to have seen Sian O'Callaghan. You don't go into such a situation thinking, *He's a serial killer.* Now, not only had I learned he'd murdered Sian, but also that there was a second victim.

It was that person, and that second murder, that my brain automatically focused on. I was so closely engaged with Halliwell in that moment that the news of Sian's death didn't sink in; the disappointment and grief that we weren't going to find her alive after all didn't register. I'd known all along that it was a possible – if not the most likely – outcome; in a way, Halliwell only confirmed what I'd already feared.

So I compartmentalised, and I mentally put Sian's death to one side. I would deal with that horror and my personal feelings later. For now, I wanted to know: what exactly did he mean by 'another one'?

Yet I hesitated before I said anything to him. A complex array of thoughts and feelings fought inside me. From a basic human perspective, I was chilled by the implication of his words. But as a detective there was also an odd sense of disbelieving exhilaration – the idea of somebody, unbidden, confessing murder was so astonishing that I couldn't believe such a thing was actually happening. I could foresee, too, another dilemma, and at that notion my heart sank.

'Are you sure you want to tell me this?' I asked Halliwell frankly. Had he somehow forgotten I was a detective, whose job it was to hold criminals to account?

'You're the man in charge,' he replied simply.

I paused, thinking hard. What did 'another one' mean? As words alone, they were meaningless; they could have meant a cigarette. I had to find out more.

But the moment I did, I was stepping over a line again. Just as it had done that morning, my mind was racing, trying to decide what the right thing was to do.

Did I arrest him on suspicion of murder immediately? Then I'd have to caution him ('You do not have to say anything …') and take him straight back to the nick. I could do that, but at this stage I didn't know exactly what he was confessing to – and had no means of knowing without asking him more questions. Him saying 'Do you want another one?' was hardly enough to build a case against him for murder, nor was it grounds for detention. This was an unbidden, unsought confession and it seemed wrong that I should stop him in his tracks and say, 'No, thank you, Chris, don't tell me any more.'

Arresting him ran a major risk of commuting his willingness to talk. I recognised that we were back in a knife-edge moment. He appeared calm and determined, but I knew that could change at any moment, affected by my choice of words as much as anything. He was currently in a state of contrition, but I didn't get a sense that it was an unassailably robust decision on his part to confess. Who knew how long his candour would last? If I arrested him, would it last for the several hours that it would take to process him through custody? Would it endure through police officers actively telling him he didn't have to say anything? What about once he'd had his consultation with his lawyer, who would be duty bound to stop Halliwell incriminating himself in the complete absence of any evidence whatsoever? The legal advice would clearly be: 'Say nothing.'

I didn't think it would endure. Some would say that, if he changed his mind and clammed up, that was his right: his right to silence under PACE. But what about 'another one'? What about their rights? This might be the only chance I had to discover what Halliwell wanted to tell me. There was no other way to get this information: it was reposed solely in his head. Either I took this opportunity that had unexpectedly presented itself – and perhaps found justice for an unknown girl – or I didn't take it and we never found out who 'another one' was. All we would be left with were those five words.

The situation was this: Halliwell might keep talking back at the nick, but he also might not; in fact, he was very likely to stay silent once told he could and should. So could I take that chance? Was it morally right to reject the confession if it meant he got away with murder?

My mind was working quickly and I assessed the situation. Section 11.1 of PACE – the urgent interview – can be applied to preserve or prevent a loss of evidence, too. I thought it could apply in this case. After all, we were very likely to lose the evidence if I didn't speak to Halliwell in this moment and find out what he wanted to say.

So I took a deep breath and I took the plunge. 'When was it?' I asked him. It was just a question, but it took me into a brave new world.

'2003, 4 or 5,' he replied, casually.

As he said the numbers, I felt goosebumps rising on my skin. *What?* I thought in some astonishment. *You can't remember the year you killed a girl?* I tried to play it cool, however; I didn't challenge him on it.

'I don't know if you want to go for another?' Halliwell asked again, as easily as if he was suggesting a pint down the pub.

I swallowed. 'Where?'

'Eastleach, the other side of Lechlade-on-Thames.'

'Was it a similar sort of circumstances?'

'Pretty much. Out in the open.' He said he had taken a prostitute from the Manchester Road area of Swindon.

I sensed, once again, that being empathetic rather than judgmental was what was necessary to keep him in the moment. So, despite the macabre topic, there was a strangely natural element to our exchange. The bond between us seemed increasingly exceptional as Halliwell continued to speak. We were talking about double murder here, after all. He was giving me the rest of his life: a free confession to a crime for which I had no evidence, nor

215

any prior knowledge. My questions slipped out fluidly: not an interrogation but a conversation.

'Would you be able to take us back there, to the vicinity?' I asked.

'The exact spot,' he said.

I exhaled slowly. *You don't know which year you killed this girl*, I thought, *but you can take me to the exact spot where her body lies? Is that reasonable?* I didn't think so. It started to dawn on me that this was no ordinary case at all.

'I know you're not a psychiatrist,' he continued, 'but what the fuck's wrong with me? Normal people don't go around killing each other.'

I thought: *Go around killing each other?* The way he talked made it sound so habitual. Had he done this more than twice?

'Are there any more incidents, Chris?' I asked urgently. I remembered the recent sexual assault case the intel cell had told me about. 'Did you do anything in February?'

'No.'

'Only these two?' I held my breath.

Quietly, he said: 'Isn't that enough?'

It was only later I realised: *He didn't say yes …*

I didn't know if I'd be able to use any of his answers in a court case, but Halliwell was so amenable to answering questions that I took things a step further. I felt I would be missing an opportunity if I didn't ask questions while he was happy to talk. Nobody else knew what Christopher Halliwell had done but Christopher Halliwell: if I didn't ask, we might never know. He was no longer asking for a solicitor or to go back to the nick – he wanted to be here, in conversation with me: he had actively requested it. So I put the unknown girl to one side for the moment, and I asked him about the girl I'd been looking for all week.

'When we find Sian,' I said, 'are we going to find anything disturbing? Was it straight sex?'

I assumed there must have been a sexual motive; after all, he had just told me that his other victim was a prostitute. Yet his reaction was peculiar. He turned to me very earnestly and said emphatically: 'Didn't have sex.'

I was struck by his vehemence, but given the constraints of the situation – strictly speaking, I wasn't supposed to be questioning him – I felt I couldn't probe further; couldn't say, 'Why did you abduct her, then? What's this all about, Chris?' I felt if I started digging into motive, it was a real stretch.

Nevertheless, we had a rapport and I believed the right thing to do was to take the information he was prepared to give, rather than seek to contain it. A police officer's job doesn't stop the moment someone is in custody for a crime and in this case in particular – given the controversy of breaching PACE – I knew I needed to parallel-evidence his confession. My investigation hadn't halted; we were still hunting for clues.

'How was she killed?' I asked of Sian.

He spoke the words as a statement of fact, rather than with any self-realisation of the horror of what he'd done: 'Knife, in the back of the head.' He made a stabbing motion as he said it, indicating a single blow and then a levering upwards, so that the blade would split the skull. It was how you'd kill a wild animal.

I couldn't be aghast; I couldn't allow my personal feelings to put him off. So I kept on in conversation with a killer, my questions naturally leading on from what he'd said before: 'Where's the knife now?'

'Anywhere between here and Marlborough.'

'Was it a similar sort of thing before?'

'Yes, she was a prostitute – on the game.'

'You know Sian wasn't?'

'I do now.' He paused. 'What caught me? Was it the gamekeeper at Ramsbury?'

I filed that little titbit away. *Thanks very much, Chris. No, it wasn't, but it's good to know there might be a witness …*

'We've been surveilling you,' I told him.

'At Heathrow last night?'

'Yes.'

He gave a wry smile. 'I thought so. I might be sick, but I'm not fucking stupid.'

I nodded. I knew the surveillance team had had to get close yesterday evening; they must have shown out, after all.

'You can't explain this?' I asked him. I don't know what I was hoping he might say; how could anyone explain this? But he didn't try.

'I can't explain it to myself.' He smiled wryly again. 'I don't think I'll be getting community service.'

'No, you won't.' I paused, then asked again: 'Are there any others?'

He was dismissive. 'No.'

I didn't doubt him. He seemed fully contrite and I believed that he had fully unburdened himself of his offending.

Our conversation had come to a natural close. I knew what Halliwell wanted to do now: he wanted to take me to what he had intimated was the dead body of another murder victim. Yet in that moment, he was more committed to taking me there than I was to going. The thought crossed my mind: *Do I say, You know what, Chris? Let's just get you back to the nick and keep things simple?* For I knew I was breaching the police guidelines. But I also knew that he was almost certain to clam up once his lawyer heard we had no evidence of murder – no body – so how could that possibly be the right response? I felt I couldn't stop until he had led me to the deposition site. More important than PACE compliance or any future evidential presentation in court had to be the recovery of the body: because until 'another one' became a dead girl with a name and a face and a family, we didn't have a case at all.

We walked back to the car. As the three of us came down the steep chalk path, I almost did a double take. The picturesque peace of the setting had been shattered: the single-track road was chock-a-block with police vehicles; wherever we were going, we'd be going straight on as there was no room on the road to turn around now. The chopper was still up in the air and all my colleagues had eyes on us, wondering what the hell was going on.

I escorted Halliwell into the patrol car and closed the door behind him. I had only a moment to whisper to Bill Dutton: 'We're going for another one; he's offered another victim, Bill.' His face was a picture of astonishment, but we didn't have time to talk.

'Just follow us,' I told him, then I got into the car.

41

It was 13.53 as we pulled away from the White Horse and set off in our convoy of vehicles in the direction of Eastleach. As before, Danny followed Halliwell's instructions. Debs told me later that she still believed Halliwell was leading me down the garden path. After all, why would anyone confess to a murder that nobody knew they'd committed?

There was only one reason: contrition. As we drove, Halliwell became more emotional and tearful, particularly about his murder of Sian. He spoke about being a cabbie, of how women specifically requested his driving services on their nights out. 'All these girls trust me,' he sobbed. 'What the fuck's the matter with me?'

I believe I had some glimmer of comprehension as to what was happening inside his head. Christopher Halliwell had not been in trouble with the police for 25 years: he was now an upstanding member of the community. Yet he was also, secretly, a multiple murderer; clearly, he had been living a double life. How does anyone react when their worlds collide, as his had on this very day?

In hindsight, I think that moment on the mound at Barbary Castle was about much more than simply choosing whether or not to give up Sian's location. I believe he had to make a choice about what sort of person he wanted to be. Did he hold the line and carry on as a callous, cold-hearted murderer, or did he do the right thing and come across to seek rehabilitation? I think, when it came to the crunch, he chose the latter. I think he chose the good things in his life – his children, his partner – over his compulsion to kill. In asking me if he could get help, he'd had a moment of clarity: 'This has got to stop. I have got to be stopped.' I think he was relieved because he didn't have to pretend any more; I think, in that instant, in that journey in that car, he was even grateful that it was over.

Nevertheless, I spent the entire journey on tenterhooks in case he changed his mind. The conversation was sparse as we travelled, me occasionally rolling another cigarette for us both, but every now and again I would ask him a question about the unknown girl or Sian. A lot of it was to fill the silence; given how far we'd come and what we were in the midst of doing, I wasn't going to start talking about the football. I was very careful I didn't leap on him, demanding answers – it was still conversational rather than inquisitorial – so the information almost dripped out in subtle increments. I gleaned that the girl from the Manchester Road area was someone he didn't know; he confirmed that he had murdered her and was taking us to the exact spot where she was buried.

Even as we were speaking, I was thinking, *What can I do with this information?* At times it passed through my mind that I didn't really want to hear what he had to say, because I didn't know how I was going to enter it in evidence. Nonetheless, it was better for me to know – for example – that I needed to look for a knife between here and Marlborough than not. So we stayed locked in our bond. We kept talking: two men in a critical moment in both our lives.

Our bond had a flavour now of mutual self-destruction. We'd both put ourselves into a position where we were sacrificing our lives. I knew what I was doing was controversial, and had no idea how the police, press or public would respond to it, but I couldn't stop. If I stopped at any point, I had no evidence of this second crime: I had nothing at all. Or, rather, I had the worst of all things: a clear indication of a murder, but no evidence to establish guilt.

We drew closer to Eastleach, but not so much as to enter the village itself. Instead, we drove up and down the lanes that criss-crossed the many fields in its environs. It was a landscape of endless hedgerows, anonymous fields and winding, single-track roads. There were no landmarks. Every field, every crossroads looked the same to me; it all blurred into one.

Halliwell was eager and engaged once more. His distress about his crimes on the journey had come in waves – calm one moment and tearful the next – and at this present point he was committed on this course of action. Once again, we were two blokes with a shared interest: finding a lost girl so I could bring her home.

Once again, however, Halliwell's recall let him down. He declared we were at the spot he was looking for, before saying, 'No, this isn't it.'

I wasn't surprised he was confused. Though every field must have a name on a map somewhere, they weren't signposted out here in the middle of nowhere. It only cemented my belief that Halliwell had to be the one to lead us to the location: if he withdrew his help, and the police service was put in the position of searching every field in Eastleach to find the body, we'd be doing it for decades.

Suddenly, Halliwell indicated that we were at our destination. The car pulled up in a quiet lane beside a dry stone wall. Beyond it was a tilled field.

We all surveyed the scene silently. It was little more than a blasted heath, isolated and alone. Unlike in Savernake Forest, no one had done a line search of this field; no police officer, no member of the public, had tramped up and down, calling out a name. No one had been here in years.

'Do you need to walk to it?' I asked.

Halliwell replied, 'Yes, I'll show you exactly.'

The four of us got out of the car again. We watched as Halliwell walked to the wall and climbed over. As though connected to him by invisible thread, I followed, drawn unstoppably in his direction. As I climbed over the wall, I saw the field was large, about 40 acres, covered by a reddish clay soil that was dotted with a scattering of chunky white stones. There were no trees; brambles and ivy curled atop the wall that ran around the border.

Somewhere in the back of my mind, I realised how clever he had been. The stony ground gave the field zero agricultural value: no farmer could grow crops here. If you buried a body in a ploughed field, the following spring you'd have the owner on the phone, alerting the police. But no one tended this land. No one but a killer, planting his own grim seeds.

'Steve,' I suddenly heard Debs say.

I turned around.

She was on the other side of the wall, still on the road. 'I can't get over,' she said helplessly: her ankle-length skirt wasn't designed for such activity.

The situation was so surreal that the moment was almost comic. I didn't know what to say, but somehow thought, *You're kidding me, Debs! This is the seminal moment in our detective careers and you're going to miss it?*

But she was. Only Danny and I joined Halliwell in the field.

He was intent on what he was doing. Taking his bearings from a dip in the wall, he began pacing into the middle of the field, putting one foot in front of the other. After taking a precise number of steps, he stopped and indicated that the body was beneath his feet.

I felt a shiver run down my spine. *The exact spot.* Just as he had said. He was so extraordinarily specific that I asked Danny to stand on the place he'd indicated so that we could mark it.

It was a surreal moment. Above our head the helicopter was clattering; the colossal circus of cars that had been following us had drawn up alongside the field too. By now it was mid-afternoon and the odd bright day had transmuted to create this very strange afternoon light. I felt tired and drained from the intensity of what we'd been through; I think Halliwell felt the same. He expressed a need to urinate, so I took him a little way off for some privacy.

I believe it was around then that one of my colleagues came up to us. His presence was an unexpected, jarring interruption. He came bouncing up like Tigger, and I think he actually said to Halliwell, 'Are there any more?' like an overexcited schoolboy.

I shooed him away in frustration. I was still locked in the moment with Halliwell and, frankly, my colleague seemed an irrelevance, a person from another time, another place, another life. For Halliwell's part, the interruption did not seem to register.

I don't know where the other officer went after that. In my memory, once again it was just me and Chris: the detective and the serial killer. We were away from everybody and Halliwell started to talk. He started to talk about the young woman who was buried yards away from where we were standing, whose name I did not know.

He told me he'd picked her up that night in Swindon, in that indefinable year. He'd had sex with her. He'd killed her by wrapping his hands around her neck and squeezing till all life was gone. Having stripped the girl of her clothes, he'd left her body hidden in the bushes by the wall at the edge of the field. But he'd come back the following evening: he'd spent all night digging a five-foot-deep grave, just under the place where Danny Jones was still standing. He'd placed his victim in it and covered her up with thick clay soil.

He told me he'd last visited the site about three years ago.

Three years ago: 2008. But he'd said he'd killed her much earlier in the decade.

I realised the implications. *He's been coming back to see her*. Perhaps to check that his tracks were still covered – or perhaps on a sick pilgrimage to the scene of his crime.

Now we'd found the site, it was time at last to bring him in. I told him that we'd head back to the nick now, and that he would need to tell all that he had told me to the officers who would interview him there.

'I don't want to have to talk about it again, Steve,' he said plaintively.

I caught his eye: the authoritative officer once more. 'Look, you're going to have to.'

He seemed to accede to it. I had no concerns, now, about him clamming up in custody. Before, a lawyer would have rightly said, 'You have no evidence' – on both counts. But, now, things would be different.

As the two of us stood there in that lonely field, the subject of his family came up. He may have said, 'Would you look after my girls?'

I replied, 'Yeah, I'll get them out. I'll keep them away from the press.'

I saw it as a decent exchange between two people – an act of humanity, if you will.

We had one last smoke. And as we stood there, our shoes stained with the red soil, the strange afternoon light all around us, I said to him, 'Look at the sky, Chris.'

He did; we both stared up at it. There was a very piercing blue light and the clouds were peculiarly puffy. It was so distinctive – that's why I'd remarked on it.

'Let's remember this,' I told him.

I was perhaps aware of how daft it sounded. Such was our bond in that moment, I thought I could half crack a joke about it. So what I said next wasn't malicious: it was said through fellowship, in the spirit of a bond forged in mutual self-destruction.

'You need to remember that sky,' I told Christopher Halliwell, 'because you might not be seeing it for a while.'

42

I told him someone else would read him his rights and took him back over the wall to Bill Dutton. He would organise a car to take Halliwell to the police station.

'I'll see you back at the nick for a coffee and a smoke, Chris,' I told him.

My plan was that we would meet again in a few hours' time to continue our conversation. As I interpreted it, there was a tacit understanding between us that this wasn't the end, but that we would resume. We had to get back to the nick first and do the formalities but after that I expected to see him again and put this thing to bed. There was so much we still didn't know and I wanted to enable him to give a full and frank confession as he was clearly willing to do.

I got into one of the many vehicles parked up by the field and we blue-lighted it back to the nick. Both my mind and body were reeling. I felt light-headed and in a strange hyper state: I'd had no sleep, I'd not eaten all day, and I'd just spent several hours under extreme pressure in an intense one-on-one with a double murderer. I couldn't quite believe what had happened. I'd gone out on a last roll of the dice, and I'd come back with the locations of not one but two dead bodies. The enormity of it made my head spin.

There was silence in the car on the way back, each of us lost in our own thoughts. I recall it as an overwhelming blur of complex emotions. I was sombre, because girls had been killed. I was euphoric, because we had achieved the impossible. I was anxious, because I knew what I'd done was controversial. Most of all, though, I think I was stunned.

A call came in as the car streaked through the Gloucestershire countryside and crossed back into Wiltshire. It was a member of the team, calling to let me know that they'd located Sian O'Callaghan.

She had been found about an hour after I'd left the search teams on that remote road, while Halliwell and I were on our way to Eastleach. It was the first confirmation I'd had that Halliwell had been telling me the truth that afternoon; that he had taken us to the right place. It was reassuring, in a way, to know I hadn't been duped.

Unlike the girl in the red clay field, Sian O'Callaghan had not been buried. She was found still wearing her grey dress, which had been pushed up, but her distinctive boots and bag were missing. Just as Halliwell had described, she had been violently stabbed in the head. The teams were even now tending to her, organising the transport of her body to a hospital, where a post-mortem would be conducted.

My first thought was for the family. I needed to see them as soon as possible. I knew they would be supported by their FLO, but this was a visit I needed to make in person.

I was only in the nick, therefore, for a matter of minutes. When Debs and I walked in, everyone was standing stockstill, staring at us. There was an atmosphere of sombre exultation. I recall this solemn hand-shaking parade with a line-up of senior officers; far from the condemnation I had feared, there was only congratulation. The MIR was busy: John had already assigned teams to the multitude of jobs we now had to take care of – sending diggers to Eastleach to look for the unknown girl; scouring the site where Sian had been found for forensic evidence. The place was a maelstrom with countless officers from all departments flapping about.

One of my first priorities was to direct that Halliwell's family should be taken care of: the news of his arrest would soon be out. Some people actually said, 'Bollocks to that, they can take their chances.' But I insisted. If Halliwell did have more to say, I wanted to be shown to have fulfilled my promise.

Another urgent action was that Debs's notes of what had happened with Halliwell were taken from her, in order that they could be photocopied and put to him in a PACE-compliant interview for him to sign as an accurate record of what had taken place. I instructed Bill Dutton to get Halliwell into interview at the earliest opportunity: we needed to get him on tape repeating both of his confessions. He had been taken into custody at 15.15 but I knew it would be many hours yet before any interview could happen; a solicitor had been summoned but would not arrive at the nick until 17.45, as it turned out. Nothing more could be done with Halliwell until he'd had access to legal advice.

But I wasn't concerned about Halliwell now. My only thought was for the O'Callaghans.

As a young PC, I'd had to deliver what we call 'death messages' all the time. They were usually as a result of road traffic accidents – I had to knock on the door of the victim's mum and deliver the worst news of her life. When you've done a fair number, you develop a way of dealing with the shellshock and emotion, but it never gets any easier.

The nick had been a storm of activity, but there was only stillness in the O'Callaghans' home. And that was where it hit me, as I stood in their front room before what seemed like a dozen or more people, the place packed with relatives who had been hanging on, minute by minute, throughout the agony of the past week. That was where the loss of Sian O'Callaghan became real for me. She was a 22-year-old woman and she had been robbed of her life.

The room had that umber you get in the early evening and there was a hush as I walked in. I remember standing as I addressed the room; I think I stayed for an hour, offering them the answers to any questions they wanted to ask. I knew that I was bearing the worst of all possible outcomes for them, yet they were utterly dignified. When they thanked me for bringing her back, I had no words. I'd wanted to bring her back to them alive.

I bade farewell to them shortly before 17.00, leaving them to their grief. It sounds wrong to say they were lucky, but I knew that they would, in time, find some comfort in the fact that not only had the offender been arrested, but that Sian could be given a proper burial and funeral. Many families never have that closure.

As I made my way back to Gablecross, my thoughts turned to the unidentified girl in the red clay field. How long had her family been waiting for her to come home?

As soon as I was back at the nick, I was rushed into a press conference that had been organised in my absence. I hadn't asked for one and frankly, with so much to do on behalf of the victims, sitting in front of the press was the last thing I wanted.

I blinked in the blinding camera flashes, my sleep-starved eyes sensitive to the light. The room was stuffed full of journalists; I had never, in all my years as a police officer, seen it so busy.

As I made my way to the front, there were murmurs of congratulation and a few of the journalists pumped my hand. I sensed a positive buzz – and why shouldn't there be? Only a few days after picking up what was likely to be one of those cases that ends in failure – as it would have done, had I not persuaded Halliwell to take me to Sian – we had a result; and some. I had feared all along that the media would kick us but, to their credit, now this extraordinary turn of events had transpired they gave credit where it was due.

Given the enquiry had been covered in live time by the media, I think they felt as if they'd been part of the investigation. And, of course, they had. I honestly couldn't have done it without them. Would Halliwell have been primed to confess without their coverage? I believe the answer is no.

I took a seat beside the senior officers and read the statement that had been sanctioned by the Gold Group: 'A 47-year-old man from Swindon has been arrested on suspicion of kidnap and two murders. I have been taken to the location of two bodies, neither of which has been identified, but one of which is believed to be Sian O'Callaghan ... I ask that we be given the time to recover the bodies with the dignity and respect they deserve.'

Afterwards, I thought no more of it. But – as later events would show – that hastily arranged press conference would come to take on a great significance.

At 18.25, exactly as the sun was setting, I called my team together for a debrief. The fact it was sunset was apt, for although there was still lots of work to do from here in terms of parallel-evidencing the cases and securing a conviction, the sun was setting, too, on the fast-paced enquiry that we had been chasing since Saturday night. I wanted to thank them for their incredible hard work over the past six days. Pat Geenty also relayed a message from CC Brian Moore that he had 'never felt more proud'. Neither had I; it was a fantastic team effort. Yet there was still more to do. At 18.50, we went back to work.

So I was still in my office, still reeling from the remarkable outcome of the day, when there was a rap upon my door that evening.

I glanced up; it was Bill Dutton. He entered the room with an unexpectedly frenetic energy.

'We've just offered Debs's notes of this afternoon to Halliwell,' he told me. 'Steve, as you suggested, we gave them to him to sign.'

I nodded. My heart, inexplicably, began to pound just a little bit harder. Instinctively, I found I was reading Bill's body language – and he had a familiar, bit-between-his-teeth way about him that set my own teeth abruptly on edge.

Because Bill got like that in only one situation: when he was dealing with an intractable offender who was giving him the runaround in interview.

My heart had made the link before my brain did.

Bill is dealing with Christopher Halliwell.

I felt a sudden sinking feeling, a kind of caving in of worlds; perhaps it was how Halliwell had felt that afternoon.

'And?' I said. 'And, Bill?'

'He's offering "no comment",' he told me bluntly. 'Steve – I'm sorry – Halliwell's refused to sign.'

PART 2

Truth and Justice

43

There are a million and one ways for a world to shatter. Sometimes, it's a sudden explosion – a car smash on the motorway, a plane falling out of the sky – that leaves you picking up the pieces of your life. But, on other occasions, it's far more insidious than that. It can be the thinnest of cracks that first appears, barely visible to the naked eye. Though you don't know it, the path of destruction has been set. You walk down it blindly, little knowing what lies ahead. Little knowing there is no way back.

I wasn't worried, when Bill shared the news. I was bewildered. When I'd left Halliwell at Eastleach, he had been genuinely contrite. And that feeling hadn't faded for him while he was processed through custody: when asked by the police surgeon if he knew why he was there, he'd replied, 'I have killed two people.'

From the off, I suspected his legal advice was at the root of his volte-face. But although repeated 'no comments' were the sort of nonsense I expected as a copper when dealing with two-bob burglars, this situation was hardly comparable. In fact, it was a ludicrous state of affairs: Halliwell had taken me, an entire surveillance crew and a police helicopter to two deposition sites and confessed to murder. What did he hope to achieve now in offering 'no comment'? I was frustrated to think we were being subjected to the usual charade.

As Bill and I talked, I no doubt used some Anglo-Saxon language and got extremely knocky as we concurred in our view that all lawyers were bastards. Bill knew Halliwell's solicitor of old; I gleaned that he took the view that it was rarely in his client's interest ever to offer a comment. It's all part of the standard legal advice: you offer 'no comment' until you get disclosure on what evidence the police hold. But how could Halliwell explain this? I felt confident he had an undefendable case.

I wasn't tempted to go in there myself and ask Halliwell what he was playing at, nor did I suggest reconstructing the bond we'd shared that had elicited the confession in the first place. In hindsight, perhaps I should have done. But I was aware I'd already sailed pretty close to the wind and I wanted to get everything back on track and PACE-compliant: do things the standard way. The standard way was for SIOs to stay out of the evidential chain and let the interview teams do their work, so I sent Dex and Bea back in, now armed with several reasons why Halliwell should confess again.

But it didn't work – not the first day we had him in custody, nor the second, nor the third. By that Saturday, we had unearthed the remains of the unknown girl in the Eastleach field, which vindicated my initial assessment of Halliwell: he *had* told me the truth. It made me even more determined to overcome the effect of his 'no comment' stance. I wanted these games to be over. Surely he would plead guilty. Then, after the trial, Halliwell and I could get back in a room together and continue our conversation. I sensed there was a lot more he could say.

Despite his seeming change of heart, I still believed we shared a bond. That was why, when I saw him in the magistrates' court on Saturday 26 March, I appealed to him directly to tell the truth again.

We were there to apply for a warrant of further detention; those 96 hours on the custody clock aren't given in one go, so you have to keep going back to the courts every 12 hours. It was the first time Halliwell and I had been together since Eastleach.

He looked just as I had left him. Except, I suppose, for the fact that he was standing behind strengthened glass in the dock. I stood across from him in the witness box and the two of us acknowledged each other – a look, a nod. I saw nothing that suggested anything had changed between us.

Unfortunately, there was now *someone* between us. Halliwell's lawyer – let's call him Mr Smith – joined us in the cheap-oak-panelled room. The two of us took an instant dislike to one another. He clearly thought I was some kind of crazy maverick who would do anything to get a result; I was frustrated because it seemed like he'd advised his client to say 'no comment' – ignoring the fact that we'd recovered two bodies found only at Halliwell's direction.

Yet Smith in truth was an irrelevance to me. I tuned him out in order to focus on Halliwell. We were in open court: this wasn't part of the evidential chain. I could speak to him again.

I reminded him of the mutual trust we'd shared on that extraordinary afternoon. 'Chris, I've done what I promised to do,' I told him. 'I got your family out.' I appealed to him directly: 'Give me the account that you've already given me again.'

I could sense Smith's disapproval of me speaking straight to his client, but I continued nonetheless. 'We've found the second body,' I told Halliwell. 'So you were telling me the truth. I know you want to tell the truth. Why are you reversing the confession?'

Smith got very shirty. Normally, lawyers and police officers play a particular game of politeness, but you couldn't have missed the animosity between us because it was mutual and intense. At this juncture, the reason for his animosity became evident as he made what was to my mind an extraordinary allegation against me.

'Can you assure the court,' he asked while I was under oath, 'that you haven't been monitoring my confidential conversations with my client?'

I was flabbergasted; such a thing is illegal. 'I have done nothing of the kind!' I riposted.

It was a shocking allegation, but of course Halliwell was only saying 'no comment' in interview, yet I knew from my time with him that he actually wanted to confess – and I'd now revealed that knowledge. Smith, however, believed (wrongly) I had the information only because I'd miked their consultation room. On that basis, he saw me as some kind of rabid 1970s' throwback copper.

I felt extremely calm in court, but also angry and frustrated, and I didn't hold back. I spoke again to Halliwell. 'Are you sure you're happy that you're getting the right legal advice?' I asked him bluntly.

I was frankly astonished that in these circumstances the legal advice was *not* to suggest the client offer an account. And not simply from the perspective of the case: 'Is it too late to get help?' Halliwell had asked me. He'd expressly sought rehabilitation. In my view, his rehabilitation couldn't start until he had confessed on record. All that was happening was that a three-ring circus was being created around something that had to my mind already been resolved.

Right at the end of the hearing, in a last-ditch attempt to get back to where we had been – two grown adults having an honest conversation – I made the motion of a cigarette to Halliwell, as though to say, recalling old times,

'I'll meet you for a smoke.' He gave me a thumbs-up. I hoped that meant we could soon pick up where we'd left off and that this charade would be over.

But back at the nick it was the same stonewalling and 'no comment'. I can't know, of course, what Halliwell was thinking, but I suspect after our altercation in court that Smith at least was even more determined to close up shop. Our mutual antipathy was clear and it was inadvisable for me to lead another interview. I'd never been one for playing politics but, on reflection, I think I should have handled that situation differently. But I thought it was just a load of nonsense. Halliwell was never going to get away with murder, so why prevent him from giving a full account?

I pondered what I knew of Halliwell. What had I learned of him during our interaction that could help me now to persuade him to come across again? What would make me roll over if I was in his shoes?

I thought I had the answer. It was an unusual idea, but the only one that I now thought might work.

I decided to ask his daughter if she would be prepared to help.

In that godforsaken field, Halliwell had asked me to look after his family. I genuinely believed he cared for them. In my experience, few killers are wholly evil; even if it is hidden deep inside, there is usually a smidgeon of humanity somewhere to which you can appeal. If anyone could draw out a confession from him at this stage, I thought it would be them.

When we suggested the idea, his eldest daughter readily and kindly agreed to help. I understand she knew Sian a little; I cannot imagine her feelings on discovering her father had killed a friend. In all of this, she and her siblings were victims too.

Halliwell was asked if he wanted a visit from her and to my relief he agreed. The plan could go ahead. An interview room was prepared with recording equipment to capture any confession; it is legal to do this.

And it turned out we had an unexpected bonus card to play. Not only had one daughter agreed to speak to her father in person, but his youngest girl had also written to him. We read the letter before we gave it to Halliwell. It said words to the effect of: 'You've broken enough hearts. It's time to tell the truth.'

Halliwell was given the note in his cell. When he read it, he choked back tears and became extremely emotional. I only hoped that emotion would be enough to persuade him to alleviate the distress of both his daughters and his victims' families. At this stage, we still had no idea who the second victim was. An account of the murders from Halliwell himself could reveal that vital information and give her family closure of sorts. His confession would also avoid a long, drawn-out legal process that would benefit no one but the lawyers. I wasn't concerned about his 'no comment' reflecting on me. He was clearly guilty – no court could find otherwise – and I thought he would have to plead that way. And with an uncontested trial, it wouldn't matter whether the evidence I'd secured through breaching PACE was admissible or not, because he would automatically be convicted as a result of his guilty plea. It would simply save an awful lot of time, heartache and money if he just rolled over now.

Halliwell composed himself and his eldest was shown into the interview room. Father faced daughter. They were alone.

I was on tenterhooks. Would this work?

Halliwell gazed at his daughter. He appeared genuinely upset, yet he was also very calm. As calm as he had been at Barbary Castle ...

Of his own volition, without prompting from his lawyer and without an ounce of contrition, he now said clearly: 'They will be recording this. Change your name, sell your story and make as much money as you can.'

So much for a smidgeon of humanity.

44

On Sunday, 27 March 2011, Christopher Halliwell was charged with the murder of Sian O'Callaghan. He was technically bailed for the murder of the second victim. As we didn't yet know her identity, we couldn't ask Halliwell any specific questions about her. As such, it was better to press the 'pause' button on the custody clock for that offence and bring him back for further questioning once we knew more. I was hoping that by the time we did, we would have stumbled upon some incontrovertible evidence that would have him bang to rights.

The point of charge in a case provides a moment of reflection. With Halliwell retracting his cough, I could see that there was a long road ahead. Unfortunately, the perception from senior officers invariably seems to be that at the point of charge it is all over bar the shouting. Steadily but surely, resources were cut from the enquiry until I was leading a team of just 14. It was frustrating because we faced an uphill battle. Though I was convinced Halliwell would eventually plead guilty, in the meantime we now had to build an evidential case. It wasn't so much a 'whodunnit?' as a 'can-we-*prove*-he-done-it?'

Critical to gathering evidence was to gather more intel on Halliwell himself. It was no good saying, 'He's just an evil bastard' – I wanted to understand why he had ended up the way he had.

From his family, we learned more about his background. As a child, he had spent some time in care; he was put there by his mother. She was known to be abusive, beating him from the age of three with a leather strap and employing extreme forms of discipline. There was talk of Halliwell having had drawing pins stuck in his head and his face rubbed in his food as punishment; his mother also used to press a hot iron on his hand and smile at him while he screamed. No wonder his family said he had developed a deep, lasting hatred of her. They said how similar Sian O'Callaghan and his mother had looked.

I wondered, given he had not abducted Sian in order to rape her, was this why Halliwell had snatched her?

We also learned he had worked as a butcher, and enjoyed fishing and hunting pursuits. The memory of that stabbing, slicing motion he had made as he described Sian's murder came back to me, unbidden. There was something so practised about it. His sister also said that as a boy he would often pull the legs from insects, showing little emotion as he did.

It was soon after his arrest that I took a trip out to Ashbury Avenue. As is always the case, it was an ordinary house on an ordinary street. I pulled up in an unmarked car with a building sense of anticipation. Houses are usually insightful illustrations of people's personalities and I needed to gain a deeper understanding of who this man was; I was hoping, too, that we might find the motherlode stash of blood-flecked clothes or a kill list that would tie him irreparably to his crimes.

The neighbourhood was quiet when I arrived, but the house was a hive of activity with officers already searching it. It was tidy, with a laminate-floor lounge that led through to a hexagonal conservatory he'd built himself. A rather old-fashioned oak dresser in the living room contained a quantity of loose-leaf photographs, each of which would be scrutinised for clues. There were sheaves of elaborate pencil sketches too; Halliwell had a habit of sitting in his taxi and sketching, rural landscapes in particular. They were all seized for further examination.

Throughout, it felt like a normal family house: pink bedrooms upstairs for the daughters; a bathroom halfway through a DIY upgrade; a master bedroom he shared with his partner. That was sparsely furnished, with just a bedside table and a double bed, but at its foot there were some open shelves heaving with all kinds of stuff: old handbags and wallets and the like.

A thought struck me as I viewed them. I was concerned we hadn't yet found Sian's distinctive boots and handbag. What had Halliwell done with them? The perfume bottle hadn't yet come back from forensics, but I was still taken with the notion that Halliwell might be a killer who liked to hoard trophies. As such, I took in every detail of that bedroom, on the hunt for clues. I noted there were no books on the bedside table; nothing but a yellowing scrap of lined paper on Halliwell's side. I turned and went downstairs, to where the main search was underway.

Halliwell had met his partner when he'd helped convert her garage – and this location was the most intriguing place in the house. It was a large tandem garage with an up-and-over door, but the door had been blocked up on the inside with some kind of plasterboard. You had to see it to believe it: it was absolutely stuffed to the rafters with old tins of paint, lawnmowers, fishing rods, tools, spades, gaffer tape … All the usual crap you'd expect to see, but given the reason for our presence, each everyday item took on a darker connotation.

Had he used this tape to bind a girl? Had he used that spade to bury her?

There was so much stuff in the garage I knew it would take the team a good long while to work through it – but we would leave nothing to chance. Every inch of the house would be searched, including the files on Halliwell's computer.

As the days went by, Sian's case grew stronger. Thanks to our recovery of her body, the forensics team were able to pin Halliwell to her: they found his partial DNA profile on her corpse, and her blood was identified on the car seat covers he had dumped in the wheelie bin. The barbarity of what he had done to her was chilling: the post-mortem revealed she had been stabbed twice in the head and her face was heavily bruised, consistent with punching or kicking. She had also suffered bruises and abrasions to her breasts; her left breast was bitten. She had not been raped.

For the unknown victim, however, we were in a much more difficult position when it came to securing evidence. There are four pillars to any investigative case: you get your evidence from forensics, passive data, confessions and witnesses. This nameless girl had died almost a decade ago – there were no forensics or passive data; and Halliwell had retracted his confession. Until we knew who she was, we were without witness evidence too.

A forensic archaeologist was trying to rectify our ignorance. They pored over her bones, looking for clues as to her identity. We already knew she was a woman. Now we learned she was petite – around five foot in height – and aged between 20 and 30 years old. I was informed that we had not recovered her complete skeleton. Distressingly, her feet, hands and head were all missing from her grave.

It was possible they had been moved by animal activity. It was possible that, even though the farmer didn't cultivate the field, he had raked over it and in so doing scattered the absent bones. Later, we did find some metatarsals elsewhere in the field, but of her head there was no trace at all, not a single skull fragment. The archaeologist said they could not rule out the idea that she had been deliberately decapitated.

Halliwell hadn't mentioned *that* in his account of her burial. But as time went by, I was starting to appreciate that the full unburdening I'd believed had occurred wasn't quite the truth. Things weren't lining up: there were too many discrepancies, too many suggestions of something more. It felt almost as if that day he'd experienced a freak high tide of emotion, which had washed up these two bodies on the beach. But now, in custody, those waters had receded: he was an unnavigable ocean once again. And all oceans have hidden depths. I was beginning to believe that Halliwell had some truly sinister secrets that he had deliberately chosen not to spill.

I kept remembering that he had very specifically told me that he had spent all night digging a five-foot grave for the second victim. But it had turned out that the white bones we found were buried only 20 centimetres deep. Far from taking care to conceal her, far from a night full of heaving effort, Halliwell had left her in just a scraping of ground.

How could he have got it so wrong?

I felt a creeping sense of grim realisation, the hairs lifting up on the back of my neck. I stacked up what I knew from our exchange, the building blocks falling into place with a dull thud, conclusive as the final beat of a heart.

He didn't know which year he killed her.

He didn't know how deep he buried her.

He didn't say 'yes' when I first asked him, 'Only these two?'

The inference was obvious. There *were* more than these two. He must have confused the details of this girl's burial, and death date, with that of another victim.

I felt new knowledge running through my blood. *Christopher Halliwell is a serial killer.*

45

He had the perfect cover for it. A taxi driver by night, giving him opportunity to select his victims. We had learned he did a lot of groundwork by day, giving him the perfect disposal method. Generally speaking, if you get rid of the body in a murder, you've disposed of the majority of the evidence. The fact the fate of our unknown victim had escaped notice for so long showed he was good at this. He had made a chilling comment to a colleague just a few days before his arrest: 'Who knows what or who you will find buried out there? *There could be loads of people over the years.*'

I now believed there were – and that he had killed them.

Instantly I wondered who they were, of course. When I'd first joined Wiltshire Police I'd completed a review of all outstanding mispers for the region – so I knew that, in Swindon, there was only one name on the list: Sally Ann John. She was a pretty woman who had vanished in 1995, aged 23. She worked as a prostitute and lived on Broad Street.

At that time, *so did Christopher Halliwell.*

I felt my heart racing as an idea struck me. Could Sally Ann be the girl in the field? The dates were wrong – but then again, Halliwell hadn't been sure on the year. By his own admission he used prostitutes: with he and Sally

Ann living in such close proximity, the two of them couldn't have missed each other.

As evidence continued to be collected, more unsettling questions arose. We recovered a pair of knickers from his garage that did not belong to his partner or daughters; the owner could not be identified. Another victim? The gaffer tape we'd found in the garage was seized too; we'd found similar tape in the Eastleach grave. Was this part of his modus operandi – to bind his victims with gaffer? Because he wouldn't speak, we didn't know. The bloodied tissues from Wanborough turned out to be a red herring – the DNA was not Sian's – but the perfume bottle remained of interest. Though forensics now confirmed it was not Sian's either, to my mind that didn't mean it wasn't a trophy. Why else would Halliwell have dumped it if it was not incriminating? I felt a shiver run down my spine: I suspected there was somebody dead around that bottle.

Apprehensively, I entered the DNA profile we'd found on it into the police database, but there were no hits. Whoever this girl was, she had never come to police attention.

Of course, neither had Christopher Halliwell – not for 25 years. What was perhaps most startling of all about this notion of him being a serial killer was the fact that, until he had been caught for what he'd done to Sian, no one had suspected a thing. The media had wasted no time door-stepping his neighbours and they all said Halliwell had seemed 'a smashing bloke' and 'a really nice guy'. 'I couldn't believe it when I heard!' exclaimed one.

He had fooled his nearest and dearest too. 'We had a happy, loving relationship,' his partner Heather later told the *Sun*. 'In all the time we were together he never showed any anger towards me. It never crossed my mind that he was capable of hurting me.' She added, 'I don't know why he did it. He had a good life. There was no reason for him to do it.'

Halliwell had been living a double life. Just as I kept my family away from the crimes I encountered at work, he segregated his, too. And he had clearly been convincing in his efforts to conceal his true nature, though I suppose you don't get to become a serial killer if you're a dribbling Nazi with uncontrollable anger issues. It made me wonder: if I'd met him at any other time – at a time when he hadn't been so spooked by the notion of getting caught that he crumbled – would he have been able to fool me too?

More intel came in that built the picture of a man who was highly capable of living a lie. We had a call from ITV to say they thought they had footage of Halliwell mingling with the public in Savernake Forest, 'helping' with the search for Sian. We also learned of a conversation that Halliwell had with a passenger the very morning of his arrest. He had claimed to be a 'friend of the family' of Sian O'Callaghan – 'I've known them years,' he'd said breezily, 'I'm mates with Sian's dad' – and declared of the kidnapper, 'If I found the bugger, I'd kill him.'

It begged the question: did he believe these stories he was spinning? Was he somehow able to deny to himself as well as others his true evil nature? Killers often become self-justificatory, unable to see the horror of their actions, and it made me wonder if Christopher Halliwell was such a man.

As our enquiries continued, we traced his movements leading up to Sian's murder. It became clear those loops he'd made around Swindon in the early hours of the morning *were* a trawl for potential victims – he had passed Sian O'Callaghan as she walked home alone along the High Street, *then* he had manoeuvred his car into position beside the Goddard Arms. He had made his choice. He had lain in wait for her.

And while he was hunting, he continued to present a normal face to the outside world. Just an hour before he abducted Sian, he'd texted Heather: 'I love you.' Even after the murder, he upheld the pretence: it appeared he had returned to Sian's body four times before we'd started surveilling him and, after one of these trips on the Saturday morning, mere hours after he had slaughtered Sian, he went back home and had sex with Heather. 'He was completely normal,' she later said to the *Sun* about that day. 'He was laughing and joking ... It felt like any other time we'd had sex.'

I began to realise – this was someone who was *really* good at what he did. Even in Sian's case, we had only a *partial* DNA profile, and we were probably only lucky enough to get that because he'd moved her body in a panic and had not had time to wipe her down and bury her; we'd found a book on forensics in his loft and he appeared to have studied it thoroughly. If Marcus Beresford-Smith hadn't given us the breakthrough to identify Halliwell so quickly, we wouldn't have seen him dump those car seat covers that were flecked with Sian's blood – so that evidence would not be available either. Halliwell knew enough to switch off his devices to avoid incriminating passive data, and he operated in the dead of night when there were no witnesses. If we hadn't recovered Sian and the seat covers, there would be no evidence. He would be walking free.

In the light of Halliwell's retraction of his confession, I had anxiously reviewed my decision to breach PACE. But I was now certain I had done the right thing. We would never have nailed him without recovering Sian: the blood on the seat covers wasn't enough, as it wouldn't have proved he had murdered her if there was no body. And it was clear he would never have given up her location in the nick: if I'd taken him into custody earlier, he would have stayed silent – just as he had done ever since. Now, it seemed apparent that catching him was an even more critical achievement, given there might be other victims, given he might have made a career out of killing.

On Thursday 31 March, I strode into the MIR with my usual energy. It was a much smaller room than those we'd first commandeered at the start of the enquiry; with Halliwell in custody, and notwithstanding the clear indicators of other potential crimes, we were yesterday's news and had been downsized. In fact, it was a luxury for me to be there at all: I had been granted permission to stay on as SIO, but only if I simultaneously kept up with my other work as director of intelligence. It was like being asked to work double shifts every day of the week, but it didn't matter to me.

I was fully committed to this enquiry. Only I had managed to form a connection with Halliwell and I wanted to be the one to investigate the full extent of his offending. That morning, I managed to get away from my work at HQ and returned to the MIR to discover the latest leads from the team.

I noticed a buzz about the place as soon as I walked in. Neil Southcott beckoned me over with a flushed face. There had been an update from the prison, he told me, where we were monitoring Halliwell's calls and letters. And the suspected serial killer had made a major slip-up.

Under surveillance, he had said, 'The police want to interview me about eight murders.'

Eight.

Yet I had the bodies of only two dead girls.

Who were the other six?

I felt a familiar feeling in my gut, my policeman's nose twitching. It wasn't all over bar the shouting at all.

In fact, we had barely begun.

46

I tried to think back over all the police interactions with Halliwell. Would he have got the number eight from anything said in our interviews? No: there was nothing. That specific number could only have come from inside his head, from his own certain knowledge of his own sick acts.

My SIO brain started calculating. I needed to put strategies in place to try to work out who the other victims were. There were two obvious approaches: the first was to follow lines of enquiry that would thoroughly examine Halliwell's life and background – where he'd lived, what car he had driven, were all his former partners safe and well? – and the second was to achieve what we'd been trying to do from the minute he'd been brought into custody: get him to talk to us.

I called in the National Police Improvement Agency (NPIA), which provides central expertise on specialist areas of policing, and through them engaged the services of Dr Samuel Woolcott, one of the foremost criminal psychologists in the country. I wanted his help to gain an understanding of Halliwell: insight we could apply to the forthcoming interviews we'd eventually conduct with him about the second murder. We needed ammunition to increase the likelihood of him giving us a cough. After all, the easiest way to progress the enquiry was for him to tell us the whos and whys and wherefores. Unlike him, I didn't like operating in the dark.

There were so many lines of enquiry to progress that it was incredibly frustrating we had such limited resources. There were 120 actions awaiting allocation on HOLMES, yet no officers to undertake them. Astonishingly, my impression from senior management was that they saw my pursuit of the investigation as some kind of vanity project, and insisted on reducing our numbers to minimal levels. I felt like I was banging a drum, saying, 'He's a serial killer!' but no resource was put into investigating it. It seemed to me to be politics and cost-cutting: major crime enquiries are expensive and management wanted to get back to normality, with officers going back to their normal routines. Debs and John had both gone; my new deputy was DI Tim Parker.

Despite the difficulties, my small team and I kept plugging away. 'What caught me?' Halliwell had asked. 'Was it the gamekeeper at Ramsbury?' I put out an urgent media appeal for gamekeepers, poachers and lampers to come forward with any sightings or information, and search teams headed out to Ramsbury. As with the Eastleach area, however, it was a vast rural expanse, and I didn't hold out much hope that with the minimal crew we had we would be able to cover it fully. Nevertheless, we at least had to try.

We were following up on information from Halliwell's house and car, too: we were seizing items of interest and 80 exhibits had been submitted to forensics so far. The gaffer tape and knickers were not the only leads: we also collected soil-stained spades from the garage.

His computer records, meanwhile, in line with those of other killers, demonstrated a fascination with hard-core pornography, including child abuse and bestiality. His search history exposed an interest in murder, violent sex and rape, and he had a particular predilection for bondage, with searches entered on how to tie knots. That snagged my attention: there was an unsolved murder case in Bath where the victim, Melanie Hall, had been tied with a thin blue rope, and I wondered if Halliwell could be a potential suspect in her case. Was Melanie one of the six?

As with the unidentified girl in the Eastleach field, however, the murder had taken place so long ago that evidence was scant.

We were working desperately hard to identify our unknown victim. I was very aware that around this murdered girl there was a family who had been waiting a very long time for any news of her. The media, as is their wont, had been running speculative stories as to her possible identity – Claudia Lawrence, who went missing two years to the day before Sian did, was a high-profile suggestion, though as with Sally Ann John the dates of her disappearance were outside Halliwell's suggested parameter.

Understandably, there had been a huge public response to the discovery of the second body. Distressed families were constantly calling the MIR, wondering if it was their daughter we had found; we had received 600 calls overnight. Consequently, I had issued a media statement with the few details that we knew, her age and height, wanting to put some of them out of their misery; though that misery, of course, went on in other ways. For other families, the more detailed information only made the horrible anticipation of an imminent police visit that much worse.

For my part, I didn't really indulge in speculation. I knew that for every known missing person there were countless others who were not even on the police radar. Trafficked girls and sex workers, people disconnected from their families – there was a whole swathe of people in hard-to-reach communities that we simply knew nothing about. It could be that the unknown girl was one of them.

Work on the enquiry continued at the same intense pace as March moved into April. Such was my commitment that I kept up almost the same hours that I had put in during the search for Sian; I certainly didn't take the weekends off. It was only later – weeks later, when Yvonne pointed it out – that I realised to my shame I had missed Elsie's eighteenth-birthday celebrations. We'd intended to have a family meal at a restaurant but I'd been in the MIR all weekend, chasing leads on Halliwell, and I'd been so focused on the job that I'd forgotten. I apologised profusely, but Elsie told me not to worry. She said that catching criminals like Halliwell was what she would want me to be doing.

On Monday 4 April, I was working at Gablecross again. I'd just done an in-the-can interview with Steve Brodie of the BBC, to be broadcast after Halliwell had been convicted – that's how confident I was that a guilty plea would soon be entered. A call came in for me just as we were finishing up.

Once I heard the news it was relaying, I said instantly to Steve, 'I've got to go.'

It was a very important call. Because – using DNA extracted from the deep marrow of her bones – the team had just identified the unknown girl who had lain in that red clay field for so many lonely years.

Her name was Becky.

47

There was no report of her being a missing person on the police database. We wouldn't even have been looking for her if Halliwell hadn't led me to her grave.

Immediately, we started work on victimology. Unlike the owner of the perfume bottle, Becky Godden-Edwards's DNA had come up as a match on the PNC: that's how we knew who she was. She had some convictions for soliciting, and the computer gave a last known sighting of 16 December 2002, when she'd last had contact with the police. Despite having been sporadically in trouble over a number of years before that, there were no further entries on her record after that December date.

Perhaps Halliwell was right the first time, I reflected. *Perhaps it was 2003 when he strangled her to death.* His account of her murder in that red clay field was even more chilling now I knew her name.

She was only 20 years old when she'd gone missing. Our systems didn't tell us much more than that about her, except to give the names and addresses of her parents; they had split up when Becky was six. I decided to visit her mother, Karen Edwards, first, and made my way out of the nick with a heavy heart.

It grew heavier still when I noticed a particular date on Becky's file. I would be breaking the news of her death to her mother on what would have been her twenty-ninth birthday.

As I drove through Swindon, I had no idea what to expect. For the moment, Becky Godden-Edwards was just a name on a sheet of paper. I knew she would only become real to me once I met her family and heard her story.

The Edwardses lived in the better part of Swindon in a large detached house enclosed by high walls. I pulled up to hear the barking of dogs.

In my memory, the front door was already ajar as I walked up to it. A woman pulled it wide. She was beautifully turned out – her blonde hair perfectly coiffured, her body impeccably dressed – but the moment she laid eyes on me she crumpled and burst into tears.

She recognised me from the police media briefings on TV.

She knew why I had come.

We sat down on her red sofas; a fire flickered in the grate. And I had to say those words to her – the words no parent wants to hear.

You never know what a family's reaction will be like when you deliver this message. Often, you get an aggressive response or anger taken out on you as the bearer of bad news. But Karen Edwards was just heartbroken. I think it was like a floodgate being opened. Everything she had feared, especially over the past few days once she'd known about the body in the field, had come true. It *was* her precious daughter. Becky wasn't ever coming back.

Photographs of her daughter were displayed on the mantelpiece. They made my heart catch; she looked very similar to my Elsie. It reminded me how very fragile life could be.

Becky Godden-Edwards was a young blonde woman with haunting eyes and an apparent grace and beauty. One snapshot showed her, aged 16, as a bridesmaid at her mother's wedding to new husband Charlie in 1996. She wore an emerald gown and a shy smile. I thought she and her mother looked very alike.

Karen fetched the photo; she referred to it often as we spoke. She wanted to tell me all about Becky – and I wanted to listen.

She'd had a troubled life, Karen said. As a child, she was very affectionate and loving – a happy little soul. But when she hit adolescence, things took a turn for the worse. Becky had a very feisty personality, sparky and wilful, and she wanted to experience things, as young people do. After she fell in with a bad crowd at school, she started on a slippery slope of alcohol, aerosols and worse. The psychiatrist Becky was seeing told Karen that her daughter had the emotional age of a 12-year-old: she was a child in a woman's body, and people took advantage. After a while – after her so-called friends introduced her to it – Becky became hooked on heroin.

She battled desperately to get clean. Karen remembered her saying, 'Mum, my life is a complete mess, please help me.' And Karen did. She and Charlie put her into rehab – again and again. Heroin addiction is perhaps the nastiest of vices. It robs you of everything: all you want is the next fix. Becky couldn't stay away from it. After a while, to pay for her habit, she turned to prostitution and started turning tricks in the Manchester Road area of Swindon. Her mother said she could never really accept it was happening.

Karen had last seen Becky in December 2002, after picking her up at the magistrates' court. 'She had conditions to stay at my house,' she remembered. 'On the way home she said she wanted to see her boyfriend. She begged me and said she would just be half an hour. After a while she came back out and told me she wanted to stay longer. I was in tears because I knew what was happening inside that house. She was taking drugs again and I pleaded with her to come home with me. I became firm as I knew the best place for her was at home.

'But Becky said, "I love you so much, Mum, I can't keep putting you through this. I will come back home when I'm clean."

'She got out of the car, opened the boot and took out a scraggy black bin liner containing her belongings. I knew if I insisted on taking her home, she would only run away. I'd always said to her, "You go, but you know where the door is when you want to come back." My door was always open to her. I said the same to her now.

'But Becky never walked through my door again. That was the last time I ever saw her.'

It was a desperately sad, sorry story. What I've always thought with such things is that it could be my daughter or anyone's daughter that it happens to: nobody judges people who get caught up in these nightmares, especially when they're young, naive and misled as Becky was. Some officers in the force – some people in society – seem to think there are gradations of value to life depending on how you live. I don't feel that at all, but especially so after hearing Becky's story. She was just a young girl. She didn't deserve to die this way. No one does.

'It was just a waiting game,' Karen told me. 'We talked about her as though she would turn up one day.'

She explained to me why she hadn't formally reported Becky missing to the police. It was truly shocking. Sources she trusted – throughout the entire eight years she'd been missing – kept telling Karen they'd seen her; seen a girl we now knew had been dead and buried all that time. It was so cruel, it beggared belief. Becky hadn't been reported missing, not because she hadn't been missed – but because her mother believed her still to be alive and well, but estranged from her personally after their exchange in the car.

Nevertheless, it didn't mean she stopped looking for her daughter. She'd contacted a missing persons' website for help. 'I need to contact her urgently or just know she is OK! Can anyone help?' she'd written plaintively. Most heartbreakingly of all she went out looking for Becky most nights, every single week, driving up and down Manchester Road, swinging by Becky's old haunts, driving past the Destiny & Desire nightclub – and others – until that establishment had closed back in 2004. The Swindon landscape changed, but Karen still went searching for a forlorn, familiar figure against the shifting backdrop of the red-light district. Every week, for eight years, she went out looking, hoping to catch a glimpse of a girl she had been told was still out there, somewhere, but who was seemingly not yet ready to come home.

Such a lengthy, desperate pilgrimage was enough to make you lose your mind. Later, Karen's husband Charlie told me privately that she hadn't been far off. Karen had literally been going mad searching for a girl who would never, ever have been found, but for a moment of contrition up on White Horse Hill.

Karen ushered me upstairs at one point during my visit that afternoon. And there, in a pale-pine wardrobe, in coloured bags of red and gold and green, were all the birthday and Christmas presents she had bought for Becky, every year she had been gone. Karen had never given up hope of her homecoming, and she'd bought her gifts at each celebration for when Becky came back. Now she knew: she never would. I genuinely felt her pain.

She asked for lots of information, so I told her what little I knew. I described the man who'd killed her daughter, and the lonely field where she'd lain for so long. She said something that would become very salient. She said her Becky would have fought like a wildcat if she was threatened.

I was struck by Karen's dignity, and that of Charlie and Becky's brother, as they took in the news that Becky had been murdered. I could not think of anything to say to lessen their pain, but promised Karen that I would do all I could to bring Becky's killer to justice.

I intended to do all in my power to keep my word.

48

We began to build the evidential case for Becky's murder the very next day. I released her identity to the media – requesting that they remembered she was somebody's daughter and did not focus on the more salacious elements of her story – and began a search for witnesses. From what we knew so far, Becky had last been seen alive in December 2002. We needed to trace her movements to try to narrow down the time at which she had been murdered and find out if there were any witnesses who could place her with Halliwell.

A major strand to the investigation was tracing all the working girls in Swindon. This wasn't just to see if the girls knew Becky or had ever had Halliwell as a client – I wanted to be sure they were all safe. Both of Becky's parents gave emotional tributes to their daughter and appealed for assistance with the case too.

Unfortunately, the public appeals for witnesses had to stop after this juncture: because Halliwell had been charged with Sian's murder, putting too much information into the public domain would be *sub judice* – we would be in contempt of court if we continued to make public appeals, because such public discussion of Halliwell's behaviour might prohibit his right to a fair trial. It was something I'd been conscious of even from the moment of charging him for Sian's murder and had noted it in the policy book. The Gold Group had sanctioned my decision to continue to release information about Becky, firstly to allay the concerns of those 600 families and then to seek witnesses once her identity was known.

The halt to the witness strategy now left us in a difficult position. As I've explained, with Becky's murder having taken place so long ago, there were no forensics or passive data available; no confession; and, now, limited opportunity to secure witness evidence. It felt like a catch-22 situation all over again.

That didn't mean there weren't other avenues we could explore, however. From DVLA records, we identified the vehicle Halliwell had been using between 2002 and 2003: a silver Volvo S80. We also discovered that in the course of his driving career, some 30-odd years, he had registered over 80 vehicles in his name.

It was an extraordinary number. Even for a taxi driver, who might get through more cars than most, it was unusual. But, if my suspicions were correct and he was a serial killer, you'd want to change cars frequently, wouldn't you? All the better for distancing yourself from any evidence you might have left behind, or so others didn't make the link to you if a witness happened to come forward.

Unfortunately for Halliwell, and despite the change of media strategy, witnesses *were* now coming forward. Our enquiries with the working girls very quickly confirmed he was a regular punter. Several reported that he acted in such a disturbing manner after picking them up, pacing aggressively around his car and becoming almost animalistic, that – despite being experienced girls, used to dealing with violent clients – they phoned their pimps to rescue them because he made them so fearful. I noted that the dates of these incidents were in the months running up to Sian's abduction, indicating that perhaps he had been building up to her murder. We also learned from Halliwell's ex-wife that he used to play *Grand Theft Auto* constantly, getting sexually excited when killing prostitutes in the game; it seemed he had put his predilections into practice.

The day after Becky's identity was discovered, we came across a significant snippet in Halliwell's medical records. Karen had told me: her Becky would fight like a wildcat if threatened. We now found out that, on 3 January 2003, Halliwell had gone to his GP with a suspected fractured finger and several deep scratches down his face. Signs of a struggle with a wildcat, perhaps?

At the time, Halliwell had passed off his injuries as being caused by a passenger in an unprovoked attack. That was feasible: taxi drivers are often the victims of crime and Halliwell had been assaulted on a number of other occasions. Each of those assaults had been faithfully reported to and recorded by the police. But of this supposed altercation, there was no record. If what he had said was true, why not do as he had always done and report the attack? Later, we also discovered that his work diaries showed he wasn't working that day.

Once again, Halliwell was lying.

My instinct told me that this was a momentous development. Because, if Becky *had* attacked him – if those scratches were the signs of a fight to the death – then we now had a date for her murder: 3 January 2003. It was speculative, but it was the best we had so far.

Bit by bit, we were closing in on Christopher Halliwell. And I had a plan to get even closer to the killer.

I turned to face the thickset, jowly man standing beside me. 'So, what do you think?' I asked.

Dr Samuel Woolcott looked around Halliwell's lounge with a keen, enquiring eye. He was a very earnest man, deep in his fifties but with a very modern haircut, dressed in a sharply tailored suit. It was the first time I'd met the criminal psychologist, but I knew him by reputation – and knew him to be the best.

As I observed, he paced the length of the room, rifling through items and trying to gain some insight into Halliwell. Now, Samuel spun on his heel and gave his verdict: 'He doesn't live here,' he opined.

Although it was Halliwell's home, Samuel's view was that he had not allowed himself – his true self – to occupy the house he shared with his family. His substance wasn't there. His compartmentalisation of his life was complete.

The theory was backed up by the findings of the search teams so far. Despite combing through Halliwell's house and computer, to date we hadn't found anything compellingly incriminating. We had our suspicions around the knickers, gaffer tape and spades, but Halliwell hadn't – for example – kept a sickening 'treasure map' of where his victims were buried or a store of trophies with Sian's boots stuffed inside. He was a better quality criminal than that.

I was intrigued by Samuel's opinion. Because, if Halliwell didn't 'live' here, then in all probability there would be another place he inhabited. Perhaps the trophy store I sought did exist, but Halliwell was far too clever to have located it at Ashbury Avenue. It was another line of enquiry we would pursue as a priority – yet the most important priority of all was persuading Halliwell to speak again.

That aim was even more significant now that Halliwell had appeared to disclose there were other victims. Our continued investigation wasn't just about making the path to justice for Becky and Sian smoother. Halliwell was the sole repository of information about any other victims. The effect of his refusal to disclose their murders was that there were at least six mothers, six sets of siblings, six sets of friends, who were living in a permanent state of disconnection and suspended grief. It wasn't like a missing loved one was something you ever got over. People didn't say, 'Oh, we used to have a daughter once, haven't seen her for a while ...' We needed somehow to find a breakthrough – to get Halliwell back to the place he'd been in on White Horse Hill.

That was partly why I had enlisted Samuel's help. That morning of 6 April, before heading to the house, we'd had a briefing together with a chap from the NPIA, going through everything we'd learned about Halliwell so far. I was hoping Samuel could suggest some ways to get Halliwell back into that mindset. Was there some trigger we could press to prompt him to return to that state of contrition?

Samuel had focused on what we'd learned from his family. He thought it very significant Halliwell had such a deep hatred of his mother. Apparently, if he even saw a picture of her he'd have such an extreme reaction that he would start ripping the furniture up and smashing doors and windows, then he'd lie sobbing in the corner of the room. Might it be something we could use as a lever?

Now, as we turned from the living room and started up the stairs, Samuel returned to another psychological element of the case that had intrigued him. It was his conviction – supported by what we'd already learned about Halliwell's sexual response to violence – that there was a psychosexual trigger to Halliwell's murders: essentially, he got off on killing women. The murders were motivated by Halliwell acting out a sadistic masturbatory fantasy.

Samuel outlined an added element to this theory. He explained he was convinced that a man like Halliwell, so compartmentalised, who was managing to maintain a seemingly healthy relationship with Heather, must have used some psychosexual trigger to stimulate himself for those times when he wasn't able to murder. He said it was common and probable that Halliwell would refer to his memories of murder and rely on an actual, physical trigger to recall them while masturbating. Of course, Halliwell was too clever for that trigger to be, for example, a photograph of a victim. It would have to be something that wasn't incriminating. Samuel explained that it could be anything, from the trophies I'd already considered to something as seemingly innocent as a document or reference which was not overt.

By this time, we had entered Halliwell's bedroom. With Samuel's words fresh in my mind, my eye fell again on the yellowing piece of paper beside Halliwell's bed: the only thing on his bedside table. I went over to inspect it more closely, suddenly interested in what it might be.

It was a page torn carelessly from a notebook. On the lined paper was a funny little symbol, drawn in blue ink. It was a hexagonal shape, with an oval sketched inside it.

That hexagon made an immediate impression: Halliwell's conservatory was that shape. The conservatory he had built himself. The conservatory he had constructed three years ago.

Three years ago was when he'd last visited the Eastleach grave where Becky had lain.

I felt goosebumps rising on my skin. When I'd visited Karen Edwards two days before, I'd had to tell her the news that, not only had her daughter been killed, but that I was unable to return *all* of her daughter to her. Her head was missing. Her head, in which had resided that feisty wildcat spirit, that happy little soul, had probably, barbarically, been taken by her killer.

I looked again at the paper. Six straight lines of a hexagon. One round oval.

You do the maths.

49

I gave the order to excavate the conservatory, as well as other possible sites where Halliwell had been known to dig. If he had sickeningly taken Becky's head as a trophy – as I strongly believed he had – I was going to try to find it. If I did, surely he would come across again. He couldn't 'no comment' his way out of that.

After Samuel and I had finished at Ashbury Avenue that day, we went for a pint down the pub; his colleague from the NPIA joined us too. Strange as it may sound to those not involved in the criminal world, we were all quite chipper, despite the depravity of the man we were investigating. We were all quite clear we had identified a serial killer and I think, professionally, we were all engaged with the idea that we were part of something that was quite out of the ordinary.

Over our beers we talked, understandably enough, about the unconventional way I had caught Halliwell. I'd been both relieved and abashed at the amount of positive feedback I'd received since my actions that day. The response from the public had been phenomenal. So many people had been involved in the search for Sian that there was a massive outpouring of feeling when we'd managed to collar her killer.

'Pure amazin work by the police, wiv barely anything to go by they caught the killer and possibly solved another unsolved murder within a week' was just one of the comments on social media. Of my work, someone wrote, 'That's the kind of passion police officers need.' I'd had my hand shaken in pubs and petrol stations by random members of the public who just wanted to say thank you and well done. Trust me: that doesn't happen to police officers! It was the most extraordinary case I'd ever been involved with in terms of the outpouring of gratitude and recognition from the public. A member of the Gold Group said it was 'the biggest boost to public confidence in policing' he had ever experienced.

Yet it wasn't just the public who backed me. There had been a review of the investigation by an independent officer shortly after I'd brought Halliwell in: he'd listened in silence, making notes, as I'd talked through the impossible situation in which I'd found myself and, when I'd finished, he'd sat back in his chair and exhaled in admiration. 'Christ, Steve,' he'd said, 'you deserve a QPM for that.' (A QPM is the Queen's Police Medal: the highest honour an officer can receive.)

Within my own force, our CC Brian Moore had issued a force-wide message to say how 'brilliantly' managed the enquiry was. 'I particularly extend my thanks to Detective Superintendent Steve Fulcher,' he'd written, 'for the bold and confident approach to the investigation.' I was happy that people understood not only why I'd done it, but that they agreed the end result – capturing a serial killer – was well worth the breach of guidelines.

As we discussed the case in the pub, it seemed my colleagues on the national team concurred. That day, they told me that a vacancy had just come up in the National Crime Operations Support Team and encouraged me to join them. It sounded a really interesting role, assisting coppers nationwide, as and when additional expertise was required, on murders and major crime: just the sort of hands-on operational policing I loved. I saw at once, too, how being on the national squad could help me to progress the Halliwell investigation in a countrywide capacity.

By now, we'd learned that he had lived in various places around the UK, including Liverpool and Northampton; his father had lived in Huddersfield, giving him good knowledge of and access to a range of towns in the north. In particular, he was known to be familiar with York, where Claudia Lawrence had vanished. His taxi-driving profession meant he often went further afield than Wiltshire's borders (both Becky and Sian had been left in counties beyond his hometown). I therefore wanted all other forces in the UK to be aware of his offending and the likelihood he had committed other murders, in case Halliwell could be linked to any cold cases. I knew I'd have much more impact if I was able to champion the case to them in a formal national role.

I decided to apply for the post. In due course, I learned that my application had been successful. My new job would start in June.

In the time remaining to me as SIO of Operation Mayan, I tried to make as much progress as was possible with the limited resources I had. I wanted to go right back to year zero and build up what we knew of Halliwell. In particular, I was trying to find leverage points we could use in interview.

Our investigations bore fruit. One old cellmate of his, Springer, voluntarily came forward. He was an old lag who'd spent his life in and out of jail and he and Halliwell had shared a prison cell back in 1986. Springer said that of all the many people he'd shared a cell with over the years, Halliwell was the strangest and most worrying.

When he told us what Halliwell had said to him, I could see why. On one occasion, he'd asked, 'Have you ever had sex with a woman while strangling her?' On another, he'd said chillingly, 'How many do you have to kill to be a serial killer?'

This was back in *1986*. Had he been carrying out his crimes since then?

To my mind, it made the possibility of him being involved in Sally Ann John's disappearance in 1995 even greater. We soon found other links to the missing girl too. Our interviews with the Swindon sex workers confirmed that Halliwell *had* consorted with Sally Ann; in fact, it appeared he had developed an obsessive relationship with her. An obsession that led to murder? Potentially. In a sign of how seriously I took the link, I asked the force to reopen Sally Ann's case.

We spoke to 196 sex workers in total, and a couple of crucial witnesses eventually emerged. They said Halliwell was a regular punter of Becky Godden-Edwards and that he was obsessed with her. They reported him wanting an exclusive arrangement and said he was very controlling. They described a similar pattern of behaviour to that reported with Sally Ann John.

When I heard the news, I was struck by it – because Halliwell had expressly told me that Becky was 'just' a prostitute and he hadn't known her. He had been lying – again. But why? Why was it important to him to conceal Becky's identity when he knew full well who she was? Did it explain why her body parts were missing? I was slowly starting to appreciate the truths and half-truths he had told me that day; that there were things he had said in earnest contrition and others he had deliberately disguised. A pattern – an MO – was emerging, too. Separate witnesses described these obsessive relationships he'd had with both Sally Ann and Becky. Perhaps the women had tried to break free.

Perhaps he hadn't liked it.

Yet at the same time, if this was his pattern, the murder of Sian was a conundrum: he *hadn't* had an obsessive relationship with her, to our knowledge. These were two different MOs. Was there a unifying factor? If there was, I couldn't see it – at this stage, at least.

On 15 May, a directive was issued from senior management that the few remaining additional officers working on the enquiry had to be returned to their other duties with immediate effect. I was staggered that so little priority was being placed on pursuing Halliwell's offending history.

Our skeletal crew of 14 struggled on; there were some 300 actions outstanding on HOLMES now. We heard from women who said Halliwell paid them unwelcome attention; from a taxi passenger who said he'd ignored her instructions and driven off route. She had become so concerned she'd phoned her mother and then the police to deter him.

Everything we heard told the same story. This man was dangerous. This man was intent on causing harm.

Before I left the force, I wanted to interview this man one last time.

In May 2011, Halliwell was brought out from prison for further questioning. Would the psychological levers work? Could we bring that pressure to bear?

There was only one way to find out.

50

You could hear the sirens from several streets away. In a blaring entourage, Halliwell was being driven from Long Lartin prison, where he'd been on remand for the past two months, to a police station in Worcester for the interviews.

It was a huge security operation. Halliwell was in a prison van with a cavalcade of three or four police vehicles surrounding it, the roads blocked off at every junction so he could go racing through. It was a necessary safety measure: our informants had told us there was a contract out on his head. Even hardened criminals were repulsed by his crimes and there was a plot afoot to assassinate Halliwell. We had him double-staffed at Long Lartin to minimise the danger, but he wasn't behind bars now. We'd received intel that there was a specific threat to intercept him en route to court, so every time he left the prison a full-scale protective plan had to be put in place.

Sitting in Worcester police station with my team, I wondered how Halliwell would respond when questioned. I was hoping that he'd have sat in prison for the past two months, reflecting on the way this was going, and would have decided on a different course of action from 'no comment'. He was going down for this: he'd led us to two dead bodies. Given the impossibility of mounting any defence, his best bet was surely to give a full and frank.

In particular, I'd been ruminating on what he'd said to his daughter: 'Sell your story and make as much money as you can.' If he wanted to do the best he could by them – to create the most lucrative price tag around their story, so they would benefit – then, as cold-heartedly commercial as it sounds, I thought he should cough not only to killing Sian and Becky, but to the other six murders he'd referenced while in jail. Doing so would make him a national cause célèbre.

I really wasn't in the position I'd wanted to be in for this further questioning. Over the past two months, I'd come to appreciate how cunning Halliwell was. Despite the fact we knew he'd killed two women (at least), there was not a scrap of hard, non-circumstantial evidence we could find beyond their bodies. We'd hunted high and low for a possible trophy store but to date we had been unsuccessful in locating it. There was no trace of Sian O'Callaghan's boots or handbag, no matter how hard we looked.

Nor, to my anguish, had I managed to find Becky's skull. I was convinced he had taken it and secreted it somewhere. But our excavations had revealed no sign of it. If that hexagon symbol on the notepaper beside his bed did depict its location, it wasn't the conservatory that it stood for.

I was joined on this further questioning venture by Dr Samuel Woolcott. We would be downstream-monitoring the sessions while Dex Drummond and Bea Reiss put Halliwell through his paces. The interview room was rigged with video cameras which fed footage to us in a separate room. From there, we could observe and influence the interviews by suggesting different lines of questioning.

The room we were in was large: a small, old-fashioned monitor from the 1980s the sole focus of our attention. All eyes were on the slightly fuzzy picture as we suddenly saw movement on the screen.

Halliwell was here.

I watched him with interest. He was dressed in normal clothes; no handcuffs. *How has prison changed him?* I wondered. *Has he undergone the transformation we need?*

He *was* transformed; I could see that instantly. During my interaction with Halliwell on 24 March, in the main he had been aware of his offending and weighed down by it. But that wasn't the character of the man I saw before me now. In contrast, he was cocky.

You could see it in the way he swaggered into the room, accompanied by his solicitor Mr Smith. He'd just been escorted in a three-ring circus, of course, and perhaps those efforts had buffed his ego till it shone. It certainly emanated from him, luminous as light, as he took his seat at the table in the interview room and stared confidently across it at Dex and Bea.

I held my breath. We'd put so much preparation into these sessions. Every scrap of evidence we'd been able to find, such as his GP visit on 3 January 2003, when I believed he'd sought treatment for the scratches Becky had inflicted, was going to be put to him. Every suggestion Samuel had made was going to be utilised. This was the moment of truth.

They began with a broad preamble of questioning, attempting first some basic common sense. 'Can you confirm you led us to the location where you had buried Becky Godden-Edwards?'

You know with these things within the first few seconds if they are going to be of any value. Halliwell sat easily in his chair. He barely seemed to listen to the questions. Then he opened his mouth and said, 'No comment.'

I exhaled in frustration. But Bea and Dex were well-trained and I still had some hope they might get somewhere. They next appealed to his sense of decency: 'There are people out there who are bereaved as a result of your actions: for their sake, please answer us and tell the truth.'

'No comment.'

Halliwell seemed almost to enjoy himself, as though he relished being the centre of attention. He preened a little in his chair, his body language and facial expressions communicating that he knew he had something we wanted and he wasn't giving it up. He hoarded his knowledge like treasure, like a miser counting coins.

We had him here on a three-day laydown: for three days, we would question him in all manner of ways. So I wasn't too down-hearted when this first interview failed to make him come across. We still had some aces up our sleeves. That night the team and I had a meal together to discuss tactics. Evidently his conscience wasn't going to prompt him to ease the pain of the parties he had affected. Another direction was clearly required.

The next day we tried again, using other techniques and lever points, gently testing whether there was anything that might get Halliwell to change this position. At Samuel's suggestion, we went back to his past.

'Talk us through how it felt to go into care,' we said. 'How it felt when you came out of care and had to go back to your mother.' We also asked him what he'd meant by his conversations with his former cell mate, Springer.

But to each question we received a flat: 'No comment.' He didn't vary the way he said it. There wasn't even a knowing smile behind it; he was clever enough not to offer that kind of leakage. His natural response was just what you'd expect from a serial killer. That's how you protect yourself if your life is one of murder. And I guess he was pretty confident – he'd got away with it all these years. Why cough now?

We tried to use all the psychological levers at our disposal. We asked him to do the right thing; to do himself and his family some good. We talked about the victims, Sian and Becky alike, snatched from their lives full of potential, but it caused not a ripple on the surface of his implacably still pond.

Then, we asked him about his mother. By that time, Halliwell had got into such a routine, answering every question with 'no comment', that he wasn't perturbed. The trick is not to get affected by the questions and he held that line immovably. I think he even relished it: he liked the fact we could try all we liked, but a simple 'no comment' solved every problem.

I debated at length whether to use a picture of his mother to prompt a reaction. From what we'd been told, that might break through this barrier he'd erected between himself and the truth; it might also break him entirely. So I was wary. I didn't want to completely antagonise him. My thinking at the time was that maintaining some positivity from the relationship would be beneficial in the long run. If I alienated him now, we'd never be able to rebuild the relationship following his conviction. I was thinking of those six other victims. In the absence of any hard evidence, we needed him to tell us who they were and where they were. It always came back to empathy and understanding, and the impossibility of extracting a confession by any other means. We had to keep Halliwell on side.

So I stepped back from that lever; I didn't pull that string. Nor did I go in there and speak to him myself. I regret, now, not trying in person one last time. I think on that occasion I should have done. But it didn't seem right: I was the SIO, not an interviewing officer, and with Mr Smith still involved I didn't think I'd fare any better in eliciting a confession.

By the end of the three days, no matter what questions or tactics we had tried, Halliwell had said only two words: 'No comment.' To say it was frustrating is an understatement. He could do it, because it was his right, but you can see how it makes a farce of the whole process. It used to be that questioning people was one of the fundamental pillars of an investigation, but it isn't now. Without it, detective work simply becomes a passive gathering of any evidence the criminal has been clumsy enough to leave behind. Get a clever criminal like Halliwell and you're almost completely incapable of catching him.

If I hadn't breached PACE, we wouldn't have done.

He was cocky as he swaggered out, heading back to prison. But he was less cocky when, that same month of May, we formally charged him with the murder of Becky Godden-Edwards.

Instead, he asked the officers, 'When do I plead?'

51

On 7 June 2011, I left Wiltshire Police and relinquished my position as SIO of Operation Mayan. I was confident I left the case in good hands: my deputy Tim was stepping up to lead the team, and I considered him probably the most talented officer I had ever worked with. Yet I was concerned for him that his resources were so limited – I noted in the policy book on my last day that the MIR was not being fully staffed in accordance with MIRSAP (major incident room standardised administrative procedures), which meant the team had been cut so much that actions on HOLMES were not being completed. However, the strategy adopted by the Gold Group was that Halliwell was certain to plead guilty; therefore they considered the investigation to be largely over.

Though I didn't agree with them there – what about the other six potential victims? – I did concur in the view that an early plea from Halliwell was likely. I was almost looking forward to that moment because, once he was no longer in the confines of the court system and under the influence of lawyers, he and I could reconvene and continue what we'd started in March.

I wasn't washing my hands of the other six victims in moving on to the national team – not by any means. I would be working hand in glove with SCAS (Serious Case Analysis Section) to investigate Halliwell's potential crimes, as well as reviewing the national homicide index, on which there were several hundred unsolved murders, to see if anything hit.

In some ways, it was perhaps just as well I left Mayan when I did, given my proclivity for digging up former construction sites of Halliwell's in my search for Becky's skull. For it came to light that, in his role as a freelance groundworker, Halliwell had dug the footings for Gablecross. If I'd had any more time on the enquiry, I'd have had them ripping up the floorboards of the nick.

'Alright, guv'nor, good to see you!'

I shook hands with my former colleagues as we all scooted along the back row of the courtroom in Bristol Crown Court on 28 July 2011. We were there for the PCMH (plea and case management hearing) in Halliwell's trial for the murder of Sian and Becky. It was just a pre-trial, administrative hearing, but nonetheless there was a buzz of anticipation as us coppers congregated together. There was every indication that today might be the day he pleaded guilty.

As I mingled with my fellow officers, there was a buoyant air of 'hail fellow, well met'. Having been out of the force for almost two months, it was great to catch up with people. My only slight consternation came when I learned that Tim was no longer SIO of Mayan; there'd been some politicking behind the scenes and he was off the case. In his place was a DI who was rather more inexperienced.

Despite the fact the PCMH was a simple administrative hearing, the courtroom was packed with both journalists and members of the public. Everybody wanted to see Halliwell: they wanted to see what a serial killer looked like.

He wasn't in court in person, however. Instead, he was video-linked from Long Lartin. I considered him on the screen. He looked very impassive, as though none of the hullabaloo was to do with him, yet he still had the cockiness I'd seen in May. He sat still and sedentary on the screen as the action in court played out.

There was a rustling through the court as we all stood for the judge to enter. He acknowledged the black-robed barristers before him and we all retook our seats.

By now, Halliwell's legal team had swelled in size; alongside Mr Smith was his newly appointed barrister, Richard Latham QC. Under legal aid you can get the best of the best and Halliwell had lucked out: Latham was probably one of the top five barristers in the country. He was tall and willowy thin with a very aristocratic look, and he exuded the kind of impressive confidence you'd expect him to have as a leading barrister who'd won most of his cases.

Acting on behalf of the prosecution was Ian Lawrie QC. His physical contrast to the tall, thin defence barrister was almost comic: he was shorter, with an enormous girth, grey hair and a beard. I liked him immensely: he was a very avuncular chap with a jocular personality, the type who tells amusing anecdotes with ease. It was his first case in silk; he'd only just been appointed as a Queen's Counsel.

There was a hush as the barristers stood to begin proceedings. I listened with interest to Lawrie giving an opening presentation, wondering if Halliwell would plead today as we all hoped.

But Richard Latham didn't let it get that far. I watched him hold court effortlessly as he spoke: he had a gravitas about him; everything he did had a sense of unassailable authority. I was so engaged by his evident ability that I was thrown when I unexpectedly heard my name.

'I've asked for the exclusion of Mr Fulcher from this court,' Latham began.

My forehead creased in consternation; it was the first I'd heard about it.

Latham went on, each carefully chosen word a stepping stone that led down a particular path: 'I've asked for his exclusion because I have to lay before the court the gravest allegations concerning the SIO in this case, which will require external investigation.'

It was a path that led to my own personal circle of hell.

At his words, I felt extreme heat rising from my feet right up to my face. I was aware of this flapping sensation around the court – a tidal wave of movement as people turned to look at each other and then to look at me. I felt their eyes like daggers, pricking at my fallen pride. There was consternation in court – from the press corps, my colleagues, members of the public. I couldn't see Halliwell; I felt like I couldn't see anything. There was just this sense of heat and blackness, a cloud of horror and despair descending on me and blocking out all else.

Up to this point, I had been unable to see how Halliwell's case could possibly be defended. I did now: by painting me as the bad guy. From the hero of the piece, having found the body of an abducted girl and a second victim, it seemed I would become the villain. I could see the way this was going to go: my actions at Barbary Castle and on White Horse Hill were going to be attacked in order to jeopardise the hearing of the case. I felt as if a rug had been ripped out from underneath me.

That crack in the world, the crack that had been created by an unrepeated confession, fractured further and then further still, until I was looking down into a gulf.

But it wasn't just me teetering on the edge: it was Sian, and Becky, and justice.

52

It had never occurred to me that the actual facts of the case would – apparently – not be taken into account. The issue of Halliwell's guilt or innocence wasn't in question and I'd always thought his case was undefendable. I had never anticipated that his legal team wouldn't even *try* to defend it – that they'd simply try to have it thrown out of court. But that was what was happening.

In the immediate aftermath of Latham's announcement, I fought my way out of the court, surrounded by a scrum of media with flashbulbs popping in my eyes, and so began a long period of darkness. Latham hadn't been specific about what 'allegations' he intended to raise, so I was left hanging in the breeze, thinking the worst. I was concerned he would seek to suggest that my actions were unlawful. I didn't know the particulars: there was just the raw threat.

Halliwell's solicitor had no doubt briefed him and Mr Latham must have formed his perception of me from that. I didn't know what Smith had said – but given the allegation he had made in court back in March, that I had illegally recorded his consultations with Halliwell, I had no doubt as to the portrait he had painted. He possibly even said I was exactly the sort of copper whose actions had necessitated the introduction of PACE in the first place, which was intended to stop the police from abusing their position in order to fit people up for crimes they didn't commit.

I'd been aware at the time that breaching PACE would be controversial. But PACE was put in place to protect the innocent. The defence objection was not that Halliwell was an innocent man ill-treated by the police, but that he was a guilty man who should have been protected by PACE. However, if I had adhered to PACE, we wouldn't have known him to be guilty.

I wondered if Latham was aware of the context in which I had made my choice – that I did it in the hope of saving a girl's life and then to secure the evidence of a second murder – and if he knew that I had not acted alone, behind closed doors, but in full view of 30 officers and a helicopter, with Deborah Peach along as scribe. I still believed I had acted appropriately, following the kidnap manual and Section 11.1 of PACE, but I started to doubt myself following the proclamation in court. There was very little case law on the subject.

As I've said before, PACE has been amended nine times to accommodate practical scenarios not anticipated by the guideline-writers. Was this one of those times?

I was gripped by a grim sense of foreboding. From July onwards, I wasn't able to sleep through the night without sleeping tablets. I kept waking in the small hours, plagued by fears. One of the key strengths of an SIO is being able to calculate consequences, but now it was a paralysing weakness, leaving me in a constant state of pre-emptive turmoil. I was keen to seek legal advice, to discuss the position I had taken back in March, but because I was a bound witness I couldn't talk to Lawrie, and the force didn't think I needed my own lawyer. They were remarkably breezy about the whole thing. The view relayed to me was that attacking me was a sign of desperation for an undefendable case.

I hoped they were right. It did seem a bold idea that Halliwell's legal team were going to try to persuade the judicial system to commit itself to freeing a clearly guilty double murderer. After all, even if I'd hung Halliwell over a motorway bridge and the truth had been shaken out of him like loose change, they should still prosecute him for his crimes. In that scenario, they'd rightly prosecute me too, but it still wouldn't change the fact of Halliwell's guilt. And, of course, I hadn't done that. I spoke to him. That was all.

As the months drew on and we edged into autumn, more details emerged of what position the defence were taking. They had two complaints, which would be aired in a special court hearing called a 'voir dire': a pre-trial hearing in which the judge would decide if there was merit to their arguments. The first complaint regarded my breach of PACE. Latham argued that all the evidence we had secured from the moment I breached it – so Halliwell's confession *and* the fact he had led us to the bodies – was inadmissible in court. The second argued that the police force had conducted a reckless media strategy by putting too much information into the public domain, which had prejudiced Halliwell's right to a fair trial. The latter carried a potential criminal offence if it was upheld: I could be seen to be in contempt of court.

Though I was concerned about the latter, I knew I had acted only with the sanction of the Gold Group with regards the media strategy, so it was the lesser of my concerns. In addition, the force had recently won a national award for the best-handled media case for Operation Mayan; if it was so reckless, it seemed unlikely the strategy would have been celebrated in such a public way.

I was much more worried about the implications of the first complaint. I had known from minute one that, if Halliwell did not plead guilty as I expected him to do, an admissibility argument could be raised because of the breach of PACE. Yet it wasn't automatic that any evidence gained in such a scenario was inadmissible: the decision was entirely at the discretion of the judge. Naturally I understood that we didn't want to live in a world where police officers could breach PACE willy-nilly and offer up accounts in court that were otherwise unsubstantiated. But my concern on this point had been assuaged by the fact we had recovered Sian and Becky. I could see that if we hadn't done that, and were trying to prosecute Halliwell for their murders with only my word against his that he'd confessed to the crimes, the defence would have a very strong argument for excising the evidence from trial. But it *wasn't* just my word against his. We had Sian's bruised and battered body. We had Becky's bones. And we had them only because of what I'd done. So how could it be wrong?

I was under no illusions that the implications of the judge upholding this complaint were serious. In Sian's case, I wasn't so worried, because – thanks to our having recovered her body – we had the forensic evidence to tie Halliwell to her. My concern was for Becky. The effect of being unable to appeal for witnesses meant we had a limited case. Everything we did have was circumstantial. If a jury wasn't told Halliwell had led us to her body, and we were trying to convict him solely on the basis of his having a scratched face, we weren't going to get very far.

Christmas that year was affected by the dark cloud of uncertainty. Even being with my girls didn't cheer me up. The first voir dire had been set for the end of January 2012 and I would have to wait for that event to see how my future and the future of the case would progress. I kept asking myself whether what I had done was wrong; what else could I or should I have done? What were the alternative consequences of not speaking to Halliwell? Would we have ever found Sian? I thought it very unlikely. We hadn't been searching anywhere near Uffington.

We would certainly have known nothing about Becky and she would still be in the field at Eastleach. The case against Halliwell, without having found Sian, would have been non-existent. The consequences of bringing him into custody would have been that Sian and Becky would never have been found and Halliwell would be walking free, probably suing the police over wrongful arrest in the glare of publicity and, given his propensity, other victims' lives may well have been forfeit too.

But would the judge see it that way?

I was told that a week's court time had been reserved for the hearing. This was unprecedented in my experience; normally, voir dires last a couple of hours. Debs and I had both been notified that we would be called as witnesses – though, interestingly, Debs had been summoned by the defence, not the prosecution. I pondered what that meant.

The new year dawned. The voir dire loomed at last. I wondered: would any judge in the country dismiss such a double murder case without it proceeding to trial? Could Halliwell's legal team get the case thrown out? The public reaction would be seismic. But the corollary of that verdict would be that I would be held personally responsible for the outcome. I felt sick, stressed and under immense strain. Everything hung on me and my evidence. If I could persuade the judge to admit Halliwell's confession through my testimony, then surely Halliwell would roll over and plead guilty: there was no defence to what he had done. Sian and Becky would receive justice and he'd spend the rest of his life in jail.

But what if I couldn't persuade the judge? What then?

In the small hours of the night, there was never any answer.

53

On Tuesday, 31 January 2012, I made my way into Bristol Crown Court for the voir dire. As bound witnesses always are, I was held in a small room on my own while I waited to be called to give evidence.

As I sat there, fixed in a rare moment of stillness, I let my thoughts percolate. As an SIO, you're often racing against the clock, with everyone crowding round you, part of a buzzy team all pulling together for one end. The contrast now was striking: it was just me, with a potentially life-changing few hours ahead.

I'd thought long and hard about what to say on the stand. Without legal advice, I was concerned about the implications of my testimony – both for me personally and for the case. I'd had several people say to me, 'Why don't you just say you cautioned him?'

I never considered following their suggestion for a moment. If I lied and perjured myself under oath, how did I differ from Halliwell or any other criminal? My view was simple: I could only tell the truth. I remained confident that, once the court heard my account and understood the decisions I had made and their impacting factors, justice would prevail: that Halliwell's confession would be admitted so that he could be held to account for murdering two women. Surely anything else would be a travesty of justice?

It was shortly before 2 p.m. that the usher came to collect me and escorted me to the court. It was a small, compact courtroom, its compressed feeling amplified by the sheer numbers of people crowded into it. The press gallery was full to overflowing, but the public seats were also fully occupied. I was supremely conscious of the audience: the victims' families, the media, Halliwell, Lawrie and Latham, and of course the judge.

Judge Cox was sitting on a raised bench: a diminutive woman dressed in the full red-robed regalia of her profession. I knew a little of her background; she came from the family division. This was her first-ever sitting in a criminal case.

I walked in as confidently as I could in the circumstances. There was one step up to the enclosed wooden dais that was the witness box and I navigated it carefully. There was a seat in there, for infirm witnesses, but I knew I should stand. There's a slang phrase for the process of giving evidence, 'gripping the rail', and sure enough a solid brass rail ran around the edge of the box. But I didn't let my eyes linger on it. I was far more interested in Christopher Halliwell.

He stood across from me in the dock, his presence somewhat diminished behind the strengthened glass. We made eye contact. Even at that point in time – despite what his legal team were in the midst of doing on his behalf – I still felt we shared some kind of bond. What he'd done that day in March, almost a year ago now, in giving me Becky and Sian, was something I valued: we would never have found them without that moment of honesty on his behalf. I was aware that in this forthcoming exchange I would be speaking as much to him as to the judge; I would have to choose my words carefully. I still hoped we would get beyond these legal contortions and end up back in conversation one day. The six other victims deserved being given a fighting chance of being found.

At that moment, however, I was fighting principally for Becky and for Sian.

The usher brought me a plastic cup of water, which is always the first test of character for any witness. If your hand wobbled and the water went everywhere, you were a goner: the barristers would scent blood. Strangely enough, though, I found as I took the cup that I wasn't nervous any more. Instead, I felt calm and alert. I found that I was almost back in the mental state I'd assumed during that extraordinary time with Halliwell: my mind was working very clearly and I felt on top of my game.

It is a lonely job being an SIO, notwithstanding the team around you. But I think standing in that witness box was perhaps the loneliest moment of my career. It was my decision-making that was under scrutiny, my vocation that hung in the balance and my sole accountability for the success or failure of the prosecution. I felt a mixture of trepidation and relief that the time had come at last to give an account of my actions. I expected a rough ride and a vigorous test of my reasoning – yet I also held the belief that truth and justice would out.

Lawrie rose from his chair to begin the questioning. I felt reassured seeing the familiar twinkle in his eye and his avuncular manner set me at ease.

'Can you give your full name and rank to the court please, Mr Fulcher?'

'Stephen John Fulcher, detective superintendent,' I replied. My voice was confident and steady.

Lawrie talked me through the case in some detail, highlighting to the court that this was a crime-in-action investigation right up until the moment the search teams actually discovered Sian's dead body at the bottom of that sloping bank.

Lawrie asked me, 'Had you formed any view as to Sian's physical condition [before then]?'

'My fear was that she could well be dead,' I replied frankly, '... I feared that, but I hoped that she was alive. And my duty in these circumstances was quite clear, it was to work to find and protect Sian, if I could.'

'... Is that because of the nature of this investigation of crime in action?' asked Lawrie.

'Because of the nature of the investigation of crime in action – and it's what any parent would want a police officer to do for their child,' I answered. I still believe that to be true.

Naturally, he soon addressed the breach of PACE and the lack of a formal police caution.

'Can I just deal with this please,' Lawrie said easily, as though it was a simple matter that we just needed to clear up. 'It would appear from this record that before you spoke to [Halliwell] or indeed at any stage when you were speaking to him that you don't appear to have given him [a] caution, is that correct?'

I held my head high. 'That's correct,' I said clearly.

'Do you accept that you didn't give a caution?'

'Yes, I didn't caution him.'

Although I was focused on Lawrie, I couldn't help but be aware of Latham too. I believe at that juncture he turned several pages over in his lever-arch file at once, as though the content within them had just become frustratingly redundant. At the back of my mind a realisation hit me: *Perhaps he thought I was going to lie.* 'Oh yeah, I did caution him. It was Debs who messed up when she didn't write it down.' *That* was why Debs had been called as a defence witness, I realised – so that when I perjured myself and lied about my actions, he could call her and call my evidence into question. I think my integrity rather took the wind out of his sails. At any rate, after I had given my evidence, Debs was stood down as a witness and not called. It meant her account of the exchange between Halliwell and myself was never heard in court.

Lawrie, understandably, pressed me on the issue. 'Can you help us [with] why it is you didn't caution him?' he queried, giving me a chance to state my case.

'Yes.' I took a deep breath. My entire argument hung on my reply. 'He'd been arrested, he'd been cautioned, he'd been interviewed by my officers ... The key issue was saving Sian's life and my view was that opening a conversation by telling him he didn't have to say anything at that point in time was unlikely to achieve that. My view was that her right to life was more important than having a PACE-compliant interview.'

As I said the words, it seemed to me that the issue at stake was a no-brainer. I hoped the judge would agree. A ruling against the course of action I had taken in these circumstances would send the message that it was better to let victims die than to breach the rights of those who had killed them. It sounded bonkers: surely we as a society could not make that decision?

Lawrie questioned me for some two hours, taking me through my previously submitted formal statements. Yet this was the easy bit. As the prosecution rested and Richard Latham stood to begin his cross-examination, I took a sip of water to dampen my dry throat.

Watching Latham stand up was like watching a feline hunter uncurl itself before it began to stalk its prey. He must have been around six foot four; even his height was intimidating. But it was the sharpness of his brain that I feared more. I knew how barristers worked: they led you down a particular path, guiding you there with seeming innocence, then once you had made the concession they sought, they turned around and declared, 'As a consequence of you saying x, the corollary is y, therefore, Your Honour, you should reject the evidence and Halliwell should walk.' So I viewed him with some trepidation as he began to put his questions to me.

He raised the meeting I had had with Pat Geenty to discuss the media strategy and my fear that putting pressure on Halliwell might cause him to commit suicide.

'This was your primary concern at this meeting, wasn't it,' Latham asserted, 'that Halliwell would do something to himself and therefore, in the most brutal of ways, obstruct your enquiry?'

I was conscious of Halliwell in the dock. Unlike at the PCMH, he seemed engaged in proceedings. I believe he was genuinely interested in what I had to say; it was the first time I'd explained to him why I'd acted as I had.

'No,' I replied of the assertion that I'd cared only about the case. 'Quite genuinely, I [had] a duty of care to Christopher Halliwell ... I don't take such a brutal view as you described ... We had a duty of care.'

I was speaking almost directly to Halliwell – attempting to communicate, I suppose, that we had tried to do right by him; hoping he would still do right by us.

'You believed [Sian O'Callaghan] was dead, didn't you?' Latham stated with his unshakeable authority. I focused on the question: if I gaily admitted that, he would move to say there was no justification for the urgent interview – if I believed Sian to be dead, the argument that her right to life trumped Halliwell's rights under PACE was null and void. But although I had at times during the investigation *feared* she was dead, I did not *believe* it – to do so would have been utterly remiss of me.

'... Although I feared she was dead, I recognised that my primary duty remained to work to save Sian until all hope was exhausted,' I replied. '... The fundamental first and only objective of this police operation is to save the child's life.'

'... Mr Fulcher,' Latham began, before referencing the minutes of the meeting I'd had with Geenty, '... There is nothing within this note ... which suggests you are concerned that she might still be alive.'

'... I think you're missing the point here,' I riposted. 'The point is what I thought, feared or even believed is irrelevant to the execution of my duties as a police officer and my responsibilities to Sian O'Callaghan. I might very well have feared that she was dead ... but my duty at that time, and Mr Geenty's duty and [that of] every officer in Wiltshire Police ... [was] to take that last opportunity to save Sian's life, if we could do it.'

The difficulty with the cross-examination was that I didn't have free rein to set out the timeline of events in a linear way. Latham's job, of course, was to boil my actions down to the bare facts: this officer breached PACE, therefore he's a wrong 'un and we shouldn't accept the evidence. He didn't want the judge to hear a clear, logical, sequential story so she could appreciate the catch-22 position in which I'd found myself, whereby there was no other way to save Sian's life other than to act in the way I had.

'[Halliwell] said a number of things,' Latham began, setting off on a new line of questioning. 'He didn't want to say anything, which was his right, yes?'

'Yes,' I acknowledged.

'He wanted a solicitor, which was his right ...'

'Quite.'

'... and he wanted to be taken to a police station ...'

'That's right.'

'... which is where in anything other than extraordinary circumstances he ought to go, correct?'

'Quite. These are, of course, extraordinary circumstances,' I argued.

Latham fixed me with a look above his half-moon spectacles. 'Well, you turned them into extraordinary circumstances, didn't you?' he bluntly said.

I tried to present my case as passionately as I could. 'This [was] a matter of life and death, notwithstanding your view that I already thought she was dead. I didn't *know* she was dead ... The least I can do – the least I can do – is speak to him myself and appeal to him ... in order to preserve Sian's life ... I'm fully aware of PACE, of course I am, as you'd expect me to be. The choice is adhere to PACE ... and never find Sian and never find Becky ... or to take steps that I considered reasonable in the circumstances ... I say my responsibility as the senior police officer responsible for Sian, responsible in that moment in time for her life or her death, the least I could do is to speak to him in person. And that's what I did.'

I felt Latham's gaze like a weight.

'The end justifies [the means]?' he asked lightly.

I took the bait. 'Well, in these circumstances it does,' I concurred hotly.

It was a stupid thing to have said. If you start saying the end justifies the means you get yourself into very dodgy territory. Such was the heat of the moment I had walked into the trap.

And there were others ahead. The job of a barrister is to paint a picture in the judge's mind of a set of circumstances. Latham next picked up on the location for my interaction with Halliwell.

'... A remote area, isn't it?' he asked.

'It is remote, yeah,' I acceded.

'About as different from the custody suite of Gablecross police station as it is possible to envisage, isn't it?'

I knew what he was doing: suggesting that I'd deliberately taken Halliwell to the rural location of Barbary Castle in order to put pressure on him away from the security of the nick. Of course, the location was chosen to help Sian in the belief that she was there but, given she wasn't, Latham was now drawing inferences that weren't supported by my actual reasoning.

By this time, it was late on in the afternoon and I couldn't resist a touch of sarcasm. 'Well [it wasn't that different from the nick] under these circumstances, as it happened,' I told him, 'because there were an awful lot of police officers conducting a search.' I waited a beat, then conceded more accommodatingly: 'But in principle, yes.'

I think my tiredness was showing a little – and, perhaps, my frustration that he was fighting this battle on behalf of a clearly guilty man. We talked of Halliwell coming into custody and I referenced, off the cuff, '... the medical examination, during which, of course, he told the doctor that he is in because he killed two women ...'

Latham hurriedly intervened – he wanted to limit what was heard in court regarding his client's guilt and Halliwell's further admission to a second party. 'Mr Fulcher,' he interrupted, '... you are doing yourself a disservice in speaking as you do and you might think about it.'

He turned to the judge after a brief glance at his watch. 'My Lady, I note the time. I'm going to be a little time yet.'

My heart sank; my ordeal was not over.

'It may be as Mr Fulcher has had a long day in the witness box – and has got a little excited it would be better if we broke off until tomorrow morning.'

The judge concurred.

My battle to see justice done was not done yet.

54

Latham and I began our verbal duel again at 10.03 a.m the following day, Wednesday 1 February. And I believe I achieved something that morning. Naturally we once again discussed the issues at hand and I valiantly argued that Sian's rights had to be prioritised over those of Halliwell. It was a strangely personal interaction – I was supposed to be convincing the judge, but I found myself fixing my gaze on Latham's long thin face as the two of us batted the issue back and forth.

We had been going for quite some time when Latham said, 'You weren't sailing close to the wind, you made a decision to sail right into the wind, didn't you?'

'My judgment was that Sian's life was more important.'

'... Than PACE?' Latham asked disbelievingly, as though PACE was the be-all and end-all.

'*Yes*,' I said emphatically. Of course it was. Of course a girl's life took precedence over guidelines.

There was a strange – yet familiar – sensation. The day before, I had felt I was back in that intense mental zone I'd accessed during my time with Halliwell. Now, a similar tipping point to that before Halliwell had said, 'Have you got a car? We'll go,' shimmered between me and the black-robed barrister. I remember it distinctly: Latham paused and dropped his half-moon glasses onto the tip of his nose so he could look over them at me.

The two of us locked gazes and there was an exchange – of understanding, of comprehension – in the seconds that passed.

'A moral decision,' he pronounced.

In that instant, I believe he understood. He understood that I was an honourable man and I wasn't trying to talk my way out of something. Despite portrayals to the contrary, I wasn't a maverick copper. I was simply telling the unvarnished truth, giving an account of how I had tried to resolve an impossible situation for which there was no legal precedent, and I was presenting those exact facts to the court so it could make its choice.

'Yes,' I said, confirming his assertion. 'A necessary decision, in my contention.'

However, even though I believe that Latham understood at that juncture *why* I'd done what I had done, it still didn't mean he was going to allow the evidence in. He had to act in the best interests of his client. The gossamer-thin truce between us tore in two.

'But you're not entitled to do that [not give a caution] with somebody who's been arrested, are you?' he said.

I spoke plainly. 'The issue is that the law necessarily leads to the worst of all outcomes, which is the death of the party who you're trying to save, who has been abducted by the party you're talking to. I believe that PACE is broad enough to enable these facts to be judged in a court like this and for somebody to make that objective judgment.'

'But there is a difference,' Latham said, '... a fundamental difference between making a decision, a moral decision as you effectively describe it, in order to gain intelligence information which may, *may* save someone's life. There's all the difference in the world between that and translating the intelligence you get into admissible evidence in a criminal trial, isn't there?'

'Yes, there is,' I acknowledged.

'Yes,' he said in satisfaction.

'But in these particular circumstances, in which the result of that conversation was so dramatic, insofar as he took me to two bodies ...'

Latham cut me off. He didn't want the court to consider Halliwell's guilt: he only wanted the issue of the breach of PACE and the admissibility of the evidence under inspection.

'Yes, we know,' he said dismissively, as though the discovery of the girls' bodies was not of any importance, 'we know what happened, but that's back to the end justifying the means and go hang with PACE, isn't it? Isn't it?'

'I personally believe,' I said, 'that British justice is broader than that and is capable of assimilating the circumstances and the impossible decision that I had to make.'

'... So,' said Latham, taking me metaphorically by the hand and leading me down a path he'd picked out, 'I mean, within reason, you were entitled to do anything in the agony of the moment to get the answer you wanted from Mr Halliwell?'

'Within reason,' I said cautiously.

'Yeah. Threaten him?'

'No,' I said emphatically. I would never do that.

'Well,' responded Latham provocatively, 'why draw the line there if somebody's life's at stake and it's a moral decision?'

'My view is that asking him the question, "Will you take me to Sian O'Callaghan?" is a perfectly reasonable proportionate issue in the circumstances.'

'But you did, in fact, threaten him, didn't you?'

I felt the blood drain from my face. I hadn't threatened Halliwell; I truly hadn't. My old mentor Howard Bostock would have had my guts for garters. I had approached him only in an empathetic, if authoritative manner.

'No,' I replied. I repeated it for emphasis. 'No, I didn't.'

Latham looked up in theatrical consternation, ready to play his ace card. 'You made it quite clear that he was going to be vilified, didn't you? … You spoke about vilification, you used the word twice, didn't you?'

I could hear my heart pounding in my ears. I could only tell the truth: 'I did.'

Latham asked me, with demonstrative naivety, 'Unless you told the media about what he had or hadn't done, the media would have no idea of whether it was appropriate to vilify him … would they?'

I smiled wryly. 'It doesn't quite work like that, unfortunately … The media … are, after all, free … Even before I left Gablecross police station, certain journalists were on the phone asking me what … had occurred.'

The video of Halliwell's arrest was already in their hands before I'd left the station. They had his identity. It would have been a Christopher Jefferies scenario all over again. In raising vilification with Halliwell, my concerns had been two-fold, and neither was a threat. The first was that, if he was innocent, he didn't want to endure unwarranted vitriol from the press; the second that, if he was guilty, in leading me to Sian the vilification would potentially be less severe given he had done the right thing. Both of those motivations showed only a care for Christopher Halliwell. The illogical nature of Latham's argument infuriated me. How could mentioning the media be construed as a threat? If you were guilty, I would argue that the media's disapproval of a murderer's actions was justified. If you were innocent, such a so-called 'threat' would hardly be enough to compel you to cough to an abduction you hadn't committed.

Latham moved on, having powerfully planted the seed of the threat in the judge's mind. '[Halliwell had] been arrested for kidnap, and shortly after you set off on that hour-long drive [from Barbary Castle], it became apparent

301

to you that you were the SIO of a murder, rather than a kidnapping, [didn't] it?'

'Yes, that's right,' I conceded. I'd had hope for Sian until the confirmation of her murder, but I'd known from the way Halliwell was talking that it was almost certain she was dead.

'As soon as he made that clear to you ... he should have been arrested for murder, shouldn't he? Shouldn't he?'

I shook my head in disbelief. Latham's assertion was that, if my suspicion of Sian's death was aroused en route from Barbary Castle to Uffington – *before* Halliwell had identified her location – I should have arrested him, cautioned him and taken him straight back to the nick. I could see why he would want me to do such a thing, because if we hadn't found Sian we'd have no evidence to convict his client. But the corollary of his argument was that I should have left Sian to the mercy of wild animals. I couldn't believe Latham could even argue it.

'Not in my view in these circumstances,' I replied. On the stand, I gave my rationale: 'My reason for [not arresting him for murder in that instant] was this: if I lose that moment, that agreement, that inclination on his part to take [me to Sian] ... by taking him out of that moment in time, then he might very well not [reveal her location once back at the nick].'

'Yes,' Latham had replied gravely. 'So again, we're back to the means and end, aren't we, I'm afraid?'

'There is a means and end,' I simply said.

It was mid-morning before he got onto the matter about which I was most concerned: the admission evidence relating to Becky. Latham was forthright.

'The need for an urgent interview had concluded at that stage ... Any question of getting yourself under the umbrella of C11.1 [Code C, Section 11.1] has gone, hasn't it?'

'No, not in my contention,' I argued. 'The C11.1 is, as you know, about saving life and immediate threat to life, it's also about preserving or preventing a loss of evidence and my view at that time was that if there is evidence to be gained as a consequence of Mr Halliwell wishing to speak further, that C11.1 could conceivably still apply and I worked on that basis.'

'... [The situation] warranted a caution as soon as you realised he was talking about something quite else. You should have said, "Look, we'll talk about this at the police station later." That's what you should have said, shouldn't you?'

'Well, I don't agree,' I said plainly. '... I think that my role as a detective is to gather such evidence as can come my way ... I recognised at the time that we would doubtless have this discussion [about admissibility]. My view was that ... the court would hear the circumstances and would decide whether my actions were reasonable in the circumstances or not and whether this information should be admitted as evidence or otherwise. But my decision was quite clear, that rather than not have the information and therefore not find Becky [it was better to proceed] ... No murder detective is going to not seek to pursue that line.'

Latham now brought up the second complaint of the defence team: what information I had put into the public domain as part of the media strategy, which they argued now precluded Halliwell's right to a fair trial. The focus was on the strategy post-arrest and centred on that harried, hurried press conference I had given on the same day I'd caught Halliwell, when I had been rushed from breaking the news of Sian's death to her family into the full glare of the media spotlight. 'A 47-year-old man from Swindon has been arrested on suspicion of kidnap and two murders,' I had said at the time, reading the lines the Gold Group had approved. 'I have been taken to the location of two bodies, neither of which has been identified, but one of which is believed to be

Sian O'Callaghan.' At the time I made the statement, I did not know Halliwell was going to retract his confession. I had spoken plainly and merely told the truth, working to inform the public. Latham now said that statement contained a key pillar in the prosecution's case against Halliwell and the information should never have been revealed.

'You were putting into the public domain something which should be *sub judice*,' Latham argued.

'I don't believe so, no. I don't believe that's the case.'

It had been the truth. *Can the truth be prejudicial?* I wondered.

'So you reveal, do you, to the press and to the world at large before a trial starts what someone has done, that you intend to use as part of the prosecution case against them?'

'... It's not an issue that I considered at the time.'

'No, you didn't, you didn't think it through, did you, Mr Fulcher?'

'I can't say that I spent a huge amount of time considering the issue,' I conceded; I had had rather more pressing matters on my mind at the time, '... I agree that I didn't spend a lot of time thinking through the implications of the script that was given to me.'

'... To your intense annoyance,' Latham said, segueing into a different but still salient subject, 'you discovered that Mr Halliwell had decided that he didn't want to answer any questions in interview.'

'Yes, true,' I concurred.

'Yes. And it became a matter of considerable frustration to you, didn't it?'

'It was frustrating, yeah.'

'Yeah,' said Latham, 'because it wasn't part of the deal, was it?'

I wasn't sure I had heard him correctly: what was he talking about? 'The deal?' I asked in confusion.

'The deal you'd done with him that you would look after his family and get them out of Swindon.'

What?

That wasn't a deal, I thought, *that was an act of humanity* ... But I appreciated such reasoning might sound daft to the court. Whoever heard of a detective acting in such a considerate way towards a double murderer? It certainly didn't fit the image of the threatening maverick that Latham was attempting to conjure with his cross-examination. Crucially, Halliwell and I had only had that conversation about his family at the very end of our interaction, once he had given up the locations of the girls. It wasn't an inducement to compel him to confess. It wasn't a 'deal' such as Latham had described.

'You were very cross at what had happened since he'd arrived at the police station, weren't you?' Latham said.

'I was frustrated, yes.'

'... You began to realise, during the several days during which he was interviewed, that if he said nothing more, then what you had done on the twenty-fourth was going to place you and your investigation in a very difficult position, wasn't it?'

'No, that wasn't the calculation I made,' I told him. I spoke frankly – spoke as I am sure a great many members of the public would have done. 'I thought it was utterly ridiculous that an individual who's taken me and 12 [vehicles] in a surveillance convoy to two dead bodies should seek to find some mechanism, some quirk of the law, some loophole ... that would get him away from the fact that he's a multiple murderer.'

'So PACE, in your view, is a loophole?' Latham asked archly.

'No.' I sighed, feeling I had fallen into a trap again. '... [I simply say] that when it comes to dealing with threats to life, [PACE] doesn't always necessarily work in the interest of the victim whose life is threatened.'

My words hung in the air in the courtroom, almost visceral after such a heated debate, as though they were puffs of steam summoned by our strength of argument.

In response, Latham paused, briefly, and then said, 'I've no other questions, my Lady.'

Ian Lawrie stood to re-examine, but our exchange was short. He confirmed with me that the so-called 'deal' came only after Halliwell had made his confession, and I reiterated that I had taken Debs along 'to record any conversations that occurred as accurately as possible', as well as my reasons for acting as I had.

Lawrie shuffled through his papers one last time, then looked up at me. 'Mr Fulcher, you are free to go.'

The judge assented: I was excused as a witness at 12.10. I felt mentally and emotionally drained after two days of intense testimony. I didn't glance at Halliwell or anybody else as I left, I just turned on my heel and made my way swiftly outside to the court steps, into a fine bright day. I felt light, lighter than I had in six months, and even experienced a slight elation after the pressure of the courtroom. Having spent the past two days recounting the reasoning behind my actions and the facts of the case, I felt newfound hope that all would be well. It seemed ridiculous that the fact of a murderer confessing his crimes and taking me to where he had buried his victims could be ruled as inadmissible evidence. I felt hopeful that the judge would not throw a murder case out of court on the basis of a breached guideline.

I wasn't the only officer called to testify at that voir dire in February. Although Debs's evidence had not been heard, former ACC Pat Geenty (who had since been promoted to DCC in the wake of Dave Ainsworth's suicide) took the stand that afternoon. I didn't see his testimony, but I read a transcript of it later. I was really quite touched by his impassioned support:

'Having thought myself about the circumstances of [Steve's breach of PACE], it's my belief that Detective Superintendent Fulcher was acting to save somebody's life. Was trying to do what we believe is our primary responsibility and that is to bring Sian back to her family ... that is why police officers use judgment and it's what I encourage my officers to do ... [Just] because the rules say you shouldn't do something, if you believe that there is a greater good involved in rescuing somebody, for example, then I would expect my officers to use that element of judgment to do that.'

The transcript, in fact, bore out my belief that Latham had revised his opinion of me. He quoted my stated rationale to Geenty – '[Sian's] life was more important than PACE' – and declared, 'Morally one can't criticise that statement, can one?'

'No,' Geenty replied.

'... Mr Geenty,' Latham went on, 'I am not talking about any officer ... being in any way disciplined for what he has done.'

'No, nor am I,' concurred the DCC, '... I think the decision [Steve] made was, to use the slang, a gutsy decision.'

'Yes,' agreed Halliwell's own defence barrister.

'I think it was a brave one,' said Geenty, 'and I'd like to think that I would make a similar decision in his circumstances.'

'... That's why I emphasise,' reiterated Latham, 'that there's no question here of complaining on a disciplinary basis of anything that he did, that is not what I am talking about.'

I felt it was an extraordinary position for him to take, and I was grateful for his public expression of it. When I read his words, I thought back to what Latham had said at the PCMH – that he had the gravest allegations to make about me that would require an external investigation. My honest testimony, it seemed, had changed his mind. Naturally, he was still acting for Halliwell, so even though he could comprehend my reasoning, he was still making the legal argument to say that the evidence I had gained was inadmissible. But he was also saying I hadn't done anything wrong in trying my hardest to save Sian's life and to recover Becky from that lonely field where she had lain for so long. It was an endorsement of my actions from a clever man for whom I had the greatest respect.

It was Friday before the judge was ready to give her verdict. I was in court to hear Latham give his closing argument. He stood before Judge Cox with all that aristocratic authority he had and summed up the issues as he saw them.

'This is not about truth and justice,' he proclaimed levelly.

Even as I listened, I was a little agog. Wasn't that *exactly* what the courts were about?

'This is not about guilt or innocence,' he continued. 'This is about admissibility of evidence.'

I was sat at the back of the court again, behind Lawrie and the Crown Prosecution Service lawyers. There was an apprehensive atmosphere in the room as Judge Cox prepared to pronounce. There was a feeling it could go either way.

I couldn't see what Halliwell was making of the drama; the dock was behind me. Yet I was conscious of him. When I'd entered the room, he had been busying himself in a way that suggested he was totally detached from proceedings. He could have been sitting on his own in the corner of the pub, rather than in a dock at Crown Court, learning whether or not his case was going to go to trial.

From my perch on the hard wooden bench, I surveyed the barristers. Lawrie looked concerned, I thought; Latham in control. Though it still seemed inconceivable to me that a judge would rule to let a murderer not face trial for his crimes, I shared the prosecution barrister's apprehension. After all, Latham was such a persuasive lawyer. Though breaching PACE was not an in-or-out, do-or-die criterion when it came to admissibility, the decision was now solely in the judge's hands. Allowing the evidence in or not was entirely at her discretion.

A hush fell in the court and Judge Cox began to speak. Her voice was miked, creating the disconcerting effect of it coming out of the speakers all around the court. That voice echoed all around me: no way to escape.

I can't tell you exactly when it was that I realised what had happened. She was delivering a lengthy preamble. But bit by bit – to my mind – I kept hearing phrases that sounded familiar. It seemed in my view that she'd been heavily influenced by Latham's impressive phrasing, by the verbal smoke-and-mirrors effect he'd created as he'd stated his case, and some of those good lines had seemingly resonated. She delivered her verdict in a calm, straightforward way. That was peculiar for me because, despite her matter-of-fact tone, what she was saying had the effect of an earthquake, uprooting everything I'd ever tried to do.

'While Detective Superintendent Fulcher was entitled to adopt an approach which would lead to the gathering of intelligence and information,' she pronounced, as later included in her written judgment too, 'what resulted was not, in my judgment, such as can fairly constitute admissible evidence in a criminal trial ... The confession [from Halliwell] ... would have such an adverse effect on the fairness of these proceedings that [it] ought not to be admitted.

'For all these reasons the application made on behalf of the Defendant at this voir dire is granted.'

You'd think it would be more momentous than that, when a man gets away with murder.

55

I felt faint. That heat I'd felt at the PCMH wrapped itself around me again, that heat that burns you inside and out so that you almost can't see because of the blackening before your eyes. I was in a state of some shock. In the immediate aftermath of the decision, Lawrie and the CPS lawyers ushered us coppers, Kevin Reape and the O'Callaghans downstairs for an immediate debrief; on police advice, the Edwardses were not present in court that morning – something Karen regrets to this day. In a small basement room, the lawyers acted swiftly to assuage the O'Callaghans' concerns: 'OK, we've lost the confession, but we've still got a strong case for Sian with the forensic evidence.' Neil Southcott started jibber-jabbering away, but I only heard the buzz of his conversation as from a great distance. All I could say was: 'What about Becky?'

I left the room, too caught up in my emotions to be able to stay. I was distraught. I felt guilty – but not about breaching PACE: we wouldn't have known who Becky was or where she was or have recovered her body if I hadn't taken the one opportunity Halliwell had offered to find her. I felt guilty because I hadn't managed to persuade the judge that she should admit the only evidence that proved Halliwell to be a double murderer.

I walked back upstairs into the atrium of Bristol Crown Court. I was still standing there, shell-shocked, when Elaine O'Callaghan came out of her meeting and into the lobby too.

I had no idea what she and her family might make of this, whether they would be angry or hostile towards me. I needn't have worried. She threw her arms around me and hugged me. It was one of the most touching things I'd ever experienced. She was a bereaved mother of a murder victim, but she was offering me reassurance and comfort; I thought it was extraordinary of her given what had just happened in court.

The judge ruled that she found me to be oppressive of Halliwell in our interaction at Barbary Castle – because I 'sought repeatedly to persuade him to speak ... when [Halliwell] had clearly indicated that he did not wish to'. Well, she was right in a way: the aim of the interaction *was* to persuade him to speak when he did not want to, but that did not mean it was oppressive. The seed Latham had planted that I had 'threatened' Halliwell with vilification in the media, meanwhile, had grown to a full clause in her written judgment, finding again that I was oppressive because of it. The circumstances of my repeated questions, Halliwell's recent arrest and the rural location all combined to 'affect the mind of this Defendant that he spoke when otherwise he would have stayed silent'. Her ruling seemed to suggest that such a thing was outrageous, as though we didn't want murderers to confess their crimes.

I disagreed, of course, with her finding of oppression. I even thought that what had happened on White Horse Hill between Halliwell and me confirmed my viewpoint: if I'd been oppressive, it would have been impossible for me to have created such an open relationship with him that he was prepared to offer the voluntary confession regarding Becky. He had unburdened himself to me; he had cried on my shoulder and asked for help. Those were not the actions of a man oppressed, I would wager. I was also disconcerted that she had reached her decision on whether or not I was oppressive without hearing evidence from Deborah Peach, the only close witness to what went on that day.

The fact that Halliwell's confession regarding Becky had been entirely voluntary did not make a difference to the judge, however. She found my explanation that I couldn't issue a caution for fear of making him clam up 'unacceptable'. 'Whilst the initial words from the Defendant may have been unprompted,' she wrote, 'they arise from what had already passed between them and cannot be viewed in isolation from what had gone before.' She said I should have taken Halliwell to the police station and not gone to find Becky. I say there is a fundamental flaw in the law when a detective has to refuse a voluntary confession from a suspect.

I hoped the CPS would appeal the decision. Surely they should: there were legal arguments we could make; there was common sense to apply. No one seemed to grasp what the ruling meant for policing generally – that offenders' rights now took precedence over those of victims – but it was Becky I was worried about. We couldn't give up on her case without a fight.

To my horror, though, it wasn't only her case that was under threat. With no appeal forthcoming from the CPS following the first voir dire ruling (they told me later they considered the judgment watertight), the legal juggernaut moved on to the second voir dire in April, this time hearing the claim from the defence that, because of the media strategy, Halliwell could not receive a fair trial for both Becky *and* Sian's murders. His lawyers were trying to get both cases thrown out of court.

I wanted to resign; to fall on my sword. Though I had only ever acted in the best interests of the victims and their families, the law had pronounced it didn't much like that approach. The message I was hearing loud and clear was that I had jeopardised Halliwell's conviction. I felt utterly sick. I felt I'd let a lot of people down.

Debs persuaded me not to quit. She reminded me that I'd caught a murderer. But for how long had I caught him? The idea that a man I was convinced was a serial killer might soon be back on the streets was staggering. If the judge ruled for Halliwell in the second voir dire as well, he would be walking free.

I was specifically told to stay away from the court in April. I was, however, told to travel to Bristol in case either Lawrie or Latham should wish to call me. I spent the day in the rain, just wandering the streets, wondering if Halliwell was going to get off scot-free. Wondering, too, what the corollary of the judgment would mean for me. I was potentially facing a criminal charge of being in contempt of court. Debs tried to reassure me by saying that I hadn't acted alone at the press conferences but with the full sanction of the Gold Group, with senior officers literally sitting by my side; she was adamant that I alone could not be held responsible. But I wasn't reassured.

Part of my concern was prompted by the fact that there had been a regime change at Wiltshire Police by now. CC Brian Moore – who had thanked me for my 'bold and confident' handling of Mayan – had departed and Pat Geenty was top dog. Pat and I had always got on OK but there were some other senior figures now in the mix and I was not convinced they would be supportive.

Following the first voir dire judgment, I was persona non grata in the Wiltshire force. There was no contact from senior colleagues to discuss what would happen next. Still working away from the force in my national job in Bramshill, Hampshire, I felt the isolation profoundly. I had expected the judge's ruling to come fairly swiftly for the second voir dire, but every time I asked if there had been a judgment yet, I was told by my colleagues there was no news.

Then, in May, there was an update. But not about the second voir dire: about Becky.

The CPS had decided to drop her case from the indictment. Halliwell would not face trial for murdering the beautiful young woman he had callously taken from the streets of Swindon, strangled and buried in a shallow grave. I felt extreme mental anguish; I could only imagine what her family felt. I was expressly precluded from the decision to drop her case; *I* would have fought like a wildcat to keep her on the indictment if only I'd had a seat at the table.

But the CPS feared there wasn't enough evidence to convict Halliwell without the confession. Everything else we had was circumstantial.

The injustice of it was staggering. I couldn't believe we were just rolling over and removing Becky from the indictment without an appeal. But it had happened. The decision had been made. *Halliwell was getting away with murder.*

As for Sian's case, to my knowledge that still hung in the balance too. When I asked, I was told the judgment on the second voir dire had been deferred. The longer the deferment went on, the more fearful I became. Why was it taking so long? What was Judge Cox going to say and what was my liability? Was she saying, 'Arrest that officer'? The effect of not knowing the outcome all this time was severe. I didn't know if Halliwell would walk free, if Sian would be denied justice as Becky had already been, if I would face criminal charges. My health began to suffer. Later, I would learn that the judge had actually made her ruling punctually, but this was purposely kept from me. I didn't learn the reason for that until much further down the line.

In the wake of Becky being dropped from the indictment, Becky's father lodged a complaint against me with Wiltshire Police, saying that my actions had caused Becky to be denied access to justice. I didn't blame him for doing so. I acknowledged that he would be grief-stricken and up in arms about this travesty. Of course Halliwell should be held to account for his daughter's murder.

Yet, with respect and in all fairness, his complaint against me was illogical. The nub of it was that my actions prevented Becky from getting access to justice because we'd lost the confession evidence because of my breach of PACE. But, *but* for my actions, we'd never have found Becky and she would still be in the field at Eastleach and there would *be* no case. The case was thrown out because of my actions, but wouldn't exist if I hadn't acted the way I had. It was tautological: a circle that couldn't be squared.

It didn't mean I didn't agonise over what I'd done. But I couldn't think of any other course of action that would have achieved the same end result of bringing both girls home. Halliwell had demonstrated time and again that in PACE-compliant conditions he refused to speak. He did it before my intervention and afterwards too. If I hadn't intervened, he'd have walked and we'd never have been able to convict him of Sian's murder, nor even known about Becky. The judge had specifically ruled that I couldn't take the confession relating to Becky in an urgent interview because in her view Section 11.1 of PACE did not apply on White Horse Hill. So even if I'd felt a caution was appropriate in the knife-edge circumstances – which it was not – and had cautioned him and continued our conversation, she would have still ruled the evidence inadmissible. Operating under the aegis of PACE, Becky would never have been found.

Police forces have the capability to assess complaints when they come in, to decide on a course of action. In this situation, I had hoped the officers in charge of discipline at Wiltshire Police would assess Becky's father's complaint and recognise its illogic. I had hoped they would consider the sworn opinion of their own chief constable that, in this particular case, there were no disciplinary charges to answer. But they did not: the complaint was immediately referred to the IPCC.

I accepted that. So when the investigator phoned me to say she would be handling the case, I welcomed her approach and offered to give a full and frank account to her immediately.

Yet the investigator refused it. I suspect it may have been because the IPCC investigation could not properly begin until the legal proceedings against Halliwell had been concluded, but I still thought it a strange response. As anyone can recognise, it is far better to take a witness statement close to the events being scrutinised, because human memories are fallible. But I was told she did not want to hear from me at this time.

Spring turned into summer and still I had heard nothing about the ruling from the second voir dire. The time weighed heavy. I was still working in my national job, trying to make the best of things, but it was a pretty grim time. I was sickened by the idea Sian too would not find justice, reeling from the decision to deny it to Becky, and fraught by the notion that I might be facing a criminal charge.

In July, Yvonne and I went away on holiday with our girls to Portugal. We were now three months on from the second voir dire and I was convinced there must be some dramatic outcome from the ruling. I feared it meant the judge was going to dismiss the case entirely. Someone would have to be held responsible for such a calamity; that person, I foresaw, would be me. I concluded that criminal action must be being planned against me.

On the last day of our holiday, I gathered my wife and daughters around me. I'd spent the whole vacation trying to be light-hearted for them so they didn't realise what a dark place I was in, but the time for amateur dramatics was over. I didn't want them to be upset the following day.

I told them I expected to be arrested at the airport when we flew back to the UK.

It was a difficult thing to have to say, but in some ways it came as a relief. They didn't pooh-pooh the idea. We got very practical: I gave them some advice on how to get home without me and the people they would need to call. As it turned out, I wasn't arrested but – as I would only learn much later on – my apparent paranoia was not unfounded.

Shortly after returning home, I finally received a call from the force to tell me the judge had ruled *against* the defence in the second voir dire: Halliwell would stand trial for the murder of Sian O'Callaghan. It was a huge relief. The judge found that, in releasing the information to the media as I had, there was no bad faith on my part. She also acknowledged that the Gold Group had granted me authority to conduct the press conferences, and that they had never challenged my handling of the media. Though she considered the media strategy constituted 'a serious error of judgment', the fallout was not such that Halliwell could not receive a fair trial.

I exhaled as I put the phone down. I was relieved for myself, but most of all I was thankful for the O'Callaghans and Kevin Reape. I pictured in my mind the girl I'd sought for all those desperate hours, that one week in March that now seemed a lifetime ago. Sparkling green eyes. Asymmetric hair. The smiling face of Sian O'Callaghan. Justice *would* be done for her. And, no matter the judge's ruling of oppression, I knew I had done the right thing to bring her home. I knew it was right not to have left her to the wild animals. I knew I was right to have caught her killer.

My personal relief turned out to be short-lived, however. It was only about an hour later that I received another phone call, this time from my boss on the national squad.

'Steve,' she said, 'could you please come and see me as soon as you can? I've got something to say and I'm afraid it's going to be distressing.'

I persuaded her to tell me on the phone anyway.

The words are a catchphrase these days. Turns out, they're not so funny when you're on the receiving end.

In essence, what she had to say to me was: 'You're fired.'

56

I was sacked from my role on the national team with immediate effect and returned to force; a matter of some professional disgrace. There was no hearing, nor any process of appeal. I was informed that a conference had been held in my absence by senior officers and they had concluded that, in light of the judge's rulings in the voir dires, my position was untenable.

I requested the opportunity to state my case in person, but this was denied. It seemed to me that officers wanted to close down any debate that could have been had around how the current form of PACE did not work in the best interests of victims, but instead prioritised the rights of suspects.

I landed back on Wiltshire Police's doorstep in August 2012. I was given some 'strategy and planning' role and felt very much a spare part. However, it gave me the opportunity to ask my colleagues on the force what they would have done in my position on that long-ago March day. I was still unable to sleep at night because I was constantly reassessing my decision. Yet no matter how many times I twisted the Rubik's cube of reasoning, I could find no other course of action that gave the same solution of capturing Halliwell and recovering the women.

One senior officer told me: 'I'd have got rid of Deborah Peach, ensured there were no witnesses and verballed him up. It's your word against his whether you cautioned him or not.' It was a shocking thing to say: back to the dark days of the police lying under oath and acting improperly behind closed doors; the complete opposite of what had transpired between me and Halliwell.

'What are you suggesting an SIO should do in those circumstances?' another, very senior, officer was asked.

'PACE is inviolable, it applies in every case,' he replied.

'You do understand that that would mean accepting the inevitable death of the girl we are charged with the responsibility of saving?'

He had shrugged. 'So be it.'

I found it unpardonably callous. If it was my daughter who had gone missing, I would want the police to take every reasonable step to find her, rather than abandon her to her fate.

If it was your daughter or loved one, what would you want the police to do?

I hadn't been back in the force long when I received a phone call from Karen Edwards. It transpired that she fully supported my actions. I went to see her and she expressed her shock that Becky had been dropped from the indictment. She had been asked by the police to keep the news absolutely confidential – she couldn't even talk to her best friend about it – and the pressure was taking its toll; she felt sick to her stomach. I assured her that I would do all I could to secure justice for Becky.

I therefore suggested to my superiors that I became SIO for Operation Mayan once more and stated my case passionately. In the absence of the confession evidence, it was more important than ever that we pursued the investigation – and not just for Becky, but for the other six victims Halliwell himself had mentioned.

I had no confidence this was happening at present. I'd learned that, the previous year, a witness had come forward to report seeing Halliwell digging at a second field in Eastleach; searchers had identified a grave-sized hole – the possible burial site of a third victim? Yet the team had not excavated the site for several months. It demonstrated there was no urgency to the operation any more, even though it had proved a false lead in the end. There could have been a third girl buried there; a third family desperately waiting for news.

However, to my disappointment, my request to return as SIO was vetoed. It was not felt to be appropriate given the IPCC investigation that was still hanging over my head, still to begin. There was nothing more I could do.

In early September, I received a call from Rob Murphy, the crime correspondent for ITV, wanting to talk through the findings from the voir dire and why Becky had been dropped from the indictment. Understandably, he was having some trouble comprehending how Halliwell had got away with murder. I tried to help him, but the issues were complex so he asked if we could meet in person. I agreed to grab a quick coffee with him.

Two colleagues were in the café at the same time. I sensed they viewed the meeting with suspicion; this was at the height of Operation Elvedon, the enquiry into the cash-for-information scandal where corrupt coppers received payments from the media. As a consequence, I informed the force of the meeting as a belt-and-braces measure. Then I really thought no more about it.

On Friday 21 September, I was summoned to a senior colleague's office. As the meeting unfolded, I realised with almost visceral shock that I was being suspended from duty. They demanded my phone and warrant card, and from that moment on I was no longer an active police officer. Arrangements had been made to escort me off the premises and back to my home, where my laptop was seized; I was also banned from leaving the county. I felt like a criminal.

There was no hearing; I didn't even know the reason for my suspension. I suspect, now, it was because I'd met Rob for a coffee; I think it was a disproportionate, knee-jerk reaction given the context of Elvedon and because of a critical misapprehension from the force that a judicial order had been made to prevent the police briefing the press. It was later accepted no such order had ever been given. At no point in my suspension did they take my account, it was just 'close down the shutters, this bloke is bent, you're out on your ear'.

To say I was devastated doesn't do it justice. For someone who was driven by the job and the need to catch criminals, it was purgatory. I think suspension for police officers is particularly gruesome: all the time you're in the job, with all its faults, you are in a club of sorts, but with suspension comes exile.

The uncertainty was the worst of it: I didn't know why I was out, nor how long this would go on for. You have no power in such circumstances: decisions were being made and views espoused about me without my input. From being the puppeteer in Halliwell's case I had become the marionette myself, under other people's control – but my strings were well and truly slashed. I had no voice. I was in a process now, indefinitely suspended without word of when such a status would be lifted, nor means to break the impasse.

I drifted into a depth of despair and was prescribed antidepressants. It's hard to describe just how dark and hollow you feel in such circumstances. Without knowing the suspension was to do with Rob, the breach of PACE necessarily came to mind.

For all my belief that I'd done the right thing, it didn't change the fact that because of my actions, and mine alone, Halliwell had not been held to account for Becky's murder. It weighed heavily on me, a burden I bore with no ounce of self-pity, simply self-recrimination. I felt I'd let her down, and her mother, and the force and, in turn, Yvonne and my daughters too.

In October 2012, Halliwell pleaded guilty to Sian's murder. In the midst of all this darkness, it was the one bright spark. It was a plea that had been a long time coming, but the only one Halliwell could offer under the circumstances.

I had hoped, of course, to re-interview him at the point of conviction, but given my suspension that was off the table. He was sentenced to 25 years' imprisonment, with some time off for time already served. With only one murder conviction to his name, he could be walking free in just 12.5 years, as most prisoners serve only half their sentence before being released on parole. It only added to my sense of horror that a suspected serial killer might be free to murder again. Yet there was a worse feeling, because the suspected victims were one thing – his known victims were quite another.

And justice for Becky remained as elusive as ever.

Following the conviction, the *sub judice* reporting restrictions were lifted and the public could be told what had happened at the voir dire and why Halliwell wasn't facing trial for Becky's murder. I was expecting some backlash, and there were a few pieces that ran with a 'copper cocked it up' narrative. The broadsheets, however, picked up on what I saw as the critical issue: that this was a case where the murderer's rights had been prioritised over those of the victim. Many of the journalists assumed my suspension was as a result of my actions, as did I at the time, and I was astounded at the level of public support.

'Steve Fulcher's suspension: there's nothing intelligent about this injustice,' ran the headline in the *Telegraph*: 'The detective who broke the rules to solve a murder should not have been sanctioned.' *The Times* declared, 'A murderer's rights cannot override those of his victim.' Perhaps most movingly of all, even family members from my previous murder cases spoke out too. From the *Telegraph*: 'I am so angry about this. The idea that his skills and experience and compassion are going to be lost simply because the rules are not fit for purpose is simply outrageous. No one seems to care about the rights of victims. It is all about the rights of the criminals. Now that is even taking precedence over the right of the police to do their jobs.'

All the positive press prompted Wiltshire Police to put out a press statement: 'Wiltshire Police understand that Detective Superintendent Fulcher had to make a moral judgment in a pressured environment and Wiltshire Police continue to support his rationale and his intention to find Sian alive.' At least it was an unambiguous endorsement of my actions just before the IPCC would now begin to investigate that very rationale.

Although senior officers had deliberately chosen not to address the issues regarding PACE that the case had thrown up (although you would think they'd have a vested interest in ensuring their guidelines were fit for purpose), with the national media bringing them to public attention, Karen Edwards and her MP began a campaign to get PACE reviewed, so that no other victims or families had to endure what she was going through. Questions were asked about PACE in Parliament. The chair of the Home Affairs Select Committee requested details of the case, with a mind to officially reviewing PACE, and invited me to give evidence at the House of Commons in a discussion of the matter.

I was dissuaded from accepting his invitation by the Police Superintendents Association. They said I should not break ranks, and let the suspension and the IPCC investigation run their course. How I regret listening to that advice. In my absence, senior officers stated to the committee that the police service saw no need for there to be any revision or review of PACE.

With Halliwell convicted, the IPCC investigation into my actions began. Originally, it was only Becky's father's complaint they were examining. Now, two further charges were added. The first was the reckless handling of the media strategy for Mayan (the award-winning strategy sanctioned by the Gold Group that the judge had ruled I had conducted in good faith) – a charge I was perplexed by because, if the IPCC felt there was a case to answer, why were they investigating only me and not all the staff members who had endorsed it? – and the second was that I had met two journalists without permission.

One of these was Rob Murphy; the other Steve Brodie, from the BBC, with whom I had conducted the in-the-can interview on the day we identified Becky. It had only recently been aired, in line with the agreement we had made at the time. The interview had happened so long ago that I had difficulty remembering anything about the circumstances surrounding it. I recalled no order being given by a senior officer not to do it, which is what the force was now saying had occurred. I thought it was a petty charge to bring, and I had a presentiment that – despite the force's recent, publicly declared support for my actions at Barbary Castle – the tide was about to turn.

I tried to reassure myself. It was the *Independent* Police Complaints Commission. It didn't matter if I was disquieted by a change of personnel at Wiltshire Police. The investigation that followed would surely be balanced and in-depth, hearing from all parties to make an informed decision. I welcomed the interview, which was set for December 2012, because I was sure they would exonerate me, in particular with regard to the breach of PACE. I believed my reasoning for doing it – to save a girl's life, in accordance with Article 2 of the Human Rights Act – meant I had done nothing wrong. After all, imagine what the situation would be if Halliwell was not a killer, but had kept Sian locked up somewhere. My intervention at Barbary Castle would have led me to a live girl and I would be a hero. I felt my actions couldn't be judged on the basis of whether she was alive or not, because I was not privy to that knowledge at the time I made the call. My actions were a perfectly legitimate approach, publicly supported by Pat Geenty, Richard Latham and Wiltshire Police as being one that should not attract a disciplinary penalty. I could only hope the IPCC would agree.

57

I was interviewed in December as scheduled. I was a little disconcerted that the investigator had limited knowledge of the key issues in the case – as we spoke, it became evident that she wasn't clear on the kidnap guidelines the police must follow, i.e. prioritising the victim's life. But it was an independent investigation, so perhaps that inexperience was deliberate, so as to provide a woman-on-the-street's viewpoint.

After six hours of questioning, she said she had sufficient information. She promised her report would be delivered in January 2013. I felt relieved to have a time-frame in place.

I was still suspended with no knowledge of when or if it would be lifted. Though I had been told in September that I couldn't resume as SIO of Mayan, I'd have much rather been at work so I could see what was happening with the investigation for Becky; there was nothing but a wall of silence and I was worried nothing was being done. My passion for seeing Halliwell convicted for her murder was as strong as it had ever been.

It was the second Christmas spent with the shadow of Mayan hanging over it. I can't describe how dark that whole period was for me, and my family. This saga had been played out in the press so I felt it as a public humiliation too; I got door-stopped a couple of times by journalists, who found me bearded and looking a real shock. I know I caused those around me a lot of anxiety as I was in a state of depression that I couldn't haul myself out of. I wouldn't go as far as to say that Yvonne and Debs talked me off the ledge, but they certainly stopped me putting my foot on it.

The days melded into one. My dog Pippa and I spent them morosely in each other's company; she was never more than a few yards away from me throughout that time, as though keeping watch, and perhaps with good reason. I felt some sympathy, suddenly, for Dave Ainsworth and all those other officers who had taken the path to blissful obliteration.

In time, the suspension was lifted; it wasn't clear why. But I wasn't well enough to return to work, too depressed and anxious to be able to function.

I kept going over the events of the past two years, examining my actions with Halliwell from every angle, to see if there was anything I'd missed where I should or could have acted differently. It was a self-torturing process but one I felt necessary to undertake. No matter who I asked, no one had been able to tell me what else I could have done to achieve the same result.

January came and went, and there was no sign of the IPCC report. I returned to work in April, doing some back-office project in community safety, as I was prohibited from tackling the operational policing I'd always loved because of the continuing IPCC investigation. I couldn't have a hand in trying to hold Halliwell to account. Still there was no report. I felt apprehensive, but hoped the delay was simply a sign of the thoroughness of the study.

Given the rash way I had been suspended, I began applying for police jobs outside Wiltshire Police. I was aware, however, that any job offers would be predicated on the outcome of the IPCC enquiry.

April became May. Now I was really worried. It was just like the second voir dire ruling all over again: why the delay? I felt the guillotine hanging over my head as a physical thing, its shining blade close enough to make my neck itch. I became increasingly suspicious that the investigator was considering other charges, perhaps even submitting them to the CPS for criminal prosecution. I learned from Debs that she had not been interviewed – the one person who could describe what really went on between me and Halliwell.

That summer, the only light in the darkness was that Yvonne organised a wonderful party for our twenty-fifth wedding anniversary. The occasion put a bit of balance on what was happening. I have to say, I don't know what I'd have done without Yvonne. She was incredibly patient with me and a pillar of strength.

And I needed her. I needed her more than ever when, in September 2013 – nine months after it had first been promised – the IPCC report was finally published.

It went up on their website and released directly to the media; I did not have sight of it first. Sitting in an office at work, with Debs by my side, I opened the report and began to read.

First up was the breach of PACE. I had been really hopeful, after my December interview, that I had clearly explained why my actions were necessary *in these particular circumstances alone* and that the investigator had understood. Yet she now wrote dismissively that my reasons for breaching PACE were 'not relevant for the purposes of the investigation to determine whether ... the conduct as alleged was committed'. I felt there was a peculiar tone to the report; she said there was 'compelling evidence' to suggest I had breached PACE, when I had never denied doing so. It was as though she had only asked herself, 'Did this officer breach PACE?' *Yes.* 'Then he has a case to answer.' She wrote in a bell jar, seemingly divorced from the reality of the intense situation of trying to save Sian's life, and apparently discounting the fact that without my intervention a murderer would be walking free and two families would be without their loved ones.

She did talk about the girls though. 'Although Det Supt Fulcher has argued that arresting Mr Halliwell before Ms O'Callaghan's body was found would have been an appalling decision, a clear reasonable suspicion to arrest Mr Halliwell for her murder existed at the point he indicated he killed her.' As in the voir dire, people were actually suggesting that the preferable course of action would be to arrest Halliwell for murder and take him into custody before he identified his victim's location, leaving Sian to rot undiscovered in the ground. Beyond the inhumanity of this course of action, in the absence of her body, Halliwell would never have been convicted of her killing.

The investigator seemed to believe that criminals, once in custody, did the gentlemanly thing and confessed to their crimes. Of both Sian and Becky's cases, she said, 'It is not possible to determine what may or may not have happened if Mr Halliwell had been immediately conveyed to custody after his arrest and urgent interview.' In fact, that was the one thing we *were* able to determine – because Halliwell had never given an account of his actions under PACE-compliant conditions; not in two-and-a-half years and not even after his conviction for Sian's murder, as I had once hoped. In court he had only said one word: 'Guilty.'

I held my head in my hands as I read it. It was damning.

On the media strategy, it emerged that the Gold Group policy book sanctioning my actions had gone missing from a locked office so it could not be consulted. She acknowledged that the senior management team had not highlighted any concerns, nor acted to prevent the strategy being promulgated, and declared they should bear some responsibility. She commented there was 'no evidence' that my actions were 'anything other than ill-judged'. There was a similar lack of evidence as regards the journalist meetings: she found that I had not been instructed not to meet Rob Murphy, merely given advice, and that the force's media strategy not to consult journalists had never been communicated to me. She did not believe me when it came to the question of whether the Steve Brodie interview had been prohibited.

You might think, having set out all those statements above, that she would draw back from the brink. But she didn't. Against all three charges, notwithstanding any of the mitigating factors, the following words were written in black and white:

'There is a case to answer for gross misconduct.'

Gross misconduct. It carries only one penalty: termination of service. There was every chance I was going to lose my job; I felt sick.

Yet there was worse to come. The investigator had formed an opinion of me that I was 'dishonest' and showed a 'lack of integrity', and those viewpoints too were contained in the report. I could have laughed if I wasn't so devastated. It would have been better for me to *be* dishonest; if I'd just perjured myself at the voir dire and said I'd cautioned Halliwell, I might have got away with it. It was my honesty and integrity that had brought me to this point: my unwillingness to give up on Sian and my desire to do the right thing for the greater good.

I knew Yvonne would be reading the report online at home and that that was where I should be. Debs walked down the stairs with me and back to the car. She could see how I was feeling, I think; I was lower than I'd been at any other time.

'I know you just want all this to go away, Steve,' she said. 'But don't resign.'

It had been at the forefront of my mind. I'd had enough. How much was enough? How much more could one man take?

That March afternoon with Halliwell, I'd felt we'd shared a bond of mutual self-destruction. Two-and-a-half years later, the veracity of that sensation was confirmed. He was serving 25 years in jail, and I was staring down the barrel of dismissal from the job I loved.

Although forces are not compelled to follow recommendations made by the IPCC, I was notified within days that they would be taking all three charges forward to a disciplinary hearing scheduled for January 2014. I felt I was trapped in a Kafkaesque nightmare. Less than a year before, the force had endorsed my actions in a press statement; now, it seemed there was a case to answer for gross misconduct. But if my breach of PACE was misconduct, the corollary of the argument was that it was preferable that two girls would still be missing and their killer not held to account. That wasn't what I'd thought policing was about.

The situation was so agonising that I did something I had never done before – not on any case. I gave up. I no longer wanted to fight. I was signed off sick and was back on antidepressants and sleeping tablets. I felt that if they wanted my job, they could have it. I had such a jaded view of everything by that time that I wondered if I was going mad. I had, after all, tried to save a girl's life and had ended up with three years of misery for my trouble and been publicly flogged into the bargain. I remained devastated Becky hadn't received justice; the guilt of that hung around my neck like an albatross. It was such a dark time that a friend actually asked me, 'What's stopped you from suicide?'

I had only one, very simple answer: 'Yvonne and my two girls.'

While I had given up, however, two special women hadn't. Karen Edwards was extraordinary when she heard what was happening. She wrote an open letter in the press to Pat Geenty, asking for him to be lenient when considering what to do as she had nothing but praise for me. She wanted me reinstated and exonerated, she said. Debs, meanwhile, received permission from Pat to help with my defence.

Despite their efforts, by the time I met the lawyer who would defend me at the hearing, I planned to resign imminently, before the hearing would take place. I was merely consulting my lawyer for a last legal viewpoint.

But then an extraordinary thing happened. *He agreed with me.* Article 2 of the Human Rights Act took a prior claim over PACE: I was right to act as I had done. He was the first barrister I'd personally consulted on the issues and his support shot a bolt of adrenaline through me. He said I was very unfortunate the voir dire judgment hadn't been challenged because there was an argument for that ruling to be reversed. For the first time in a long time, I felt hope that truth and justice would be achieved. Re-energised, my resignation plan was put in abeyance and I wanted to fight again. I wanted to be exonerated after all this madness. After all, not even Halliwell's own defence barrister had thought I'd done anything wrong. Why was I now on the brink of losing my career?

I wanted to fight for other officers too. Another SIO might well find themselves in exactly the same circumstances I had done and I felt the issues needed to be debated. I didn't want anyone else to have to make the decision of whether to go rogue, or play it safe and follow the rules of PACE in the full knowledge that doing so might cause the death of the party they sought to save.

And if people were really saying that we'd prefer kidnap victims to die rather than breach the PACE rights of those who had taken them – as that senior officer had done when he declared, 'So be it' – then that needed to be brought to public attention.

The mists started to clear and the dark clouds began to lift. I tackled the boxes of evidence with as much verve as I could muster given my fragile mental state. They were extraordinary to look through, containing statements taken in spring 2011 that praised both the media strategy and my actions. They reminded me: *I caught a serial killer*. Halliwell would not be in jail if it wasn't for me. There was a letter from the national police lead on media issues, who said he wanted more detail on what we'd done so that other communications departments and SIOs could learn from us; a leading reporter wrote we were a 'shining example'. This was gross misconduct?

There was one particular document that was hugely significant – not just because of its content, but also because it was not contained in the boxes of statements supplied to me by the force. A fundamental principle of our justice system depends on the prosecuting authorities being open and honest with the material they gather: full disclosure. As an example, you might recall that the Guildford Four – the innocent people wrongly convicted of being IRA terrorists – had their convictions quashed when it was found that crucial alibi evidence had never been shown to the defence. It is a basic pillar of justice that full disclosure must be given.

Why, then, was it not revealed to me that Wiltshire Police had *twice* nominated me for a Queen's Police Medal for my actions at Barbary Castle?

'There is no doubt that without his direct intervention and engagement with the suspect the bodies of both young women would not have been located,' the nomination, written in 2011, read, '... This is but a flavour of his remarkable and sustained contribution ... [He is] a man of integrity, whose achievements not only enhanced the reputation of Wiltshire Police but upheld and demonstrated the best traditions of British policing.'

This was gross misconduct?

Yvonne cried when she read it. I didn't wonder at that. I felt like crying too.

It was around this time, as I prepared my defence, that I caught wind of something else they hadn't told me about. While waiting for the second voir dire ruling, and for the IPCC report, I had become concerned that the delays I was subject to were caused by a criminal prosecution being mounted against me. Now, I learned those fears *had* been warranted.

A file had been sent to the CPS. The charge? Malfeasance in a public office. It carries a maximum sentence of life imprisonment.

Thankfully, the CPS took the view that there wasn't a case to answer. Yet I was left reeling by how far this had gone. From two QPM nominations to life imprisonment for the same set of circumstances. I couldn't get my head around it.

Nor could I fathom the logic of the charge itself. As I understand it, malfeasance in a public office means you've done somebody some real harm by abusing your position. Well, who had I done harm to? Halliwell. Seriously: a file was put up that said I had done Halliwell a dreadful mischief by identifying the fact that he was a serial killer.

If I hadn't done what I did, he wouldn't have been exposed; instead, he's suffered the adverse consequences of serving life imprisonment for murder. It turns a serial killer into a victim – and a copper into a criminal.

Yet I could not forget that I might not be a copper for very much longer. The disciplinary hearing loomed: the toughest test of my career.

58

The hearing was to last four days; it would be held in the Gold Room at HQ. Yvonne insisted on coming along to support me and I was grateful to have her there. She wouldn't be allowed into the hearing, though. Despite a request from me that the disciplinary proceedings should be heard in public, this was denied. I was frustrated by the decision – I had nothing to hide.

When we arrived at HQ, on 20 January 2014, I bade farewell to Yvonne. It was a pretty extreme thing, entering that room alone. My wife wasn't the only one banned from entering; Debs wasn't allowed in either. I was permitted the support of one 'friend' from the Superintendents Association, but otherwise it was just me, my lawyer, my accusers and those who would decide my fate. Oh yes – and Becky's parents.

Given the disciplinary action had initially arisen as a result of Becky's father's complaint, both he and Karen Edwards were invited to attend. Karen sat behind me and my lawyer for all four days of the hearing, having put her job and all her other responsibilities on hold in order to offer me her backing. I found her support extraordinary. But, for her, what was happening to me was intrinsically bound up with the police force's valuation of her daughter. She had lost her beloved Becky and I was the person who had brought her back to her; now,

I was facing a charge of gross misconduct for doing so. She wanted to hear what the force would argue. If I was in the wrong to have recovered Becky's body, what did that say about their view of victims and their families?

I hadn't seen Karen since 2012, when we'd met at her request shortly after I'd been returned to the force; I hadn't wanted anyone to accuse me of having cultivated a relationship with her for my own selfish ends. When she saw me, she looked shocked, and I guess I did look different. The anguish and insomniac nights had taken their toll. My lawyer actually described me as a 'broken man'.

The Gold Room was on the ground floor of the building. Once upon a time, I had chaired a weekly strategic meeting for the force in it, but the layout was rather different today. It was set up like a court, with the panel of three adjudicators sat at a table, facing the defence (me and my lawyer) and the prosecution (the force's barrister and the investigator from the IPCC). From the windows, I could see my old office – but I turned my back on it, and on my old life that had vanished one day in March when I'd answered a call to find a missing girl. I took a seat at a table just behind my barrister.

Although the force had taken all three counts raised in the IPCC report forward for disciplinary action – and my lawyer and I had spent a huge amount of time preparing a defence to combat them – the very first thing that happened was that the force withdrew the charge regarding my alleged mishandling of the media. I suspect they had finally cottoned on to the fact that, because my actions had been sanctioned by the Gold Group, that made them complicit. My lawyer was damning as he pulled them up on it, saying it was 'manifestly a perverse decision' to bring the charge in the first place.

'Ask yourself the question,' my lawyer urged the panel, 'just how fair and balanced has this investigation been? Or has it got carried away? ... That charge should never have been brought and it was brought ... through the investigators ... not looking at the evidence with the impartiality that is to be connected with the word "I" in IPCC.'

The force also backpedalled on the specifics of the charge about me meeting journalists. In their paperwork for this hearing, they had accused me of breaching a judicial order in so doing; I believe that was why they had peremptorily suspended me in September 2012 without a hearing. It was only at this juncture, however, that they realised, somewhat foolishly, that no judicial order had actually been made to prevent the police speaking to journalists, so that charge was reworded too, although it remained on file as a charge of my meeting journalists without permission. It was still the breach of PACE that really got me, though.

'Detective Superintendent Fulcher,' said the chair of the panel, 'Allegation one [as regards the] treatment of Christopher Halliwell. It is alleged that your behaviour when dealing with Mr Christopher Halliwell on 24 March 2011 fell below the standards of professional behaviour set out in the ... Police Conduct Regulations 2008. Do you admit or deny the allegation?'

'I deny the allegation, sir,' I replied.

My former boss, Nigel, gave evidence that first day, testifying that he had expressly told me not to speak to Steve Brodie, something I did not recall. He admitted he gave me *no* instruction not to speak to Rob Murphy. On the second day, Chief Constable Pat Geenty testified. To his credit, he backed me, saying I was 'the most experienced and probably the best SIO in the force'. I was pleased; it seemed he was going to stand by his testimony of two years before, at the voir dire, when he had applauded my 'gutsy' and 'brave' decision-making in the way I'd handled Halliwell. Geenty reminded the panel that 'the presiding judge and Mr Latham both agreed this was not a misconduct issue'. As he was reminding them of that at my disciplinary hearing for gross misconduct, there was a certain irony.

My lawyer talked him through the breach of PACE. Geenty agreed that I acted properly in doing so. However, unexpectedly, he then offered this opinion: 'I disagree with [Steve's] judgment when it was past the location of Sian O'Callaghan. That is when I think PACE and the protection of the suspect would have become far more prominent because tragically we then knew that Sian was dead. At that point, my thinking would have changed.'

'... So it comes to this,' my lawyer summarised, 'with the Sian decision – if I can call it that – not to caution – you in fact ally with Mr Fulcher?'

'I do.'

'That is very helpful. With the Becky decision you may fall on the other side of the camp?'

'I do.'

Behind me, Karen Edwards burst into tears. I think, to her mind, the corollary of Geenty's testimony was that Becky was worthless; not important enough to save. Because we knew what happened when Halliwell went into custody: he didn't speak. If I'd arrested him the moment he started speaking of Becky's murder, as Geenty was now saying I should have done, we would never have found her; we wouldn't even have known her name, wouldn't have known that it was that pretty, wildcat woman with blonde hair and a shy smile that Halliwell meant when he said 'another one'. She'd have just been a line in my statement when I took him back to the nick: an unsolved mystery, an undiscovered grave. And Karen Edwards would still be driving the streets of Swindon every week; every week for the rest of her life.

Geenty ignored her emotion. His testimony was a volte-face on his previously expressed support – but he didn't have to justify his position. I felt betrayed, yet I wasn't surprised. I was just rather disappointed in him.

There was a more important issue here than personal loyalties, however. Geenty was essentially saying that when a suspect voluntarily confessed, a police officer should stop them ('You do not have to say anything ...') and take them into custody where their lawyer would prevent them incriminating themselves. In 30 years of PACE, nobody has ever taken a confession in this way, which I find deeply concerning. It seemed senior officers thought the right response to somebody saying. 'Do you want another murder victim?' is to say, 'No, thank you very much.' That's how far we'd come.

It was that same day that I gave my testimony. It lasted for four hours. Given my nerves had been shattered by this whole experience, I believe I gave a much less composed 'performance' than I had, say, at the voir dire. I simply wasn't the man I used to be.

Once again I talked through my decision-making. It was a story I had told so many times now, but the ending never changed and it never got any happier.

'You are central in the circumstances that led to Halliwell getting away with murder,' the force's barrister declared.

Did he not think I knew that, every minute of the day?

But we were back to circles that couldn't be squared.

My lawyer brought up the QPM nominations, which gave a glowing account of my work as an SIO. There was still an air of unreality, hearing about them, that I was now being maligned for this same course of action that senior officers had not just supported, but sought to honour me for. My lawyer had access to some internal emails which discussed the fact I had become aware of the nominations' existence – the emails recognised that my knowing of them and being able to use them at the hearing caused the force some considerable difficulty, given they exposed their hypocrisy. 'That is not to say that we should hide now its existence,' an email said 'but once again it questions the root of how it came into circulation.'

I didn't think that statement too significant at the time, but it would become very relevant.

On the third day of the hearing, there was an attempt made to enter an additional charge at the last minute, alleging I was dishonest. Thankfully, the panel was unanimous in summarily rejecting the application. I did feel the unfair, last-ditch attempt to attack me rather beautifully illustrated my belief that there was a determination to root me out of the job I loved and – as we had just heard in the force's own words in the QPM nominations – had actually been pretty good at.

Then it was time for closing statements. Having sat and listened to the evidence, I felt relieved and confident that I would be exonerated. I had heard no evidence that would justify my dismissal, nor a finding of misconduct. My lawyer, though obviously on my side, agreed:

> Is this actually misconduct at all? ... Out of ... matters where no harm was done, and I invite you to find good was in fact done, we have ended up with the suggestion that he should lose his career ... Many members of the public might say of this, 'Surely this can be dealt with in a more rational, proportionate way?'... The public aren't always wrong when they comment on policing and sometimes the police service, like other professional bodies, spins out of control and makes a mountain out of what might be a molehill. I seek to persuade you to take the bold decision, after an independent investigation which I have criticised ... we ask you to address as a serious contention that there is no misconduct here.

We were so confident that, while the panel retired to consider their findings, I went out to have a pizza with my lawyer and Yvonne. It was a celebration of sorts, though the overwhelming mood was simply one of relief. I'd been living in purgatory for two years, but I could finally leave that limbo-land and move on, getting back to a proper career – the career of service to which I had dedicated my life. I anticipated returning to the job I loved. Maybe there was even something I could do to help with Becky's case, though it would not be with Wiltshire Police. I hoped I could find another role, elsewhere. I'd had a job offer back in September, but because of the IPCC report it had been retracted. Yet it gave me faith that, once this mess was all cleared up, I would be able to move on and find a way to serve the public again, to solve crime. That was all I'd ever wanted to do.

It was getting dark by the time the hearing reconvened at 16.05. I had to stand up to hear the verdict, just like a criminal; just like Halliwell had. There was some preamble. And then:

'A message needs to be sent to the service that an SIO cannot ignore the safeguards of PACE to such an extent without being held fully to account.

'Detective Superintendent Fulcher … we find that your behaviour fell below the standard of professional behaviour in respect of duties and responsibilities. We regard the conduct as gross misconduct.'

I felt hot, and the world went black. There is only one penalty for gross misconduct: dismissal from the force.

That pact of mutual self-destruction that I'd made with Halliwell reared its ugly head. I had taken him down – but he was taking me with him.

59

The panel declared they would deliver their sanction in the morning, leaving me with the prospect of yet another sleepless night. Yvonne and I were remarkably sanguine as we drove home. All along I'd feared the worst, and now the worst had happened. It offered a strange sort of freedom.

That night, as Pippa watched with her head balanced on her paws, I packed up the few scraps of work equipment that I had at home, ready to return them to the force the next day. Pippa had been my constant companion through all this misery. But it was almost as though the darkness that had infiltrated the household had had a physical effect on her: she'd recently developed a huge cancerous tumour on her neck. It made my heart hurt to see it.

The very last item I placed in the box that night was the only piece of uniform I still owned: my hat. It was a classic peaked policeman's cap, with silver braid and a badge. I held it in my hands for just a beat, the superintendents' braid reminding me of my pride upon receiving that promotion so many years before. But another man had worn that hat, a lifetime ago. I placed it in the box and turned out the light in my study.

I returned to HQ for sentence in the morning. The panel spent some time running through the evidence they had heard and the reasons for the decision they had reached. As they did so, I still found it difficult to reconcile myself to their verdict of gross misconduct, but you reach a point where if everyone says you are wrong, eventually you have to accept it. Perhaps the hardest thing was to hear their review of my 'exemplary' service before I'd intervened to catch Halliwell. '[Detective Superintendent Fulcher] has received three crown court commendations and one chief constable's commendation and has no findings of misconduct. His record to date has been unblemished.'

Well, it wasn't any more.

The surprise came at the end of their pronouncements. A sentence of a final written warning was applied to each of the two charges. I was taken aback, but kept my face impassive. It was only once I'd left the room that I burst out laughing. That wasn't what the penalty for gross misconduct was; and to apply two so-called final written warnings was a nonsense in itself. After all, if I incurred a final warning for the first charge, when the second was applied I should have been immediately sacked.

It was only subsequently that I appreciated just how politically astute the sentence was. Given the mass outpouring of public support for my actions, to sack me for trying to save a girl's life could have become a political hot potato. They had neatly avoided that scenario by ruining my reputation, but not following through with the penalty that should have been applied.

In the interests of balance, let me say this: I can understand the panel not wanting to give carte blanche to officers up and down the country to breach PACE. But that was never what this was about. It was these circumstances alone that were relevant. In my opinion, what should have happened, now the case had raised the issues, was that police chiefs should have sat down with proper legal advice for a debate. Does Article 2 trump PACE?

Should we prioritise victims over suspects? Have we got a problem in accepting voluntary confessions because the current legal system doesn't allow them to occur? Instead, they made me a scapegoat for something they found too difficult to address. As a result, though, they *have* made a ruling: suspects' rights *should* be placed above all else, including truth, justice and victims. It's just they did it behind closed doors. Part of my reason for writing this book is to bring their verdict into the light.

I didn't know what to do following the sentence, nor how to feel. I couldn't think straight. In hindsight, I should have appealed, but I think my lawyer defined success as me having kept my job, and I was too broken by it even to consider carrying on the fight.

Nor was it only the panel's finding that had ripped the rug out from under me. Immediately following the disciplinary hearing, as though she'd just been hanging on to see me through it, Pippa passed away. Whether rightly or wrongly, I retain a sense of guilt that she lost her life in the midst of this debacle. I still miss her greatly.

The force had been expecting a sentence of dismissal, too, so there was some consternation over what to do with me. What can you do with an officer who is guilty of gross misconduct but mysteriously hasn't been fired? They suggested some lip-service role 'counting pencils in a back office'. Almost immediately, however, I realised I was lucky to have even that.

'It questions the root of how it came into circulation,' an email from the force had said of my QPM nominations in my disciplinary hearing, affronted by the fact I had been able to present evidence that demonstrated the force's full support of my actions. Far from saying, as I think they should have done, 'We have a real problem with disclosure here, we're not giving up all the evidence that is relevant to the case; if this was a criminal case it would be a perversion to the course of justice,' they were instead focused only on who the 'mole' might be. I received the QPM nomination documents from a fellow officer. Deborah Peach had emailed them to him, after he had given her the order to do so.

In an act that still scandalises me, the force now started discipline proceedings against Debs for obeying the order of a senior officer. Yes, it caused the force embarrassment that I had the nominations, but they should never have tried to suppress them in the first place. As with me, Debs was not afforded the opportunity to explain the situation.

By that time, Debs was the chief constable's staff officer and was leading the force's work on the national policing portfolio on missing children and adults, which involved her giving critical briefings at the Home Office. Just days after the proceedings began, Debs was briefing a government minister and government policy advisers in a series of meetings. The chief constable continued to rely on her trust and judgment to brief him and represent him at high-level meetings. Yet back in the force, despite continuing to work hard on the chief's missing children and adults portfolio, Debs suffered the Coventry treatment and petty actions, such as being told to clear her desk and being moved to a grim office. She was also banned from the chief officer corridor, so she had to request permission to walk down the corridor to get to her meetings with the chief constable.

As time went on and other developments occurred, she decided that she no longer wanted to work among people who could treat her in this way. After 26 years of service, she handed in her resignation.

It made my position untenable. How could I keep my job when friends were losing theirs because they'd been caught up in what I saw as a witch-hunt to bring me down? But it was a huge decision to make – it meant walking away from a final-salary police pension; worth, at a conservative estimate, about half a million pounds. I was only three years away from being eligible, and I was worried about the financial future of my family if I walked away. Not to mention, of course, resigning meant I would no longer be a serving police officer, which was all I had ever wanted. I wasn't sure I knew how to be anything else.

As an SIO, I had excelled at calculating consequences and making decisions. Now, I was incapable, my nerves completely shot away. The events of the past three years had systemically crushed my ability and confidence to think and reason. Though I was working for a force that had sought my sacking – and I was unable to transfer out, now, because of the finding of gross misconduct – I found I was trapped, suffering from a kind of Stockholm syndrome where even though these people had tried to destroy me, I stayed with them.

In the end, it was my brilliant wife who forced my hand. One afternoon, she came to me with an ultimatum.

'Steve,' my wife of 25 years told me, 'it's me or the job.'

It was an Yvonne I'd never seen in all those years. I think she saw much more clearly than I did at that time.

'What about the money?' I asked.

Yvonne scoffed. 'I don't care about the money,' she said.

She was right, of course. Money is irrelevant if you find yourself under a train, which is the way I was going. Which was better: to have my sanity, health, family and marriage – or a pension pot and a badge? It was a no-brainer.

It's the best thing my wife has ever done for me – and the best decision I have ever made.

On 2 May 2014, I walked into work with a neatly typed letter in my hand. I strode down the corridor towards the chief constable's office. Once, I had paced along it with an energy born of the necessity of catching a criminal, but there was none of that in my stride that day. I passed offices I'd worked in; colleagues I respected. But it was a world that was closed to me now. I knew the hierarchy would never let me near operational policing again. I knew I'd only become bitter and frustrated as I watched SIOs and officers around me doing the job I'd loved. If I didn't take this step, I was destined to sit in the corner somewhere, preferably out of sight, definitely without prospects: an example to all that this was what happened to someone who came up against the rules.

My hand trembled, but only for a moment, as I left the envelope in the in-tray outside Pat Geenty's office. I had done the job for nearly 30 years. I had loved the job as long. But, with a twist of my heels, I turned my back on it and walked away. Inside the envelope was a letter containing a simple sentence.

I hereby tender my resignation …

60

In the summer of 2016, I received a message from the Crown Prosecution Service. I was in Somalia at the time, where I now worked. I had no choice in the location: it turns out that ex-coppers with a record of gross misconduct aren't all that employable in the UK. Despite hundreds of applications, I couldn't get a job anywhere but a warzone. In some ways, though, with what I'd survived in the past few years, it was a less stressful work environment than you might expect. I didn't need the antidepressants and sleeping tablets that had sustained me while in the force.

Despite my new surroundings, however, the UK criminal system hadn't quite finished with me yet.

The message from the CPS asked if I would be prepared to make the 22-hour journey back home; they would pay for it. It turned out that they needed my assistance.

They wondered if I could help bring Christopher Halliwell to justice for the murder of Becky Godden-Edwards.

In the wake of my disciplinary hearing in 2014, a new SIO had been appointed to Operation Mayan. It was an officer I admired: DCI Sean Memory. Immediately, he picked up the HOLMES account on which I'd left so many actions outstanding in June 2011, ready for the subsequent SIOs to follow up, and he started getting results. He circulated the index number of the silver Volvo we'd long known Halliwell had driven at the time of Becky's murder, appealing for witnesses; he finally got the soil on the spades we'd seized from Ashbury Avenue tested by forensics; and, perhaps most significantly of all, he found Halliwell's trophy store.

It was in Ramsbury, after all. At the bottom of a pond that was eight-foot deep, they found something we'd been searching for since 19 March 2011: Sian O'Callaghan's distinctive boots.

Yet that wasn't all. As officers searched the surrounding woodland, they started digging. Halliwell had been busy. Buried around the pond were more items of women's clothing. *Did they belong to the six other victims?* I'd wondered when I'd heard.

But I had the maths wrong. Around the pond where Sian O'Callaghan's boots had been dumped were not six other items of women's clothing. There were 60.

Halliwell might have been far more prolific than even I had feared.

If I'd been in charge, I'd have arranged a public viewing of the clothing. You might get a mother coming along who recognised a sweater, or a father who recalled a particular skirt. Just think of the investigative leads that could come from it. To my knowledge, this wasn't done. One mother did get to see the items, however. Karen Edwards nodded in emotional recognition when she saw a woollen cream cardigan that she believed had once belonged to her daughter Becky.

Karen Edwards had been campaigning tirelessly for Becky over the past few years. She really is the most impressive person I have ever met. I'd often wondered at what point she would jack it in, but she never did. I suppose it's something you never get over: your daughter being brutally killed and her killer getting off on a legal technicality. Karen channelled the most extraordinary amount of energy into her campaign. Though the police had washed their hands of any review of PACE, Karen Edwards campaigned to change it, presenting a petition to Downing Street with 42,000 signatures.

That was not all. Karen did not approve of the way Wiltshire Police had handled her daughter's case. It was all well and good Sean Memory finally getting some leads going in 2014, but Becky had been found in 2011. Everything Sean did on becoming SIO should have been done by others much earlier. It was a critical point because Becky was only dropped from the indictment in May 2012. If the police had been properly investigating in the intervening year, the CPS may have felt there was sufficient evidence to continue with her case, especially given Halliwell would have been tried for Sian's murder simultaneously, and he may have been convicted for Becky's murder then. The inaction, in my view, was a grotesque neglect of duty. Added to which, I learned from Karen that she'd actually had a meeting with the force in which they'd said: 'Would you be satisfied with the fact Halliwell's going to jail for a long time for Sian's murder? He'll never stand trial for killing Becky because there is insufficient evidence.' They were essentially asking her if it was OK for them to knock the case on the head. They misunderstood who Karen is and her strength of character. Of course she said no and urged them to continue.

Karen felt so strongly about the inaction that she complained to Her Majesty's Inspectorate of Constabulary (HMIC): 'I would like answers as to why only now have there been new developments in this case and why evidence that the police had since ... Detective Superintendent Fulcher [was] SIO was not acted upon,' she wrote, and added, '... I consider an inordinate amount of time and effort was put into the disciplinary investigation ... of Stephen Fulcher; had such effort been put into investigating the evidence ... Mr Halliwell would have been justly prosecuted for my daughter's murder.'

HMIC responded that Karen should complain to the IPCC. However, given she knew that they would rather her daughter had never been found, she declined.

Sean's efforts, belated though they were, soon bore fruit. Red clay soil on a spade from Halliwell's garage was deemed to be identical to that in the Eastleach field. More of Becky's friends had come forward with witness sightings. One remembered her getting into a car with Halliwell on a cold January night, a night on which Becky had rowed with him through the car window, then shrugged her shoulders, got into his vehicle, slammed the door and vanished from sight. Records also showed that Halliwell had logged a call with the RAC at 5.25 a.m. on 3 January 2003 – his Volvo had run out of fuel a few miles from the field where he'd buried Becky.

Sean even tried to get a cough out of Halliwell by re-interviewing him. This time, he didn't say 'no comment'. This time – perhaps mindful of the discovery of his trophy store – he wanted to strike a deal.

'If I wrap this up in the next few hours,' Christopher Halliwell had said cockily, 'any other charges against me that will be brought – because there's bits in the past ... car thefts, break-ins, bits and pieces, some more serious – will clearing this up be enough to stop everything else?'

Naturally, Sean declined this attempt to escape justice for any future murders that might come to light, so Halliwell did not roll over.

Yet, despite all his efforts, Sean and the CPS had a problem. The entire case was circumstantial. Becky being seen getting into Halliwell's car didn't mean he killed her. The RAC report put him in the vicinity of the field, but that didn't mean he'd buried her there. The red clay soil was unique but, even if he'd been digging there, he was a groundworker; that was what he did. Those scratches down his face: it couldn't be proved that Becky had inflicted them. The issue was this: though they knew Halliwell was her killer, the CPS couldn't prove he had murdered her on the strength of the circumstantial evidence alone.

How could they solve the problem?

The can was kicked down the road for a good long while. They had the RAC report, the GP's account, the witnesses and the soil on the spade in August 2014; and many of those puzzle pieces even earlier than that. An extraordinary delay followed, but Becky's family were never going to let this drop. Eventually, after two more long years, the powers-that-be deemed the case was almost ready to come to court.

Yet they still needed a killer piece of evidence to convict him.

They needed the confession he had given me.

Would I return to the UK, the CPS asked, to attend a pre-trial hearing that would rule if the evidence was admissible, after all?

I had never given up hope of getting justice for the lost girl I'd found buried in that field. I'd felt guilty and distressed about it all these years. Of course I would come back. Of course I would speak out. I wanted to do all I could to put Halliwell down.

On Thursday, 21 July 2016, Yvonne and I climbed the steps of Bristol Crown Court. We were four-and-a-half years on from the voir dire ruling that had left me reeling. I was anticipating a rerun of that hearing, but without the same pressure. I had already lost. I only hoped for Becky's sake that this time we would win.

The judge hearing the case was Judge Griffith Williams, who had been brought out of retirement especially for it. Unlike in Sian's case and the earlier voir dire, Halliwell had already entered a plea at this stage in proceedings, saying 'not guilty' to the charge of Becky's murder. Perhaps he knew the case against him was non-existent without the confession and hoped, if it was ruled inadmissible a second time, that he could get away with murder even at trial. Why hold your hands up if you don't have to? With only Sian's conviction to his name, he could be out in another ten years.

There was another major difference from Sian's case too: Halliwell was representing himself. There was no Richard Latham; no Mr Smith. Of course, no barrister worth his salt would allow a High Court judgment to be reversed without appeals upon appeals. But Halliwell had no barrister now.

I was ushered alone into a small windowless room to wait to be called to give evidence. I had only the briefest of meetings with prosecuting counsel. The barrister for the CPS was Nicholas Haggan QC, a short, stout, bald man in his late fifties. He came to thank me for coming, but most of all to check me out. Obviously he understood that I'd lost my career over this, so I think he wanted to know if I was the loose cannon characterised by the finding of gross misconduct, or a disaffected bloke who wanted to rip the walls down. Was I furious or a troublemaker – or both?

Of course, in the privacy of my own home I might well vent at the hypocrisy and self-serving politics that had brought me here, but to Haggan I presented the entirely reasonable, water-under-the-bridge front. Becky's case was too important for me not to. I remember one of the people involved said to me frankly, 'We wouldn't have blamed you if you'd told us all to fuck off.' But this wasn't about me; it never had been. This was about getting justice for a murdered girl who had died brutally at the age of 20.

I took a seat in the room and waited. As a bound witness, I was entirely alone. Yvonne had come to support me – she had a vested interest in the case now too, after all that had gone on – but she sat in the courtroom, listening as Haggan appealed to the judge to now admit the evidence.

I sat in that room for two days, without being called once. Haggan later said to me that it was enough just to have me in the courthouse to provide the leverage he needed: to say that this wasn't going to go away and that the ex-detective who had caught a serial killer was still actively engaged in holding him to account.

Towards the end of the afternoon on the Friday, there was a knock at the door. A woman popped her head around it: it was Teresa, who had been Karen's second FLO.

'Steve,' she said. Her voice had a burble to it, as though there was an excitement inside her that was irrepressibly bubbling up. 'Steve, he's gonna let it all in. All of the confession evidence!'

It was *the* moment. The moment after which everything changed. The future shifted and shimmered before my eyes as a whole new world of possibilities opened up. I was too stunned to acknowledge it at first, but moments after Teresa had told me the news, Yvonne stumbled into the room, all giddy and excited, to share the same message, and then Sean Memory ran through the door to say the same. I began to believe it, then. It felt like the first step out of this pit of misery, as though we'd been with Becky in that shallow grave of hers and were now reaching with her towards the light. Ahead lay a different path, a path that at times I'd never thought I'd see. The chance for vindication, exoneration – but most of all justice.

61

'What happened to Rebecca?' Haggan QC asked the jury with dramatic flair, on the first day of Halliwell's trial for the murder of Becky Godden-Edwards at Bristol Crown Court in September 2016. 'We, the prosecution, say the short answer to that question is that she was murdered.

'This defendant, Christopher Halliwell, confessed to the police that ... he had taken a girl from the streets of Swindon. He told the police he had sex with her and then he killed her by strangling her ... Not only that, but the defendant took the police to the location.

'Had the defendant not told the police where he had buried that girl from the streets of Swindon, you might think that Rebecca's remains to this day would be in that field.'

As opening statements went in murder trials, it was pretty conclusive stuff.

As a bound witness, I wasn't in court to hear it – I was back in that windowless room, waiting to be called to give evidence – but Haggan's statement reflected what I had always said: if Halliwell had not confessed, and if I had not taken that confession in his sole moment of contrition, we'd never have found Becky and he would never have faced trial for her murder. I felt vindicated.

If we didn't want killers to get away with killing, I was right to do what I did.

There was a certain irony in the fact that this opening statement told the jury, from minute one, exactly what Judge Cox had previously ruled no jury could possibly hear. He wasn't talking about soil-stained spades and RAC callouts: he was talking only of the confession. It underlined how critical that evidence was. After all, if the police and the CPS could have run the case without involving me, they would, wouldn't they, after everything that had happened?

Despite the enormity of the legal decision, my reaction was merely: this is nonsense. The effective reversal of Judge Cox's ruling in a pre-trial review, which went mostly unreported, meant that now we were five years down the line, the evidence was back in, and what had happened to me in the meantime was forgotten. Yet I didn't hold a grudge; I felt chipper, knowing that, at long last, the killer I had caught was facing trial. It had been a long time coming – for everyone involved.

Becky's parents, of course, attended the trial. Yvonne took two weeks off work to be there. Movingly, Elaine O'Callaghan and Kevin Reape also came. My understanding is they attended to show Halliwell they were still strong; they knew, too, that their loved one was likely to be heavily referenced during the trial. As such, they were also representing Sian.

Despite pleading not guilty, Halliwell had not submitted a detailed defence case statement. It meant no one knew exactly what he was going to say. How was he going to explain how he had led me to Becky's body if he wasn't her killer? It had got me thinking, with some excitement: perhaps he wasn't going to try. A seed had long ago been planted in my mind by Halliwell himself, and it now took root: 'Sell your story and make as much money as you can,' he had said. What if he wasn't going to use this time in court, in front of the world's media, to defend himself – but instead to make himself notorious? What if he was going to use the moment to cough to all his other crimes?

It wasn't as crazy an idea as it sounds. With the confession evidence now ruled admissible, it was almost certain that he was going to be found guilty, meaning he was staring down the barrel of a full life sentence. And if you're going to serve life anyway, why not go out with a bang before the doors slam shut behind you? Be front-page news around the world. Why not be a Ted Bundy, the American serial killer who'd confessed to 30 murders shortly before his execution? Bundy, too, had represented himself in court. For decades, he had got away with murder: he would kidnap, kill and then bury his victims in remote rural locations. He was also known to have decapitated some of them and kept their heads as trophies – just as I believed Halliwell had done with Becky. The parallels were rife.

Perhaps fantastically, I even wondered if he'd been waiting for me to question him before he told the truth. What with everything that had happened, he and I had been kept apart – we never had continued that frank conversation with a coffee and a fag, smoking roll-ups as he spilled his secrets. But now we *would* meet again.

Yet I wouldn't be asking the questions this time. Halliwell, acting as his own defence barrister, would be the one cross-examining me. I wondered: could we turn that conversation into a cough?

As I sat in the windowless room, a buzz of anticipation began building in my belly. Maybe this would be the thing that set the whole case on fire. It would be huge. I mean, there were *60* items of women's clothing in his trophy store. If he wanted to, Halliwell could become even bigger than Bundy. I only hoped he was smart enough to realise it – to realise, too, what was in it for him. 'Is it too late to get help?' he had asked me. In his darkest moments, in the quiet of the night, did he still desire that rehabilitation? Perhaps this would be the moment things – for both of us – could only get better.

'Mr Fulcher to court': the message finally came over the tannoy, and an usher stood at the door to escort me. I got to my feet promptly, a million different thoughts in my head. I hadn't seen Halliwell since the voir dire ruling in February 2012; both of our lives had irreparably altered since then. I had no idea what he'd been doing or thinking in the intervening years. Had going down for Sian's murder changed him? The sentence I'd been given in my own trial had certainly changed me.

The court was only 100 yards or so away, at the end of a carpeted corridor. The usher opened the door for me and I walked on through.

Immediately in front of me were the jury and above them the press gallery. It was packed to the rafters. To my right was the judge, an elderly gentleman wearing wire-framed glasses and a bright-red robe. And to my left was Christopher Halliwell.

He stood behind strengthened glass in the dock, surrounded by security guards. Sallow complexion, deep-set eyes. He wasn't as skinny as I remembered, and I thought he'd lost more of his hair. Then again, it had been nearly five years since I'd seen him; I probably looked different too. Actually, I think I'd aged more than he had in those years.

An energy passed between us as we locked eyes. It was hard to categorise. I still had this vague idea that this could be the moment where we could turn what had frankly been a debacle into something really quite powerful. Five years before, he had voluntarily given me

Becky. Was he about to commit himself to unburdening his other crimes?

I stepped into the witness box and swore the oath. Haggan rose from his place and began to lead me through my statement, which I'd written on 1 April 2011. It seemed insane that five-and-a-half years on, the murderer I had caught back then had still not been held to account.

'He told me that he had killed her by strangling her,' I said plainly. 'Halliwell said that he had ... returned the following night and had spent all night digging a five-foot-deep grave.'

Halliwell sat passively as I recounted that afternoon we'd shared.

It was a somewhat low-key, uncoloured way of giving the evidence I'd been banned from sharing for so long. You might think that perhaps there should have been a sense of jubilation at finally being able to tell a jury what Halliwell had told me, but of course there was not. Karen Edwards watched in the courtroom, hearing me describe her daughter's last moments. How could there be any jubilation in that?

Haggan finished with me and the judge turned to Halliwell. 'Have you got any questions?'

'Yes, I have,' Christopher Halliwell replied.

I shifted on the stand. *This is where it is going to get interesting*, I thought. Was Halliwell ready to pick up where we'd left off?

As Halliwell began to speak, just as I had felt at Barbary Castle, I didn't know which way this was going to go. He stood in the dock, behind the glass, to ask his questions. There would be no pacing of the courtroom for him, not for this convicted killer, but nevertheless I felt there was a certain drama in the way he spoke. He reminded me of an amateur actor from an afternoon TV show.

As we looked at each other and traded questions and answers, it was almost as though the intervening years hadn't passed. It was just me and him, locked in a moment. I called him Christopher at one juncture, and he interrupted to correct me; it was Chris. Was that a sign that we were getting back to our bond?

He had prepared his questions thoroughly. Just like a professional barrister, he wanted to lead me down a particular path ...

'[The grave] wasn't five foot deep, was it?' he queried.

'No, it wasn't,' I agreed. 'But that's what you told me at the time.'

'You know from your enquiries,' Halliwell said, 'that I spent most of my working life as a groundworker or building [labourer]. So in that capacity I knew the difference between a five-foot hole and a six-inch hole. Doesn't that stand out?'

Just above my ribcage, my heart began to beat harder, faster. *Blimey*, I thought, *we're actually going to play this out as I'd envisaged.* In highlighting the discrepancy between what he'd said and the true depth of Becky's grave, he was bringing to the jury's attention the very thing that had first made me realise he was a serial killer. *He wants to confess*, I thought heatedly. *This is how we're going to get there.* If I'd written the script myself I couldn't have come up with a better segue.

'It does stand out,' I agreed cautiously. I thought I'd help him – give him an easy way to come across. 'What I inferred from that is that Becky is one of your victims, as is Sian, and you got confused about the nature of this deposition. You described very clearly a five-foot hole.' I took a deep breath, and I went for it: 'That led me to conclude that there are other victims.'

My comment caused consternation in the court. The jury all sat bolt upright and the press were scribing away, steam rising from their pencils.

It affected Halliwell too. His mouth dropped open and I think he even took a step back to express his shock. It was only then that I realised: he hadn't planned to lead me here at all. In his eyes I saw panic, as if to say, *No! That wasn't what I was trying to get out of you!*

I realised then that my hope that he would cough had just been a forlorn fantasy, born out of my frustration and a kind of grief that we had never got to the bottom of his offending.

I wish I could have seized the initiative and pressed my point home. But I was nervous of inciting the opprobrium of yet another judge; I couldn't turn the tables and start saying, 'And why don't you tell me about who those other victims are?' And, of course, today wasn't about the other victims. It was about getting Becky's conviction home. So I kept schtum and let Halliwell recover his equilibrium.

'OK, if you say so!' he blustered. 'Or does it suggest that maybe I really didn't know?'

I sighed; I got impatient with him then. If he wasn't going to cough, what was this charade of a court case about? I probably demonstrated that I was no longer seeking to empathise and was actually just annoyed.

Halliwell turned away from me to address the court. 'By the end of this process you will know the truth,' he announced dramatically. 'You won't like it but you will know the truth … It is going to leave a hell of a lot more questions unanswered.'

He turned back to me and fixed me with those piercing blue eyes of his. He spoke pointedly and, in a mirror image of how I'd felt at the PCMH, when Latham had revealed how he was going to get Halliwell off the hook, I felt a sharp tipping point. I suddenly realised what his defence was going to be.

'The first time I was in that field,' said Christopher Halliwell, 'was when I was there with *you*.'

62

In his twisted mind, I guess it made sense. There were two of us in that field. One of us had to be the killer. If he was going to claim it wasn't him, the corollary was it must be me. I'd fitted him up. It was the detective wot dunnit. That would give you the headline of the year.

Yet he didn't take the opportunity to grill me on it; perhaps he was saving the revelation of his defence for when he took the stand himself. Instead, he rushed to the end of the cross-examination. He had a rehearsed line, or so it seemed to me, and he was desperate to get it out.

'Oh, and by the way,' Halliwell said lightly, 'it was a pleasure ruining your career, you corrupt bastard.'

He sounded bitter. And why wouldn't he be? He'd had five-and-a-half years to reflect on the fact that, but for confessing to me, none of this would have happened. I reckon he'd been kicking himself all that time. But for meeting me, he'd have got away with it. After all, events had proved that no other officer should, would or could have done as I did. I guess our paths crossed for a particular purpose.

I treated his words with the contempt they deserved. 'I'm sure,' was all I said.

As it happens, I don't blame Halliwell for ruining my career. He didn't: he's never once complained about his PACE rights being breached, nor did his legal counsel.

Despite the fact he hadn't had a hand in it, Halliwell had obviously taken note of my fall from grace. That was evident not only in his words, but also in his manner. What had happened to me added fuel to his fire, to his belief that he was hard done by. He was self-righteous and clearly shared the outrage of the IPCC that he was brought to justice at all. Over the past five years, he'd been given to believe that the notion of breaching PACE was a greater offence than murdering women. No wonder he was bitter.

After little more than an hour, it was over. The whole experience had been very short. I suspect we'd both been hoping for more from it, but in the end it was pathetic. As I stepped down from the witness box, I simply thought, *Is that it? After five-and-a-half years, that's it?*

It felt like a missed opportunity. By Halliwell's own admission there were at least six more murders we should talk to him about, but he'd had neither the good grace nor the breadth of thought to get beyond his bitter-and-twisted position to see the benefit in coming across. As a result, I felt rather hard done by too.

Yvonne and I took the next day off from court. But the day after that we came back for more, heading up to the public gallery together to take our seats. The whole court was buzzing because Halliwell was about to take the stand.

Ever since his thinly veiled hint during my crossexamination, I'd been convinced he was going to try to finger me for the job. I wasn't worried about the consequences of that – although, given the madness of everything that has happened to me, I probably should have been – I simply anticipated that it would create some hot-air news coverage. The journalists were certainly out in full force: the courtroom was absolutely rammed, so much so that I ended up perched on a windowsill, and an usher tried to kick me out.

'I'm not going anywhere,' I said firmly. No way was I missing this.

In the end, we found seats in the perfect place: right in Halliwell's line of sight.

He gave evidence from the witness box, and there was a murmur of interest as he stepped down from the dock and crossed the courtroom. As he took the affirmation – 'The evidence I give shall be the truth, the whole truth and nothing but the truth' – I wondered what 'truth' he was really going to come out with.

To my surprise, he began by admitting he had slaughtered Sian O'Callaghan. I was suddenly pleased her family and Kevin had heeded the lawyers' advice to stay away from court that day in case Sian's murder was discussed.

'I want to start by saying I am telling the truth,' Halliwell said earnestly. 'I have no reason to lie ... I have no real prospect of getting out [of jail] and I deserve every day anyway. What happened between me and Sian – my actions were brutal.'

Was it me, or did he fix me with a look with his next words, as he stared straight into the public gallery?

'I come here to tell the truth. I already said ... you won't like what you are going to hear.'

The basis of his argument was essentially: 'My honesty is illustrated by the fact I admit I killed Sian. If I was guilty of Becky's murder too, obviously I would do the same.'

Yet Halliwell was talking himself into a trap. Both Haggan and the judge warned him – because in bringing up Sian's case himself, it gave Haggan open season to present the facts of her murder. Bearing in mind Halliwell had pled guilty in 2012, those facts had never been put before a court. But Halliwell didn't seem bright enough to understand that – and in his following testimony, his own version of reality soon took over from the truth.

He tried to portray himself as an honest, reasonable bloke, and the murder of Sian O'Callaghan as some kind of aberration that he was terribly sorry about. To fit the story, he described her killing as an accident – caused by Sian herself when she started attacking him in his car. He claimed she'd kicked off because she was drunk and that was why she'd ended up with a knife in the back of her head. I genuinely believe he thought he was offering a rational explanation that the jury would buy: 'She kicked off, therefore I am perfectly justified, am I not, in stabbing her in the head twice?'

I believe the judge intervened at this point. 'So you pleaded guilty to murder and now you're saying it wasn't murder at all, it was self-defence?'

Halliwell stuck to his story – even when Haggan stepped up to tell him he was lying. Haggan, in fact, went right back to first principles, quizzing Halliwell on the time of the pick-up, the route they'd taken – details that had never been heard before. It only served to emphasise how much we didn't know and how much Halliwell had held back.

'When did she kick off?' Haggan asked.

'Almost immediately,' explained Halliwell earnestly.

'What did you do about that?'

'I stabbed her in the head.'

In this way, through his questioning, Haggan got Halliwell to admit that he'd murdered Sian within a couple of minutes of her getting into the car.

All that time we'd been searching for her, *all* that time, it seemed she had already been dead.

There really was nothing more we could have done to save her.

The timing of the murder raised other questions though. Why would he kill her within a couple of minutes of her getting in the car? For what purpose?

Haggan had an answer – he inferred it, at least. He showed the jury a series of photographs of Sian's recovered body; I had not seen them in that sequence before. Halliwell had told me that he'd rolled her down that sloping bank, but it appeared from the photographs that she had been deliberately arranged. The manipulation of her clothing – her bra and dress had both been pushed up her body; her bra strap had been cut – made it clear there was a sexual element to the way she'd been positioned. He'd bitten her breast. And, Haggan now revealed, he'd cut a hole in the anal area of her knickers too and lowered them to her ankles.

By Halliwell's own admission, Sian had been dead while he did all these things. I'd mentally compared him, earlier, to serial killer Ted Bundy. Bundy had confessed that he would often return to his victims after they had died in order to perform sexual acts with their decomposing bodies – until putrefaction forced him to stop.

The inference here was clear. Halliwell, perhaps, was not so different.

ANPR records showed that he'd returned to Sian four times after he'd slaughtered her on that Saturday morning. *Four times.* From what Haggan was showing the jury, the suggestion of what he had been doing with her during those visits was clear.

'Didn't have sex,' Halliwell had told me. I could remember it clearly. He'd been so vehement – so much so that I had noted it at the time. Sian's post-mortem had borne out those words, so I hadn't dug deeper. Now that he'd revealed the timing of her murder, however, that earnestness took on a different meaning. I'd taken it for truth, but it was only more deception. This was something he had wanted to hide.

I thought of his controlling nature, the way we'd been told he interacted with Sally Ann John and Becky Godden-Edwards: those obsessive relationships where he'd demanded exclusivity. As the creator of a woman's corpse, it gave him ultimate control. Was that what this was all about?

As Haggan talked through it with the jury, the necro-philiac motive for Halliwell's murders was laid bare. For Halliwell's part, he seemed impassive, not engaged with the horrors of what he had done. Even when Haggan put the specifics of Sian's murder to him – 'So you stabbed her brutally in the back of the neck and lifted the blade up to prise the back of her skull off?' – he agreed as though it was a normal thing. There was no conscience that correlated between what he had done and the effect it had had; there was no, 'Oh fuck me, is that what I *did*?' Strangely enough, I think he was so self-centred that the impact of his actions didn't occur to him. There was seemingly no comprehension of the fact he'd destroyed a young girl's life, and deeply affected the lives of those who loved her. He just didn't seem to take responsibility for that.

As he had done with me, Halliwell seemed not to accept the notion that there was a sexual motive to his crimes. He'd deliberately denied it with me. I think that is self-protection: if you're into something like necro-philia, you'll get a far harder time in prison. Maybe, too, it was another form of control. This was one last secret he didn't want to share; perhaps the most precious coin of all in his collection.

But he'd told us now: Sian died within two minutes of getting in his car. Yet he'd returned to her four times: to cut her bra, to cut her knickers, to leave that bite upon her breast. We knew he'd gone out hunting, looping round the streets of Swindon. Now, sickeningly, it seemed we knew what he'd been hunting for.

63

Haggan moved the questioning on to Becky. This was the trial for her murder, after all. As though now locked in a pattern, Halliwell continued to make denials. He denied ever knowing Becky, despite the fact that several witnesses had testified he was obsessed with her. He blustered and obfuscated: the honest man no more.

He struck me as narcissistic. *If I deny it, it didn't happen.* He seemed confident he was convincing the jury and, in some ways, I could understand that, given his history. For decades he'd successfully led a double life and the untruths tripped off his tongue with ease.

All this while, he kept staring at me. To be fair, it was hard for him not to – the jury were seated below the public gallery, so to address them he had to look in my direction. I was surprised by his antipathy towards me, by the depth of it, because as his evidence continued he was positively fulminating in his hatred of me – so much so that it actually undermined his testimony; it was hard for the jury to buy the honest, reasonable bloke line when they could see the aggressive vitriol he was directing towards me.

He even brought it into his defence. He said he'd made up the confession in an act of revenge: 'I only told *Fulcher* that I'd murdered her in order to ruin his career!' He spat my name out. He was suggesting that he'd only said,

'Do you want another one?' because he knew I hadn't cautioned him, and it was all an elaborate fit-up to bring me down.

Haggan fixed him with a look. 'You're seriously going to run the risk of life imprisonment for a murder you haven't committed in order to screw up the career of a policeman that you've taken a dislike to?' he said disbelievingly. 'Why would you take such an exception to the bloke?'

Halliwell glared at me again. 'Because he threatened my family,' he asserted.

'In what way did he threaten your family?'

'I'm not prepared to say.'

Halliwell simply couldn't disguise his fury at me for having brought him down. The funny thing was, I'd been about to give up, that day at Barbary Castle. He'd have only needed to keep schtum for another 20 seconds. Now he knew that if he'd just held the line, he'd have been walking free, and probably have a few more victims under his belt. Watching him glower at me, it was evident he'd been festering about that all these years.

'You really hate Mr Fulcher, don't you?' Haggan asked him at one point. 'You address Sean Memory as Mr Memory, but you don't refer to Mr Fulcher as anything other than *Fulcher*.'

Halliwell grimaced at me. 'I *loathe* him,' he concurred.

As I watched him, locking eyes with him as I had done a lifetime ago, I felt something snap inside me. It dislodged itself and floated away: a forlorn, near-forgotten hope gently leaving my heart. Like a woman's last breath, it vanished seamlessly into the ether. Because I knew, from the bile and bitterness he blasted in my direction, that the conversation we had once started would never be continued now. Strange and even foolish as it may sound, I had always believed, through all the madness, that at some point common sense would prevail and Halliwell and I would end up sat opposite each other again, having a smoke and a chat. Because I hadn't invented the bond between us; without it, he would never have confessed Becky's murder to me. I'd always thought we'd had unfinished business, but it would always remain that way now.

And with that hope went my hope for all the other victims. I don't believe we'll ever find them, now; not unless someone stumbles on them. I don't believe Halliwell is ever going to confess. All the research suggests that the majority of serial killers don't. Plus, Halliwell has added ammunition not to: thanks to the way people went after me, he has been given to feel self-righteous that I am the villain of the piece, rather than him. It psychologically justifies his position to stay silent. I think that's perhaps the most scandalous thing of all in everything that's happened.

Haggan kept on with his cross-examination, and I sat more upright in my seat. From the way Halliwell had been acting towards me, it seemed we must be only seconds away from him pointing the finger and saying I'd killed Becky, not him. I braced myself.

But at the last minute, he pulled back from the brink. I'm convinced that's what he planned to say, but he wobbled. Just like at Barbary Castle, he caved. I suspect, without legal advice, he lacked the confidence to know what he could say in court; in fact, he could have said whatever he liked, but he didn't seem too sure. Instead of fingering me, he came up with an excuse from the book of excuses. He tried to blame the murder on some mysterious drug dealers.

'In March 2003, I received a phone call from the men. They said something had gone wrong and they needed to get rid of something. When I picked them up, one of them opened the boot and they put a large sports bag inside. I didn't ask any questions. I assumed it was either drugs, money, possibly weapons.'

He said he drove them to the red clay field in Eastleach. 'It was only later one of the men told me they had buried a prostitute from Swindon. I thought he was messing about. But I wondered for years: was it true?'

He said that was why he'd taken me to Eastleach. 'I got to the field, jumped over the wall ... what I said was, "She's here, she's five foot underground." But I didn't know where she was.'

'Can you name these drug dealers?' Haggan asked him wearily. I think everyone in court was rolling their eyes in disbelief; it was such a lame argument.

'No chance!' Halliwell replied. He said he was afraid of 'repercussions' for his family.

Haggan quizzed him further, and it became apparent he was making it up as he went along.

'This is a complete fabrication,' Haggan exclaimed to the jury. 'A last throw of the dice to avoid a whole life term.'

I could taste the tang of disappointment. I'd spent years telling people what a good criminal Halliwell was – smart around forensics, no passive data, cleverly operating with no witnesses – but he didn't live up to the description.

And that was it. That was all he had. I'd come into the trial with so many hopes of what might happen, but it was just a charade, after all. The chance to do something worthwhile had passed and all that was left was a murderer trying to make a mockery of justice.

The jury took less than two hours to reach their verdict, on Monday, 19 September 2016. I wasn't in court to see it. I knew there'd be a lot of interest from the media on the court steps afterwards, and I felt I was in a strange position, being the detective who'd caught him, but also the copper who'd been forced out of the force. I wasn't the SIO: Sean was. I didn't fancy the undignified scrum, so I stayed away.

I spent the day in Sidmouth, on my own because Yvonne had gone to court. It was an Indian summer's day, with a bright blue sky and sunshine.

I spent the time before the verdict mooching around the seaside town, feeling like I'd stepped back in time to the 1930s. It's the type of place where the air sings with the crack of boules on the community green and the suck of the sea on the stones. Everyone was wearing white and there was even a classic car rally outside the apartment. It felt like the kind of place where old-school values were always upheld, where coppers caught criminals and malevolent men never got away with murder. It felt like the right place to be on this day.

I was sitting on the balcony, overlooking the sea, when my smartphone came to life with a call.

After five-and-a-half years, after all that had happened, in the end there was just one word.

Guilty.

Epilogue

The judge sentenced Christopher Halliwell to a full life term for the murder of Becky Godden-Edwards. It means he will never be released from prison. I think it was a very astute move on the judge's part. It would be morally unconscionable to let a man like Halliwell out on the streets again.

Halliwell said only, 'Thank you,' as the judge told him he was going down for life. It was a far cry from his behaviour on the day he'd been found guilty. Like the evil man he is, he had purposely stopped and smiled at Karen and her family as he'd been led away. I wonder if he's got much to smile about in his cell these days.

For me personally, there was only a muted exoneration in the judge's comments; I had hoped he would go further. He said to Halliwell, 'You very briefly allowed the little conscience you have to prompt your confession. I consider that but for that confession, there is every prospect that Rebecca's remains would not have been found.' He had recognised what I had said all along: there has only ever been one moment of contrition in Christopher Halliwell's life; if I hadn't acted on it, Becky would never have received justice. Importantly, the judge added, 'I am satisfied that the confession to the murder of Becky was not the consequence of oppression.'

Something I found notable in the written judgment was that there was no crown court commendation for Wiltshire Police, such as you normally find. Yet that was only right. In the wake of the guilty verdict, the force put out press statements that claimed 'diligent and professional' police work had brought Halliwell to justice, but that simply wasn't true. How could it be, when they had asked Karen Edwards to be satisfied with Halliwell only going down for Sian's murder? Their press puffs also asserted that new evidence, such as the soil on the spade, was what had convicted him in the end. Yet most of that 'new' evidence had been around for at least two years; some for as long as five. That was why Karen Edwards had complained to HMIC in 2014: because all the evidence was there years ago, but no investigation had been conducted. Personally, I think there needs to be an enquiry asking why.

Wiltshire Police have stated publicly that Becky's case was 'rigorously reviewed' and 'any new lines of enquiry or evidence fully investigated'. I would invite them to prove that claim by showing the public the HOLMES account, which would track what investigation was made and when. The records will speak for themselves.

Becky, however, did at least receive justice in the end. The people I am more concerned for now are Halliwell's other victims.

In the first few days of Halliwell's trial in September 2016, I caught up with some former colleagues from Wiltshire Police. They were pleased Halliwell's case had come to court; there was a 'Friday feeling' about it finally being over. 'We're going to knock this on the head now,' they told me. As far as they were concerned, the Halliwell case was closed.

Sadly for them, I then made my comment in court about the other victims – and the press picked up on it. I believe it forced their hand because, after the verdict, in direct contrast to officers' privately expressed opinions, the SIO now gave interviews that said: 'I will now go away and look at the timeline of Christopher Halliwell ... I'll look to other police forces to find out if they have missing people in very similar circumstances ... I'm definitely concerned ... I am open-minded there may be others.'

I was staggered. It was as though the idea had only just struck them that an investigation into Halliwell's other possible crimes might be needed. I think it's scandalous. From the tenor of their own statements, it seems they hadn't been investigating this for five-and-a-half years – not even after the discovery of the 60 items of women's clothing in Halliwell's trophy store.

Yet it wasn't just the trophy store they did not appear to be investigating. In Karen's complaint letter to HMIC, dated 5 August 2014, she had written: 'Many members of the public have given me information... I handed this information to the police. No action has been taken.'

This information was the sort that could help crack a case. One witness came forward to say they were sure they had seen Halliwell and still-missing Claudia Lawrence together. Given the description of a man connected with Claudia's case is identical to Halliwell *and* she went missing on the same day of the year as Sian O'Callaghan – 19 March, but two years earlier in 2009 – you might think that witness statement would be taken, but it never has been to my knowledge. Wiltshire Police have since issued a statement saying, 'There is no evidence, no evidence whatsoever, to link him to any other murder in this country.' But there is only no evidence because they haven't spoken to the witness.

Nor was that the only item of interest. Karen also passed on information regarding another woman, Linda Razzell – who *also* vanished on 19 March (in 2002) and whose body has never been found. I think that key date of 19 March is significant. Our enquiries into Halliwell's background revealed he had been dumped by a girlfriend on that same date in the 1980s. With his attitude to women such as it is, one can perhaps view these potential murders as a long-running ritualistic act of revenge.

The evidence in Linda's case came from two witnesses, who said that Linda was having an affair with Halliwell before she vanished; an affair in which he had acted obsessively, just as other witnesses had described him doing with both Becky and Sally Ann John. They said Halliwell used to sit sketching her in his car opposite this gloomy alleyway through which Linda used to walk on her way to work – an alleyway where her mobile phone was later found on the day she vanished.

Unlike Claudia Lawrence and Sally Ann John, however, Linda's case isn't unsolved. Even as I write, her estranged husband Glyn Razzell is serving a life sentence for her murder.

This rather ups the ante on that failure to investigate. There is plenty of information online about Glyn's case, but in brief I will summarise here. The passive data shows him to be nowhere near Linda's house on the day she vanished, but on the other side of town. When interviewed, Glyn – unlike Halliwell – gave a full account of his movements, informing the police that he had walked past their own nick at the relevant time. He urged them to check their CCTV to verify his account – but the force's own machines weren't working. For 15 years Glyn has maintained his innocence. The only thing that convicted him was some forensic evidence that reportedly showed Linda's blood in his car – forensic evidence that was not found on the first examination of the vehicle, nor on the second, but only on the third attempt. Glyn has tried several times to have his case reviewed, but those critical forensic results have never been released to his defence team by the force.

Now, I've never met Glyn. I don't know whether he is guilty or innocent. I don't know whether Halliwell murdered Linda or not; and even if these witnesses are interviewed and their statements finally taken, it doesn't move us any further forward in terms of pinning Halliwell to the crime. But that isn't the point here. The point is, there are witnesses who have come forward to say a convicted killer and a missing woman were in a relationship, and nobody in the police service has taken their statements. They have therefore de facto suppressed something that might undermine the safety of a conviction of a person serving a life sentence.

Can Glyn's conviction really be said to be safe in the light of Halliwell? Why have the police not re-examined the case given this new information? At the end of the day, however, it doesn't matter *why* they haven't done it, what matters is that they haven't. Because this is so much more than just a neglect of duty.

As I understand it, within the last few weeks of the time of writing, a detective sergeant has finally been asked to review it. That is good news – but it still doesn't explain the unforgivable delay. There is currently a man serving a life sentence for a murder he may not have committed – any issues regarding that should be processed with alacrity. I think Wiltshire Police are extremely vulnerable on this. Only time will tell what may happen next.

As for Sally Ann John, the pretty woman with whom Halliwell was said to be obsessed, who vanished 22 years ago, the police closed her case after I reopened it. Recently, they opened it again, this time as a murder enquiry, and in February 2017 officers began digging at two properties in Broad Street, where she and Halliwell both lived. I'm gratified they seem to be taking the case more seriously at last – although I very much doubt they will find anything; I believe Halliwell is too good to have left any evidence in his own backyard. Yet their action now only serves to highlight their inaction in the previous six years. Why didn't Wiltshire Police dig up Broad Street back in 2011? Why has it taken more than half a decade for them to properly investigate Sally Ann's known link to Halliwell?

A relative of Sally Ann's said to the *Sun*: 'Of course we have wondered about Halliwell, but we've been stone-walled by the police in the past. I have been told categorically by the police that he's not been in the frame for it. But now the police seem to be doing something. I've not been too impressed with the police but they do seem to be making an effort now, although it's a bit late ... We've been waiting for answers for 22 years now.'

And those words illustrate the thing that really incenses me about Wiltshire Police's attitude. Because whoever the six – or the sixty – other victims are, they are real people, with mothers and fathers and siblings and friends. People's lives have been wrecked, for the rest of time, by whatever has happened to their relative. Sally Ann's mother still appeals for help finding her 'bright and beautiful' daughter; Claudia Lawrence's father describes the pain of losing his child as 'torture'. 'It's like a cancer,' he told the *Daily Mail*. 'It eats into you. And it just gets worse and worse because there's no resolution until we know what happened to Claudia.' A police investigation that fails to scrutinise every possible clue is one that fails families. It fails victims.

I am certain that somewhere, in some remote corner of the world, there is a five-foot hole with a dead woman at the bottom of it: the victim Halliwell confused for Becky when he described that five-foot grave. What are the police doing to find her? What are they doing for the owner of the perfume bottle? Their actions seem so uncaring and substandard, and I personally feel they should be held to account. I'll of course be accused of being bitter because of what happened to me, but what happened to me is frankly inconsequential. The issues I'm raising are bigger than that.

And the same goes for another element to this case that no one has yet addressed. In referring my actions to the IPCC, the police force has shot itself in the foot. Because what I did – championing a victim's right to life over PACE – has now been ruled gross misconduct by the IPCC and the police are not left with an alternative tactical plan. No other officer can now take the step I did. I can't tell you how many letters I've received from members of the public, saying, 'If it was my daughter who'd gone missing, I'd want you to do what you did.' Well, that's great, but no one will be getting that again. I'm not sure the public realise that.

That's why I wanted to write this book, because there is a fundamental public interest issue at stake. It's why I want to be exonerated, too. I have to be. Because if I am wrong, and this is public policy – that an offender's right to silence trumps the victim's right to life – then everyone needs to understand that.

Of course, it wasn't only Sian I found when I broke the rules. I found Becky, too. That raises another question about what the public want their police force to do.

Bear in mind that if a criminal is any good, the only source of information is reposed in the perpetrator's mind. Yet PACE means it's the one area detectives can't go. There is an endemic problem with PACE that prevents voluntary confessions being accepted – because everything about it, from the right to silence to the right to a lawyer who will actively stop you from incriminating yourself, is engineered so that criminals don't cough. Since PACE was introduced it has essentially blocked off interviewing suspects as an investigative avenue. As such, modern policing has become a passive, box-ticking exercise, with coppers picking up the clues a careless criminal has left behind. A trained monkey could do it; you don't need a detective. It means, evidently, that coppers will only ever catch clumsy criminals. The good-quality ones, like Halliwell, will be able to act with impunity – exactly as he did, until I caught him by breaching PACE.

So I argue that PACE requires review. No one wants to go back to the old days where the police sometimes ran roughshod over the rules, but the pendulum has swung too far in favour of the criminal. Far from protecting the innocent, as PACE was originally designed to do, it in fact serves more to protect the guilty. And it creates a world where victims die and criminals get off scot-free. If that's the world we live in, then, I'm almost pleased I'm no longer a detective.

Since the verdict in Becky's murder trial, Karen Edwards has taken up a new campaign: she wants justice for me too. 'I will not rest until I have cleared Steve Fulcher's name,' she told the *Daily Mail*. 'He should have never suffered the terrible consequences, loss of reputation and career for [bringing Becky home].'

I guess that's the thing that gets me. Because it didn't have to be a choice. This wasn't an either/or scenario: I keep my career or I find the girls and convict Halliwell. It was only the powers that be that made it that way.

Perhaps the greatest irony of all this is that I was really good at my job. If I hadn't managed to get a cough out of Halliwell, none of what followed would have occurred. My Achilles' heel turned out to be my aptitude. The tragedy is that I called every bit of that complex, near-impossible investigation right *and* we got the right result, yet I still ended up in the cart.

One of the very saddest things, I think, is that this should have been the proudest moment not only of my career, but also that of my colleagues. Instead, it's been turned into a ghastly, tainted mess. I've never had the opportunity to say to my team, after everything, how bloody brilliant they were. But they were – Jess and Bill and John and Debs and Marcus Beresford-Smith ... and the rest. They were amazing. I could not have done what I did without them. We *all* caught a serial killer, in the end. Yet no one has been given the credit. On the contrary, press reports on the case inevitably mention a 'police blunder'. But I don't think the police called this wrong at all: the evidence I gathered that day convicted a killer.

The IPCC persist in publishing their report into my actions. This despite my written requests to remove it on the basis that it is demonstrably flawed, factually incorrect and defamatory. It contains discipline issues that have been disproved and withdrawn. It maintains the allega-tion of oppression, which His Honour Sir John Griffith Williams dismissed and the scurrilous, blackened-name, charge of dishonesty.

Though I think it wrong, it doesn't keep me up at night now. I can't let it. My sleepless nights are a thing of the past: I have moved on. I do occasionally fulminate, and get angry, and then I remind myself: the only prisoner of that mindset is me. And, unlike Halliwell, I don't have to spend the rest of my life behind bars.

People have said to me, 'If we could get you exoner-ated, would you take your job back?' The answer is no. Even if the political prevailing wind prompted them to ask me, I would never go back. I'm interested in the work I'm doing in Africa, where I feel I'm making a difference, doing something that will have a palpable, lasting effect for people who appreciate my support.

I gave 28 years of my life to the police force. But I can see in hindsight that I had my priorities all wrong. All those late nights, all those cancelled plans, all those birthdays of my daughters that I missed – it was all for nothing. I was so focused on helping victims' families that I forgot about my own. This case has shown me what is important, and that's Yvonne and my girls, above all else. We live in a tiny house now, trying to make ends meet, but it's a happy home – and that makes me the richest man I know.

On 23 September 2016, the day Halliwell was sentenced, Karen and Charlie Edwards and Yvonne and I met for lunch in an Italian restaurant to celebrate the news. We sat outside in a little courtyard, where the chill of the afternoon had come on. And we talked about our daughters: about Elsie and Jennifer and Becky. I felt a sense of apology, talking about my living girls, but Karen has such a wonderful way of describing Becky that it was almost as if she was with us that afternoon, in that way that lost loved ones sometimes can be when we conjure them with words. Karen remembers her daughter for who she was, flaws and all, and loves her just the same – as any mother would. And we toasted her daughter. We toasted her Becky. No longer forgotten in a distant field, but back with her family at last.

I can still remember clearly the days following Sian O'Callaghan's disappearance. I remember talking to Christopher Halliwell on that windswept hill, on that day that had far-reaching consequences for us both.

I think of him now, locked up for Sian and Becky's murders. We got him in the end. We caught our killer. But, these days, I don't think of him often. As Yvonne and I watch our daughters, so bright and beautiful, on their visits home to us, full of the excitement of their independent lives and bursting to tell us of their new discoveries, I am much more likely to think of Becky and of Sian. And of the other girls whose lives have been cut short, the ones whose bodies are still missing.

In some ways, I'm glad I don't know who they are, so they don't trouble my conscience at our failure to get closer to the truth. I believe Halliwell, if I'd asked him, would have told me at one time. But all that now is ashes. I no longer believe we'll ever know their names.

I am the detective who caught a serial killer. I am the detective who was found guilty of gross misconduct for doing so. But I've written off my career; put it down to bad luck. If I've brought some resolution to the families and held a killer to account at the cost of my career, I'd say that's cheap at the price.

There is another comfort, too. If my suspicions are right, if the evidence in the trophy store suggests a truth that still lies hidden, then Christopher Halliwell had a prolific propensity to murder – perhaps as often as once or twice a year. Which means the corollary of my actions is that I've saved at least five women by now in acting as I did. That's five daughters who haven't been killed; five families without an empty seat at the table this Christmas; five families able to see their children grow up and grow old. And that's worthwhile, isn't it? That's not a bad legacy to leave.

So, if you ask me, I'll only ever have one answer. If you gave me the choice: I'd do it all again.

Acknowledgements

I would like to thank Yvonne and my family and friends for their unfailing faith, and especially Karen Edwards, who provided her full support throughout, at extraordinary cost to herself, and without which I would not have survived this experience.

My gratitude also goes to Deborah Peach. Debs and I wrote the original manuscript of this story as a catharsis; our fates have been intrinsically linked together in our pursuit of justice.

Thank you to Richard Armitage for his spiritual guidance, and to my professional colleagues and friends – they know who they are – who provided wise counsel in the dark times.

I am grateful for the talent and dedication Kate Moore has provided in writing this book, enabling my story to be articulated to a wider audience. At Ebury Press, thank you to the whole publishing team, in particular my editor, Sara Cywinski, and Charlotte Cole, who project-managed the book. Last but not least, thank you to Robert Smith, my literary agent.

About the Author

Stephen Fulcher was born and bred in Coventry. He joined the police force in 1986 and rose through the ranks to become a detective superintendent, working for Sussex CID, Special Branch at Gatwick and the Force Intelligence Bureau before joining Wiltshire Police in 2003. During his time in the force he helped solve countless major crime cases, leading many as the senior investigating officer, and received three crown court commendations and one chief constable's commendation. He holds a master's degree in applied criminology and police management from Cambridge University.

Having now left the police force, Steve works with UK government agencies, training local police officers in political hotspots such as Libya and Somalia.

This is his first book.